SOCIAL STRATIFICATION:

Research and Theory for the 1970s

SOCIAL STRATIFICATION:

Research and Theory for the 1970s

Edited by Edward O. Laumann

The Bobbs-Merrill Company, Inc.
Indianapolis   New York

Copyright © 1970 by The Bobbs-Merrill Company, Inc.
Printed in the United States of America
Library of Congress Catalog Number 77-135769

ISBN 0-672-51402-8
ISBN 0-672-61195-3 (pbk)
Second Printing

List of Contributors

EDWARD O. LAUMANN is associate professor of sociology at the University of Michigan. He is presently on sabbatical leave at the Institut für vergleichende Sozialforschung of the Universität zu Köln.

TALCOTT PARSONS is professor of social relations at Harvard University. He will become professor emeritus this year and enjoys an international reputation as scholar and teacher.

JAMES KIMBERLY is associate professor of sociology and Director of Graduate Studies at Emory University.

PAUL SIEGEL is an assistant professor of sociology at the University of Michigan and Associate Director of the Department's Social Organization-Human Ecology Program.

ROBERT W. HODGE is professor of sociology at the University of Michigan and Acting Director of the Center for Research in Social Organization. Last year he was Simon Research Fellow at the University of Manchester (Manchester, England).

STANLEY LIEBERSON, a professor of sociology at the University of Washington, is Director of its Center for Studies in Demography and Ecology.

DONALD TREIMAN, recently of the University of Wisconsin, has been appointed an associate professor of the Department of Sociology at Columbia University.

ROBERT HAUSER is assistant professor of sociology at the University of Wisconsin (Madison) and Co-director of the Department's Methodology Training Program.

THOMAS PULLUM, assistant professor at the University of Chicago, is an associate of the Population Research and Training Center.

HARRIET ZUCKERMAN is an assistant professor of sociology at Columbia University and is associated with the Bureau of Applied Social Research.

BRUCE WARREN, who has recently completed his doctoral dissertation, is an assistant professor of sociology at Eastern Michigan University.

Contents

SOCIAL STRATIFICATION:

Research and Theory for the 1970s

Editor's Foreword

EDWARD O. LAUMANN
University of Michigan

Each contributor to this special issue of *Sociological Inquiry* was asked to write a more or less freewheeling, speculative essay on a given topic in his area of speciality in stratification theory and/or research with the accent to be on critically assessing recent developments in the area and anticipating the lines along which future work might profitably go. With the exception of the first contributor (but only in the strict physical sense), all are relatively young men or women who, in my opinion, have already made or are likely to make significant contributions to our understanding of social inequality over the next decade. Naturally, given the space limitations, we have by no means exhausted all the possible contributors or significant research areas that could have been included. I shall have a further word or two to say about these "neglected" topics in the concluding sections of the foreword. I would like to take this opportunity to express my appreciation to all the contributors for their excellent cooperation in meeting all the specifications and guidelines that others* and I suggested. The result, I hope, is a series of essays which, while on highly disparate topics, enjoys an underlying interrelatedness that enhances their mutual relevance and usefulness.

While I have followed a certain logic in ordering the papers—that is, from general theoretical treatments to more empirically and methodologically oriented discussions, especially of American but also of cross-national comparative studies—the reader should feel free to follow his own interests and priorities, as each article is a self-contained piece. The first two papers by Parsons and Kimberly are broadly conceived theoretical treatments deriving from rather different theoretical and empirical starting points although both share a common "functionalist" perspective (cf. Stinchcombe, 1968, especially Chapter 3). Parsons's two-part article represents a major reexamination and extension of his earlier work in which he applied the action frame of reference (cf. Parsons, 1951, 1964, 1966; Parsons and Shils, 1951; Black, 1961; Parsons, *et al.,* 1961: especially 130–179) to the study of social stratification. Especially intriguing for me in this new formulation is his analytic effort, almost in Marxian dialectic terms, to treat equality-inequality as a fundamental axis of strain in *all* relatively complex social

---

*I gratefully acknowledge the assistance of the following people who made invaluable critical comments on various contributions: Otis Dudley Duncan, Andrew Effrat, Paul Hare, Victor Lidz, Leon Mayhew, David McFarland, James C. Moore, Paul Siegel, and William G. Spady.

3

systems, and his efforts to describe the various mechanisms (e.g., the process of justification) by which this inherent disequilibrating strain is "handled." This represents a major departure in his thinking which previously treated inequality-equality nonanalytically and more in terms of an historic institutional shift in emphasis from preindustrial to industrial societies. He also poses some serious objections to the relevance of classic definitions of *class* (e.g., Marxian and Weberian) in the analysis of modern societies arguing, somewhat akin to Stinchcombe's (1965: especially 180–185) position, that the unit of class stratification can no longer be usefully taken to be the family but a man's complex of ascribed and achieved collectivity memberships, including his organizational memberships. While this fundamental insight may come to be generally accepted, it will have to await a systematic rethinking of our whole approach to status measurement and corresponding reorganization of current research practices before it can bear much fruit. His comments relating the concept of prestige to the concept of influence as a generalized medium of exchange and its consequent location in his analytic scheme are also well worth noting. For those fully initiated into the action framework, his discussion in Part II of the relevance of the equality-inequality dichotomy to the pattern variables and the AGIL paradigm will be of special interest.

While Parsons's paper sketches in broad strokes a number of fundamental theoretical (or more accurately, conceptual) issues and some proposed lines of investigation where resolutions might be found at the societal level of analysis, Kimberly's paper surveys the accumulating body of empirical and theoretical work on status systems in small groups and attempts to tease out its implications for our understanding of certain stratification processes, most notably the emergence and stabilization of status systems and status equilibration in more complex social systems. Being fully conversant with the Stanford group's work (cf. Berger, *et al.,* 1966) and that of other social psychological theorists, he attempts to identify some possible bridges between what we have learned about microstructural processes in small groups and macrostructural theories of stratification (e.g., Davis and Moore, 1945). Until recently (cf. Homans, 1961; Blau, 1964) these two research and theoretical traditions have unfortunately tended to develop quite independently of one another. By identifying and contrasting the assumptions and postulates of various theorists, Kimberly is able to show more precisely the crucial ways in which they differ from one another and, consequently, the ways in which their empirical deductions may be expected to differ. We are, as a result, in a better position to mount research that will have significant bearing on our theorizing about status systems.

While the remaining contributors are also concerned with examining various theoretical models or, more modestly, general hypotheses relevant to their research domains, none is as concerned as Parsons and Kimberly with general theoretical accounts of social inequality. From the standpoint of "coverage" of the field, it is worth noting here that none of the authors presents an essentially Marxist (or "conflict") approach to the analysis of stratification (as opposed to the well represented functional or "descriptive" approaches). I must frankly acknowledge this omission as a major weakness and simply ask the reader to refer to some of the following authors (including Feuer, 1959; Bottomore, 1964, 1968; B. Moore, 1966; Ossowski, 1963; Dahrendorf, 1959; Lenski, 1966; and Petras and Zeitlin, 1967) for a redress of this imbalance.

In Hauser's stimulating discussion of educational stratification in the United States, we are treated to a critical assessment of what we presently know about the impact of such factors as intellectual ability and family background on a person's educational achievement, the significance of the "quality" of one's schooling on subsequent "success," and the role educational achievement plays in allocating people to various occupational positions. All variables are reviewed as they bear on a system of national accounts for educational stratification whereby we may be in a better position to evaluate various policy alternatives for improving the performance of our educational system in this critical allocative task. While the complex conceptual and methodological apparatus developed by Hauser on the basis of his and others' work will not be familiar to everyone, it is well worth the reader's effort to attempt to come to terms with his approach, as it immeasurably improves one's ability to analyze and evaluate critically a crucial area of public policy.

The paper by Warren on religious factors in the determination of socioeconomic status in the United States utilizes a similar methodological approach to evaluate the role religious differences play in affecting the distribution of socioeconomic status and, conversely, the role socioeconomic status plays in changes of religious preference. Since Weber's (1958) famous essay on the "Protestant Ethic and the Spirit of Capitalism," there have been great controversies raging over the relative advantage of being a Protestant or Catholic in achieving worldly success (e.g., Samuelsson, 1957). While his hypothesis is really only an historical proposition that Protestantism was especially conducive to the development and spread of early rational-bourgeois capitalistic economic activity in western Europe in the sixteenth to eighteenth centuries, it has often been regarded as having contemporary relevance in explaining the presumed differences in worldly success of Protestants and Catholics in the United States. Upon reviewing the available evidence, Warren concludes, just as Weber argued although his argument has often been ignored by subsequent commentators, that the simple dichotomy of Protestant versus Catholic is likely to mask significant differences among Protestant denominations (cf. Laumann, 1969) that must be taken into account if one is to develop an adequate description of the role religious values and beliefs may play in worldly success.

Siegel's paper poses the fascinating and theoretically important question of whether there are subcultural variants on the general culture of a society that are somehow reflective of the distinctive common experiences of socially recognized categories of persons. The case in point is the determination of the existence of a distinctive Negro subculture that arises out of this group's historical experiences in America and present concentrations in occupations in the lower reaches of the socioeconomic status system. The Negroes' unfortunate relations to the American status system would lead us to expect that their evaluations of occupations (in terms of their prestige) should in some sense reflect their own experiences as distinct from those of the modal culture. In fact there are no differences in the ways Negroes allocate occupational prestige from the ways in which whites do (cf. Liebow, 1967). That is, they allocate prestige according to the ways whites are rewarded and not according to the ways Negroes are rewarded. In a stimulating concluding section, Siegel explores some of the theoretical and empirical consequences of this empirically unambiguous but theoretically awkward fact.

Stanley Lieberson's deceptively simple and brief essay broadens the discussion of religious and racial differences and their relation to social inequality in the United States to consider a more general treatment of ethnic stratification, using "ethnic" in its broadest reference, in comparison to other forms of stratification, such as those premised on economic, age or sex characteristics, from a cross-national perspective. His central thesis is that only ethnic groups, in contradistinction to other forms of stratification, are likely to generate a movement toward creating a separate nation-state; that is, "political separatism offers a solution to disadvantaged groups in an ethnic stratification system that is not possible for groups disadvantaged on the basis of age, sex or economic stratification." In examining the bases for this assertion, Lieberson informs us about certain central elements in the various forms of stratification and their mutual impact.

The paper by Hodge on social integration, psychological well-being and their socioeconomic correlates picks up on an important theme briefly discussed in Lieberson's paper, *viz.,* the consequences of a person's being simultaneously located on multiple hierarchies of social inequality. Hodge's paper falls into two parts: first, he presents some data from several national studies in the United States showing that various aspects of people's social integration (e.g., social participation in various kinds of informal and formal associations) and psychological well-being (including feelings of powerlessness and psychosomatic symptoms) are differentially related to various frequently used component indicators of socioeconomic status. The thrust of the argument is to demonstrate that a single summary indicator of socioeconomic status (e.g., the Warner or Hollingshead Index) combining such components as educational attainment, occupational status, and income will prove unsatisfactory because its component parts have different consequences for the same variable. What is especially interesting here, however, is not only its obvious implied methodological suggestion to treat component indicators separately in analysis, but also his effort to relate the results to a theoretical analysis of the ways in which various forms of stratification serve to integrate people into the society in functionally different ways. Secondly, and perhaps more important, is his clarification of some of the issues involved in the analysis of status inconsistency and mobility effects by the use of a regression model in which he can show that certain formulations of the effects of inconsistency and mobility are wholly redundant and only represent a logically possible way of interpreting the linear additive effects of the variables used to define them.

Moving to a comparative societal perspective and a much-needed corrective to the overemphasis of American sociologists on the American case, Treiman's excellent article first notes some of the difficulties of comparative analysis and then proceeds, after describing the advantages of path analysis (cf. Duncan, 1966) in circumventing some of these difficulties, to develop a number of systematically interrelated propositions relating various aspects of stratification systems to one another and to other institutional features of societies, especially those related to changes wrought by the processes of industrialization and urbanization. Some of these propositions enjoy empirical support, while most represent promising working hypotheses yet to be tested. Of special interest here is Treiman's efforts to delineate in a systematic fashion the ways in which systems of inequality *change* in response to certain macrostructural changes and, in turn, how these systems of inequality may have consequences for other institutional subsystems. From the bibliography cited it is clear that economists have been the most active contributors to comparative studies of stratification. It is also clear from the embarrassingly rich set of unvalidated propositions Treiman suggests that the time is more than ripe for persons of a more sociological frame of mind to mount comparative research. Such investigators could hardly be better advised than to follow some of Treiman's excellent suggestions.

In a major change of focus from the preceding articles, which have principally addressed themselves to the societal level of analysis, Zuckerman's discussion of stratification in American science applies the analytic apparatus of sociological theories of social inequality to describe the internal differentiation of a particular occupational group of considerable contemporary interest. Her discussion may almost be taken to be the prototypical empirical case in point to Parsons's discussion of the inherent dynamic tension between equality and inequality and the role of justification as a mechanism by which inequality in access to facilities and rewards may be defended in all complex social systems, even those stressing in their ideology the egalitarian notion of a community of peers.

Finally, we have Pullum's critical expository essay on the work of a group of mathematically oriented sociologists, who have only recently begun to appear in any number. Much of their work has been confined to more esoteric journals and difficult-to-obtain working papers than those normally "consumed" by the general sociological fraternity; and, consequently, their work has had less impact on our thinking—in this case, especially, about occupational mobility—than it deserves. While Pullum treats a number of relatively unfamiliar mathematical techniques that are not easy to comprehend in a casual reading, he has taken as his goals— and I think he has been very successful in achieving them—to inform the mathematically unsophisticated and uninitiated of developments in this field in terms that they can understand, and to provide a map to the literature for those who wish to pursue these matters in greater detail. For the initiated he has a number of critical contributions to make that they should find most useful.

As mentioned at the beginning, given the limited space available, many topics conventionally covered in discussions of social inequality had to be all too briefly alluded to or ignored entirely. We have already noted our failure to include a Marxist approach and the perspective of the radical critique of modern society as it relates to inequality, but we can comfort ourselves that these omissions are readily rectified by consulting the literature utilizing these perspectives. While some of the articles are at least implicitly relevant to public policy discussions, the accent has been on current developments in research and theory rather than on critical evaluations of specific policy alternatives. Again, given the many value positions and substantive issues involved, there are probably better forums than this journal (for example, *The Public Interest*) for discussing such matters. But there are at least three research areas about whose neglect in this collection I feel especially apologetic, as they certainly do deserve attention in this context in which we are attempting to anticipate promising developments in the seventies.

The first relates to some of the classic concerns regarding the impact of stratification position on the individual's personality and on social attitudes and behavior (cf. Lasswell, 1965, 1969). For the past twenty-five years or more, we have been refining our measurement techniques and accumulating evidence of demonstrable empirical relationships between the most diverse phenomena and various indicators of social inequality. For example, substantial relationships have been shown to exist between status position(s) and childrearing techniques (cf. Bronfenbrenner, 1958; Kohn, 1969), mental and physical well-being (cf. Hollingshead and Redlich, 1958; Srole, *et al.,* 1962; Kadushin, 1964), kinship and fertility (cf. Goode,

1962; Wrong, 1958), political attitudes and behavior (cf. Converse, 1958), class values (cf. Hyman, 1953; Kohn, 1969), and work satisfaction and values (cf. Blauner, 1960)—to mention but a few. I think that the concatenation of these accumulating research findings and recent theoretical developments places us at a point where a successful synthesis of these diverse materials might be undertaken.

The second area has to do with power phenomena as they relate to hierarchies of inequality. Parsons and Kimberly do make some highly relevant observations here, but by and large a much more extended treatment of the structuring of community and societal power systems and their interrelationships with other hierarchies of inequality (cf. Keller, 1963) would have been helpful in rounding out our discussion of inequality.

Finally, we can only note, with the exception of Siegel's article and a brief section in Parsons's article, the absence of any systematic discussion of status groups and their associated styles of life—including consumption patterns (cf. Laumann and House, 1970), daily rounds (cf. Liebow, 1967; Gans, 1962; Suttles, 1968; Lewis, 1959) and interactions across status boundaries (cf. Laumann, 1966; Shils, 1968). If anything, we enjoy an embarrassment of riches in the many excellent ethnographic accounts of the "quality of life" of people who live at different levels in the hierarchies of inequality. Indeed, it is at this level of analysis that status differentiation takes on its most "concrete" meanings. But the ideographic character of many of these studies has considerably hampered their having any cumulative contribution to our understanding the more general phenomena of status-linked behavior. We need to begin posing more general questions by which these disparate studies may gain mutual relevance. For example, we might inquire into the conditions under which we may expect the emergence and perpetuation of relatively crystallized groups possessing distinctive subcultures at some variance with the "modal" culture. In short, what are the conditions of cultural and structural pluralism and how are systems of inequality related to these conditions? Can more than superficially differentiated groups be sustained in modern societies in the face of mass means of education and communication and broadly required participation in the various institutional spheres of work, politics and community life (cf. Gordon, 1964)?

REFERENCES

Berger, Joseph, Morris Zelditch, Jr., and Bo Anderson
1966   Sociological Theories in Progress. Volume One. Boston: Houghton Mifflin Co.

Bernstein, Basil
1964   "Social class, speech systems and psycho-therapy." British Journal of Sociology 15 (March): 54–64.

Black, Max
1961 The Social Theories of Talcott Parsons. Englewood Cliffs, New Jersey: Prentice-Hall, Inc.

Blau, Peter
1964 Exchange and Power in Social Life. New York: John Wiley and Sons, Inc.

Blau, Peter, and Otis Dudley Duncan
1967 The American Occupational Structure. New York: John Wiley and Sons, Inc.

Blauner, Robert
1960 "Work satisfaction and industrial trends in modern society." In Walter Galenson and S. M. Lipset (eds.), Labor and Trade Unionism: An Interdisciplinary Reader. New York: John Wiley and Sons, Inc.

Bottomore, T. B.
1964 Elites and Society. New York: Basic Books.
1968 Classes in Modern Society. New York: Vintage Books.

Bronfenbrenner, Urie
1958 "Socialization and social class through time and space." Pp. 400–425 in E. E. Maccoby, et al. (eds.), Readings in Social Psychology. New York: Henry Holt and Co.

Converse, Philip
1958 "The shifting role of class in political attitudes and behavior." Pp. 388–399 in Eleanor Maccoby, et al. (eds.), Readings in Social Psychology. Third Edition. New York: Henry Holt and Co.

Dahrendorf, Ralf
1959 Class and Class Conflict in Industrial Society. Stanford: Stanford University Press.

Davis, Kingsley, and Wilbert E. Moore
1945 "Some principles of stratification." American Sociological Review 10 (April): 242–249.

Duncan, Otis Dudley
1966 "Path analysis: sociological examples." American Journal of Sociology 72 (July): 1–16.

Feuer, Lewis S.
1959 Basic Writings on Politics and Philosophy: Karl Marx and Friedrich Engels. Garden City, N.Y.: Doubleday and Co.

Gans, Herbert J.
1962 The Urban Villagers, Group and Class in the Life of Italian-Americans. New York: Free Press.

Goode, William J.
1962 "Marital satisfaction and instability: a cross-cultural class analysis of divorce rates." International Social Science Journal 14: 507–526.

Gordon, Milton M.
1964 Assimilation in American Life. New York: Oxford University Press.

Hollingshead, August, and Frederick C. Redlich
1958 Mental Illness and Social Class. New York: John Wiley and Sons, Inc.

Homans, George C.
1961 Social Behavior: Its Elementary Forms. New York: Harcourt, Brace and World.

Hyman, Herbert H.
1953 "The value systems of different classes: a social psychological contribution to the analysis of stratification." Pp. 426–442 in Reinhard Bendix and Seymour M. Lipset (eds.), Class, Status and Power. Glencoe, Illinois: Free Press.

Kadushin, Charles
1964   "Social class and the experience of ill health." Sociological Inquiry 34 (Winter): 67–80.

Keller, Suzanne
1963   Beyond the Ruling Class: Strategic Elites in Modern Society. New York: Random House.

Kohn, Melvin L.
1969   Class and Conformity. Homewood, Illinois: The Dorsey Press.

Lasswell, Thomas E.
1965   Class and Stratum. Boston: Houghton Mifflin Co.
1969   "Social stratification: 1964–1968." The Annals of the American Academy of Political and Social Science 384 (July): 104–134.

Laumann, Edward O.
1966   Prestige and Association in an Urban Community. Indianapolis: Bobbs-Merrill Co.
1969   "The social structure of religious and ethno-religious groups in a metropolitan community." American Sociological Review 34 (April): 182–197.

Laumann, Edward O., and James S. House
1970   "Living room styles and social attributes: the patterning of material artifacts in a modern urban community." Sociology and Social Research 54 (April): 321–342.

Lewis, Oscar
1959   Five Families. New York: Basic Books.

Lenski, Gerhard
1966   Power and Privilege: A Theory of Stratification. New York: McGraw-Hill Book Co.

Liebow, Elliot
1967   Tally's Corner. A Study of Negro Streetcorner Men. Boston: Little, Brown and Co.

Moore, Barrington, Jr.
1966   Social Origins of Dictatorship and Democracy, Lord and Peasant in the Making of the Modern World. Boston: Beacon.

Ossowski, Stanislaw
1963   Class Structure in the Social Consciousness. London: Routledge and Kegan Paul.

Parsons, Talcott
1951   The Social System. Glencoe, Illinois: Free Press.
1964   Essays in Sociological Theory. Revised Edition. New York: Free Press of Glencoe.
1966   Societies: Evolutionary and Comparative Perspectives. Englewood Cliffs, New Jersey: Prentice-Hall, Inc.

Parsons, Talcott, and Edward Shils
1951   Toward a General Theory of Action. Cambridge: Harvard University Press.

Parsons, Talcott, Edward Shils, Kaspar D. Naegele and Jesse R. Pitts
1961   Theories of Society: Foundations of Modern Sociological Theory. New York: Free Press, especially 30–79.

Petras, James, and Maurice Zeitlin
1967   "Miners and agrarian radicalism." American Sociological Review 32 (August): 578–586.

Samuelsson, Kurt
1957   Religion and Economic Action. New York: Harper Torchbooks.

Shils, Edward
1968   "Deference." Pp. 104–132 in J. A. Jackson (ed.), Social Stratification, Socio-
        logical Studies, I. Cambridge, England: Cambridge University Press.

Srole, Leo, Thomas S. Langner, Stanley T. Michael, Marvin K. Opler and Thomas
    A. C. Rennie
1962   Mental Health in the Metropolis. Volume One. New York: McGraw-Hill Book
        Co.

Stinchcombe, Arthur L.
1965   "Social structure and organizations." Pp. 142–193 in James G. March (ed.),
        Handbook of Organizations. Chicago: Rand McNally and Co.
1968   Constructing Social Theories. New York: Harcourt, Brace and World, Inc.

Suttles, Gerald, D.
1968   The Social Order of the Slum: Ethnicity and Territory in the Inner City.
        Chicago: University of Chicago Press.

Weber, Max
1958   The Protestant Ethnic and the Spirit of Capitalism. Translated by Talcott
        Parsons. New York: Charles Scribner and Sons.

Wrong, Dennis H.
1958   "Trends in class fertility in western nations." The Canadian Journal of Eco-
        nomics and Political Science 24 (May): 216–229.

Equality and Inequality in Modern Society, or Social Stratification Revisited

TALCOTT PARSONS
Harvard University

This paper attempts both to "bring up to date" the author's conception of social stratification as set forth in two previous general papers written in 1940 and 1953, and to broaden the field of consideration by giving special attention to the forces pressing toward equality in various respects, as well as the bases of inequality. The position taken is that the erosion of the legitimacy of the traditional bases of inequality has brought to a new level of prominence value-commitment to an essential equality of status of all members of modern societal communities.

Inequalities, among units of societal structure which are essential in such fields as economic productivity, authority and power, and culturally based competence, must be justified in terms of their contribution to societal functioning. The balancing of the respects in which all members of the societal community and many of its collective subunits must be held to be equal with the imperatives of inequality constitutes one of the primary foci of the problem of integration in modern society. A few suggestions about the mechanisms by which this integrative process can operate are presented.

The editor of this issue has suggested that I attempt to reconsider my "generalized analytical approach" to the theory of social stratification after a first attempt, published in 1940[1] and a second attempt published in 1953. In between, I have dealt with the topic in an essay on Marx's views of stratification (cf. Parsons, 1954: Chapter XV). Naturally problems of stratification have also been touched upon at many other points in my published work.

Both of the two earlier papers were rather directly concerned with the problem of stratification in the sense of the bases of hierarchical status or rank among societal units. This time I should like to attempt to broaden the base and speak of the problem of the nature and determinants of the balances between trends and forces making for equality and for inequality in society—for current purposes, essentially modern society.

A strong stimulus in this direction was given a few years ago by Seymour Martin Lipset when he wrote, first in *Political Man* and then, with greater elaboration, in *The First New Nation,* of the problems in American society of balancing equality and what he called "elitism" (cf. Lipset, 1960, 1963,

---

[1] Both are reprinted in Parsons (1954: Chapter XIX).

13

1966). In this connection Lipset made the suggestion that this dichotomy might be defined as a pattern variable. This suggestion did not appeal to me on grounds that it did not seem to fit in the pattern variable scheme. A suggestion of how it may relate to the scheme will, however, be made at the end of this paper.

In terms of empirically substantive significance, however, the Lipset formulation was much more appealing and has been a focus of consideration for some time. If my interpretation is correct, the concept of "elitism" in the modern, especially American, setting, refers primarily to what has been called the "achievement" complex—which as a focus of inequality has tended to replace aristocracy and other ascriptive bases during the last few generations. For purposes of the present paper, I should like to try to balance my concern with the factor of stratification as inequality, with an equivalent concern for the factor of equality.

Sociological interest has tended to focus on inequality and its forms, causes, and justifications. There has been, however, for several centuries now, a trend to the institutionalization of continually extending bases of equality. This came to an important partial culmination in the eighteenth century, which happened to be the founding period of the politically independent American variant of Western society. Such cultural influences as the conceptions of natural rights or the rights of man had a profound effect on the normative definition of the nature of the new society and received a particularly important embodiment in the Bill of Rights, which was built into the United States Constitution as the first ten amendments. The egalitarian focus of this system of "rights" was unmistakable. It was also, however, closely associated with the nearly contemporary emphases of the French Revolution on the concept of citizenship. In the United States this could, to a degree impossible in the Europe of that time, be dissociated from religious and ethnic bases of the solidarity of societal communities, since the pattern of separation of church and state and denominational pluralism in the religious sphere was already well launched. This "liberalizing" tendency was reinforced by the beginnings of the attenuation of the assumption that the new American societal community was "essentially" Anglo-Saxon. Though English remained the common language for the whole society, the ethnic and religious diversity of the elements entering the society by immigration strongly reinforced the pluralistic potentials which were present in the cultural tradition. Indeed, the Negro, recently the most difficult element to include, has, after a long and tragic history, begun to change status quite markedly in the direction of equality. Though there is a good deal of scepticism on this score, the indications of the trend point, in my judgment, to broadly successful inclusion after much further tension and struggle over a protracted period. Thus we can say that two of the most deep-seated ascriptive bases of inequality, religion and ethnicity, have lost much of their force in a society which in both respects has become notably pluralistic in composition.

There are two further contexts in which historically central foci of ascription have come to be greatly modified, namely, local and regional particularism and social class. Both present very complex problems which can only be alluded to here. With respect to the first, I may quote Daniel Bell's statement that only in the last generation or so has the United States become a "national" society (cf. Bell, 1968: 19). One of the striking phenomena has been the immense increase in geographical mobility, not only for more or less permanent residence, but also, facilitated by ease, speed and relative cheapness of travel, for more temporary purposes, both recreational and occupational as well as others. Added to this is the new technology of communication, both person-to-person varieties, and the mass media, which are directed to nonspecific "audiences."

It was first noticed that these changes have brought about an immense increase in the mobility of the factors of production in the economic sense. The most notable is labor, although there is clearly still much "localism" in labor markets.[2] An even more dramatic change has occurred with respect to capital as a factor of production, especially through the ramified system of banking, credit arrangements, and securities markets, highly dependent as these are on the new communication system.

What is true of the factors of production in the economic sense can, however, be generalized to the factors of the other primary categories of "contribution" to societal functioning from the primary subsystems, namely, collective effectiveness, community solidarity, and the integrity of maintenance of value-commitments (cf. Parsons, 1969). All of them have come to be immensely more highly "mobilized," in the sense of assessibility to "mobilization" in the more active meaning. I may illustrate with reference to the case of solidarity, which is of special concern to the present paper. As I have argued elsewhere, the two most critical "factors of solidarity," corresponding to labor and capital as factors of production, are firm policy decisions of organized collectivities, private as well as governmental, and the commitments of units of the society to "valued association," which means to the socially organized collective frameworks within which the implementation of more general value-commitments can be carried out. Here mobility of policy decisions as a factor means an increase in the "extent of the market," within which what we have called "interest-demands" may be presumed to have a reasonable chance of "influencing"—in our technical sense—the binding decisions which are necessary for effective imple-

---

[2] This is one of the several phenomena of what may perhaps be called "residual" ascriptiveness in modern societies, to which Leon Mayhew (1968) calls attention in his illuminating paper "Ascription in Modern Societies." In general I heartily subscribe to this analysis.

mentation. In spite of the importance of the hierarchy of authority in any "politically organized" society, this broadened "extent" includes a wider range of alternative sources of bindingness as well as greater influence of "constituencies" on more centralized organs of decision.

In the field of what we call "valued association," similar considerations apply. Particularly important here is the increasing pluralization of modern society so that, not only with respect to geographical location, but also on several other bases, the unit, individual or collective, has a manifold of open alternatives among the associations to which he will make commitments. A particularly salient example is the double choice, first of type of occupation, second of employing organization. Another, of perhaps equal salience, is the hard-fought freedom of choice of marriage partner.

The more general upshot is that, not only with respect to economic production, but also with respect to all the other primary categories of contribution, there has been an immense broadening of the range from which factors may be drawn to bring about the valued outputs we speak of as contributions. Put in negative terms, the most obvious source of this increased mobility of factors lies in emancipation from ascriptive restrictions which have previously been operative, among which the territorial reference has always been prominent. More positively, however, we would like to link this with the outcome of processes of differentiation by which the factors, by which we mean human actors making decisions in roles, have shifted their focus of concern from the inexorably given conditions under which they had to operate, to concern for the "meaningfulness" of the goals which they sought and the functions they could *choose* to contribute to.

This has, in turn, led to an important shift in the structure of the very important relation which Shils and others have referred to as that between center and periphery. Centralization is a very controversial issue in modern discussions and of course centrality of geographical location is only one of the relevant concrete references, but always a vital one. Increased mobility in the senses referred to inherently creates some new forces making for what we may call *concentration* of opportunity and responsibility for valued contribution, though there are also sources of a tendency to decentralization. In any case, however, the weakening of ascriptive bases of centralization changes the character of whatever "centers" survive or appear. Thus every politically organized society must have a governmental "capital" in a specific location. In very many preindustrial societies, however, there were no clear productive centers in the economic sense. The question of centralization of the foci of solidarity is highly complex. With the general process of emancipation from the more massive historic ascriptions, there has been a tendency for macrosolidarities to oscillate between religious and governmental anchorages. There is perhaps a valid sense in which the Reformation was made almost inevitable by the fact that the center of Catholicism was unalterably anchored in the city of Rome, but that the main focus of Western society, in terms of governmental power, of economic productivity and the like had, by the sixteenth century, migrated north of the Alps. On the other hand, the new level of differentiated pluralism has made possible differentiation of territorial centralities by functions. Early "nationalism" tended to favor extreme concentration—not only for the government but for the whole cultural system. Thus, for example, no other location of academic appointment in France has been closely competitive with those located in Paris. In the United States, however, both the Boston area and that of San Francisco Bay and part of the Middle West are at least competitive with, not only Washington, the seat of government, but also New York, the economic and the nonacademic cultural capital of the country.

This complicated matter of territorial concentration of functions is of course dynamically related to that which has ordinarily been called the context of "class." It has also, by and large, been the most recent primary focus of attention, especially as crystallized by the many versions and nuances of "Marxian" thought.

The thesis I should like to state as underlying the present analysis is that class in this sense represents a transitional phase in the development of the stratification systems which have become prominent in modern societies since the industrial revolution. The historically important pattern immediately preceding was that which divided a territorial population into two basic groups, the aristocracy and the "common people." We are, of course, aware of the many nuances involved, but this long remained the basic division.

The essential break in this arrangement had its roots in the fact that, since the Middle Ages, the urban sector of European society was characterized by a third group later called "bourgeois." This group has been widely held to have displaced the landed aristocracy in that, no longer land, but industrial capital became the primary controlling means of production, and the industrialization process generated a new subordinate class, the "workers" or proletariat.

Relative to the prevailing picture of early modern European society, this pattern involved two primary shifts. On the one hand, the newly dominant class had a position grounded in ownership of the newly important means of production; and, on the other, while it could be argued that the landed base of aristocratic predominance was rooted in the political power of government, of which aristocracies were an adjunct, government now came to be conceived to be dependent on the organization of the economy: it became the "executive committee of the bourgeoisie." Despite these shifts, however, two factors carried over. The first was the conception that "in the last analysis" the stratification system must be conceived as a *two*-level affair, and the second that "membership" in each of the two classes was basically determined by status of birth, as in the case of aristocracy.

Both of these constant "givens" have now been brought into question. The "ascription" of superior status to ownership of property has largely broken down in favor of a highly diversified occupational structure which no longer displays a clear division between the "controllers" and the subordinate class. This occupational structure is characterized by a fine gradation of prestige statuses with respect to which authority-power relations have come to be differentiated as one among several rationales of status-differentiation. Moreover, there is, especially perhaps through education, a far looser connection between adult position in the occupational world and status by birth than was assumed by the Marxian analysis. There has, however, remained a substantial component of ascribed status by family origin, though the "isolation" of the nuclear family has substantially reduced it, as have the other factors of mobilization just discussed.

Especially in view of the fact that modern societies generally—and the United States especially—are to a high degree "activistically" oriented in their values, this very general reduction in the ascriptive components of their social structure has opened up important new potentialities for inequality. These lie above all in two fields. First, modern society is characterized by an altogether new scale of organization, which is spreading not only in government but also through the private sector. Indeed, though with dubious correctness, "bureaucracy" is often said to be the dominant characteristic of modern society. However that may be, the prevalence of large-scale organization certainly makes for inequalities in authority and power. The second obvious potentiality is the greatly increased role of many kinds of competence, which invites the possibility of differentiating over a far wider range than, in general, was possible under simpler conditions. These factors have been institutionalized—for the individual, in the achievement complex, where achievement may involve either attaining a position of power or utilizing a special and superior competence, or both.

At the same time, the decline of ascription in certain respects weakens inherited bases of equality as well as of inequality—the decline of ethnic and religious homogeneity and of localism presenting good examples. Since the problem of equality is inherently central to the value systems of the whole of modern society, it is not surprising that a new level of intensity of concern with it has arisen in our time. Perhaps it is not too much to say that not since the later eighteenth century have defenders of various modes of social inequality been put so much on the defensive.

EQUALITY AND SOCIAL CLASS

It will be necessary, later on to spell out rather fully the contexts in which in modern society's egalitarian principles have been or are tending to become institutionalized. First, however, I should like to suggest that the most recent phase of the process has gone far enough so that there has been a shifting of burden of proof. The inequalities constituting a stratification system have previously tended to occupy the center of attention, with institutionalization of equalities regarded as manifestations of a need to curb excesses of inequality. Now the tendency is to emphasize the respects in which societal units, but especially persons, are and should be treated as equals, and to place the burden of proof not only on the explanation, but above all the justification of components of inequality. The most general principle seems clear, namely, that grounds of justification must refer to functional needs of the various action systems which are objects of analysis.

Here, however, it is essential to remember that one of the salient features of modern societies is the pluralistic character of their structures, so that, however great the concentration of attention on a society as a whole, plural social system references must always be kept in mind.

In spite of this shift of emphasis, I shall here maintain my older view that the institutionalization of stratification, or more precisely of relations of inequality of status, constitutes an essential aspect in the solution of the problem of order in social systems through the legitimation of essential inequalities; but the same holds, *pari passu,* for the institutionalization of patterns of equality. Claims to equality of status, that is, must also be legitimized, and sometimes the problem of grounding such claims becomes complicated and subtle. What I am doing is to suggest the formulation of a dual, "dialectically" structured aspect of the "problem of order" rather than, as in the earlier papers, to treat equality as the limiting case where stratificatory differences disappear. Alternatively put, all societies institutionalize some balance between equality and inequality.

We have outlined above the secular trend to the weakening of many of the historic bases of ascriptive status such as religion, ethnicity, territorial location, and class in its older senses. In general, these changes have favored the rise to prominence of collectivities and roles (organized about functional specificity and universalistic standards of selection and performance) to a paramount position in the occupational system and in most modern authority structures. Such structures are related to the problem of equality through the principle of equality of opportunity. Even here, however, the kinship system retains an important residual status in favoring ascriptive continuities from generation to generation. It is difficult to see how these can be drastically reduced from the present level without virtually eliminating the family itself.

There is thus a sense in which the prototype of the collective structures within which the functionally specific and achieved types of inequality are least admissible is the family, which occupies an interestingly ambiguous position in modern societies. The range of obligatory solidarity and hence only very specifically justified inequality, as on the basis of age, has been enormously pared down by contrast with evolutionarily earlier kinship systems, in the residential nuclear family now constituting the main unit. In spite of the necessary difference of ascribed role by generation and sex, and, somewhat less essential, birth order and interval, internally the modern family is in some sense prototypically egalitarian. Since, however, its constituent membership roles cannot be neatly fitted into any of the more instrumental specific-function structures of a modern society, the very survival of the family as a solidary unit serves as an agency of the perpetuation of some ascriptive discriminations which are in principle objectionable to a purely egalitarian ethic. This dilemma, of course, has been well known at least since Plato.

Put in pattern-variable terms, the problem arises from the facts that the family is both primarily diffuse rather than specific in function and that it is built on "quality," i.e., ascriptiveness, especially with respect to the status of children. A brief elaboration of these points may be helpful. The status of a child is less problematical in that neither his role nor his personality can, in the early years, have differentiated sufficiently to enable him to occupy other than primarily an ascribed status or to stand in functionally diffuse relations, by any standard, to his parents and siblings. The process of differentiation, with its other attendant features, is long and complex. The marriage relation is structurally quite different. It is, as Durkheim was one of the early observers to appreciate, in some respects the prototype of associational structure, as distinguished either from ascription or from hierarchical ranking. The institutionalization of the right of personal choice of marriage partner has gone very far indeed, as has the definition of husband and wife as basically equals and hence of their relationship as basically "consensual."

At the same time, for the partners, it is diffuse in the sense that, whatever other involvements the partners may have, e.g., in occupation, community affairs, etc., they are thrown back on each other in contexts both of daily living and of more ultimate personal security.[3] The fact that spouses are the almost universal primary beneficiaries of personal property arrangements emphasizes this point.

The fact that the typical marriage is expected to be complemented by parenthood and that therefore the ascriptive component comes to be heavily accented in the partners' relation to their children, in a sense skews the relationship away from the associational pattern. The recent tendency, however, has been to deemphasize the inherently hierarchical component of the generation difference within the family, and, in halting and tentative ways to try to "include" the children in the associational aspect, in ways which

---

[3] Take, for instance, the marriage vow, "for better, for worse, for richer, for poorer, in sickness and in health . . . "

accentuate the associational relation of the parents to each other. From this point of view, the good family becomes in part a training ground in the arts of participation, not only granting children, according to the maturing of their capacities, rights to participate, but training them in the responsible use of these rights (cf. Weinstein and Platt, 1969). From one point of view, even though the recent increase in emphasis on independence training and participation weakens the hold of ascriptive features of identification with parental status, from another, it may increase the status-differentiating influence of the family, in that the children of higher status parents derive special competitive advantages from their socialization, precisely in the form of capacities for more independent and more responsible action, so that their chances of maintaining or improving the parental level of status are actually improved, relative to children of less "advantaged" homes. This need not be a matter of family income level or access to the "best" schools and colleges, though it is rather highly correlated with such factors (cf. Spady, 1967). Hence the seeming paradox arises, that the ascription of children by birth to the families established by the parental marriage, accentuates the child's competitive advantage in the institutions governed by the value of equality of opportunity, rather than compensating for status disadvantages.[4]

If the above is true of the substantially "democratized" family, the question naturally arises of whether similar things are not true of other solidary groupings, the constitutive basis of which is either only partially or not at all that of kinship. Ethnic groups are the prototype of the category partially constituted by kinship relations. They, of course, often coincide with religious and "national" groups. All of these, however, are internally stratified in the normal case, so that the problems of the scope and nature of mechanisms of mobility apply within them. Between such groups there is a problem concerning the extent to which such membership has implications for status in the system of stratification. This is often highly equivocal. The status of the Negro in the United States is a particularly massive example, but even here such phenomena as the "black bourgeoisie" make it clear that ethnic status is only one of the determinants of general "class" status, even though it may be the overwhelmingly important one for large numbers (cf. Parsons, 1965).

On the other hand, there are important classes of associational groups in the constitution of which kinship is a minimal factor, if it is present at all. Thus apart from the admittedly important question of the class and ethnic composition of residential neighborhoods, school classes and youth peer

---

[4] This is a rather striking case of what Merton (1968) neatly calls the "Matthew Effect." Here, to symbolize cumulative tendencies to inequality, Merton uses the gospel aphorism "To him who hath shall be given, from him who hath not shall be taken away, even that which he hath."

groups are nonascriptive relative to the family; their composition stands in structural contrast to the family statuses of their members, and even where the families are relative status-equals, the status of the member in the group is often different from that in the family. This is one general and important area of the residual ascriptions of modern society which are the subject of Mayhew's article (cf. Mayhew, 1968; Parsons, 1959).

Membership in such groups and the status attained within them inevitably constitute ascriptive bases which affect future or current status-opportunities in other connections. Thus being in the "top ten percent" of the class in a high quality school or college substantially improves one individual's future opportunities compared to the case where another was near the bottom of an evaluative scale on either or both counts. Indeed the "better" the school or college, the more it may contribute to the Matthew effect, in that it may not only confer immediate "prestige" but also help train capacities and open opportunities which, if competently used, will improve the chances for achieving higher status than would otherwise be possible. Thus so long as the achievement complex and the related complexes of valuation of organizational effectiveness and authority and power persist, the "democratization" of the system through more rigorous institutionalization of equality of opportunity does not alone solve the problem of equality. What is true of families, schools, and peer groups is of course at least equally so of residential communities and occupational organizations.

Of the four primary historic foci of ascription that were briefly reviewed in the introductory section of this paper (religion, ethnicity, local and regional particularism, and social class), only the last, social class, was primarily focussed about the problem of inequality internal to a society. Here it was suggested that the crucial background lay in the institution of hereditary aristocracy, but that in the more recent version heredity of status through kinship was specially combined with property relations in the emerging industrial economy. In recent, non-Marxian discussions of class, the specific reference to the ownership of the means of production has virtually disappeared; concern with the distribution of wealth and of power, as well as with kinship, however, has remained.

In spite of its "oversimplification," the Marxian conception remains a very useful point of reference. It was not fully accurate, even in 1848, and has certainly become progressively less so for the principal modern societies. But what have been the principal changes? On the kinship side, the most important one has been the attenuation of lineages with their intergeneration solidarity, leading to an increased "isolation" of the nuclear family. The most important single shift has been from total or virtual "arrangement" of marriages to a situation of relatively high degree of individual freedom of marriage choice, not without ascriptive "preferences," but still allowing much more mixing across ascriptive lines than before. This in turn has been associated with the loosening of the ties of the family to the other three ascriptive contexts, namely, religious affiliation—indexed by the increase of "mixed" marriages—ethnicity, and local particularism. These more specific bases of class identification have tended to be replaced by more generalized "style of life" patterns related to income levels and access to consumers' goods.

On the "property" side, we can clearly no longer speak of a "capitalistic" propertied class which has replaced the earlier "feudal" landed class. The changes are principally of two types. One concerns the immense extent to which household income has come from occupational rather than property sources, extending upward in status terms from the proletarian wage worker to the very top of the occupational scale. This clearly leaves the problem of the relation of the income–receiver to the employing organization problematical, but it clearly cannot be simply dichotomized into the case of the classical "worker," who is simply paid by those who control the means of production, and the "owner," who, if he has a salary, essentially must be conceived to "pay himself." The second type of change is the relative dissociation of rights to property income from effective control of the means of production. Thus most of the recipients of corporate dividends have no more control of the enterprises in which they invest than do customers over those from which they buy.

The Marxian synthesis essentially asserted the *codetermination* of class status by economic *and* political factors—ownership of economic facilities giving *control,* in a political sense, of the firm as an organization. This in turn was conceived to be synthesized with the kinship system in its lineage aspect. The process of differentiation in modern society has, however, broken down this double synthesis, insofar as it existed at all, in classical nineteenth-century "capitalism." In consequence, not only has the mobility of economic and political resources been greatly enhanced, but the door has been opened to the involvement of factors other than the classical three of kinship solidarity, proprietorship, and political power in private organizations. One effect is to make it possible for other ascriptive factors to have a continued or even revived existence, in the enhanced independence of "minority" religious and ethnic solidarities, and also relative to the "microascriptions" of which Mayhew speaks. But the main macrosocial structure has moved much farther away from ascriptive foci, even that of class, than the Marxian analysis would have it.

At the same time, the "property" complex has become much more highly differentiated. Not only have the ownership component as claim to income and the political power component as right to control become differentiated from each other, but the variegated occupational system has developed a wide range of qualitatively different types. The most important new element is probably the injection, on a scale not even vaguely envisioned by Marx, of many kinds of trained competence as factors in effective occupational performance. This has established a set of links between the occupational system and that of education, especially higher education, which did not exist before. The growth of a vast range of white-collar occupations for which secondary education is prerequisite is one major consequence, but perhaps the most important is the emergence into a new prominence of the professions, dependent as these are on university level training.

Occupation rather than property having become the primary focus of household status, both through the prestige value of occupational positions and functions themselves and through the income and style of life they ground, there is neither a simple dichotomy nor a single neat hierarchical continuum in the status system—and least of all is there such a continuum hinging on ownership as distinguished from employed status. There is, of course, an hierarchical dimension to the occupational system, about which we will have something more to say; but, especially in the upper ranges, it is only one of several dimensions of differentiation. It is particularly important that there is no clear-cut break between an upper and a lower "class;" even the famous line between manual and nonmanual work has ceased to be of primary significance.[5]

In the light of these developments, we may suggest the usefulness of divorcing the concept of social class from its historic relation to both kinship and property as such; to define *class status,* for the unit of social structure, as position on the hierarchical dimension of the differentiation of the societal system; and to consider *social class* as an aggregate of such units, individual and/or collective, that in their own estimation and those of others in the society occupy positions of approximately equal status in this respect.

As we will argue later in the paper, class status and the "division of society into classes"—to use a phrase of Malthus'—represent a more or less successful resultant of mechanisms dealing with integrative problems of the society, notably those having to do with the balance between factors of equality and of inequality.

Certainly for the male individual as unit, the two primary foci of class status are occupation and kinship. The former is articulated with a variety of the other predominantly universalistic and functionally specific structures of the society, particularly the market system, with special reference to the very complex phenomena of the labor market and the structure of power and authority especially in specific-function organizations, and the educational system and other foci of the institutionalization of differences of kind and level of competence.

---

[5] It is well known that, in Communist countries, the higher nonmanual occupations, including those of industrial managers and scientists, are classified as belonging to the "intelligentsia," which is explicitly said to be part of the "working class." Of course theoretically in such societies there is no longer a "bourgeois" class.

Kinship, on the other hand, is for both the individual member and the social system, diffuse in function; it is the most important residual basis of diffuse solidarity and personal security. It, then, is articulated with the other principal bases of diffuse solidarity, which include the massive historic ones of ethnicity and religion and the relations between household and more extended kinship groupings, as well as those of residential neighborhood and, extending from this, a complex variety of solidarities associated with territorial localism, extending up to the societal community itself. Class status, for the unit, must include the whole complex of membership in diffusely solidary collectivities.

Diffuse solidarities, in this sense, constitute the structure of modern "communities." It is important to our general argument to be clear that there is no one community in a sociologically relevant sense but that a modern society is a very complex composite of differentiated and articulating— sometimes conflicting—units of community. This is one of the two primary respects in which such societies are "pluralistic." The typical individual participates not in one, but in several of them. He is, of course, a family member; but there are two typical family memberships for each individual, not one. Both his ethnic and his religious identification may be in part independent of family membership—e.g., he may "intermarry" both ethnically and religiously. In even modestly high-status neighborhoods, he probably lives in one which is "mixed" from such points of view, as well as heterogeneous by occupational roles. Even at the level of the societal community as a whole there is major variation, e.g., as to the degrees to which people have transnational affiliations, on the basis of kinship, occupation or other grounds.

The other primary respect in which modern societies are pluralistic has to do with the functionally specific roles of which occupation is prototypical. Besides occupation itself, which is, like marriage, in the normal case a one-at-a-time involvement, this pluralism has above all to do with memberships in more or less formalized voluntary associations, which, for the participating individual, have immensely varying modes and levels of significance.

In order to throw more light on the nature of the integrative problems involved in the class hierarchy of a modern society, we must first turn to the aspects of their structure in which the egalitarian emphasis is strong and indeed newly prominent in the most recent phase of development. We have linked the emergence of this phase with the weakening of certain aspects of historic ascription of status. It should, however, be clear that equality versus inequality and ascription versus achievement should be treated as independently variable. We are suggesting here not their identity, but specific connections between them, namely, that the weakening of historic ascriptions "opens the door" to new modes and forms both of equality and of inequality. Hence a new situation comes into being for defining the relations between them.

CONTEXTS OF THE INSTITUTIONALIZATION OF EQUALITY

The case of Constitutional rights provides the most convenient point of reference for raising the question of the status of the relatively "unconditional" egalitarian component of the modern status system. The conception of equality of opportunity then forms, from the egalitarian side, the most important institutional link, not between equality and inequality generally, but between equality and that set of components of the latter which could be most fully integrated with the equality context, via achievement and functionally justified authority.

Especially since the work of T. H. Marshall (1965), the "rights" component of patterns of equality which he calls "civil" has come to be seen as part of a broader complex, which above all, following Marshall, may be said to include both "political" and "social" components. To these, should, I think, be added another which may in a rather vague and residual sense, be called "cultural." Each of the four categories is at the same time a focus of the institutionalization of components of equality of status and of the legitimation of components of stratification.

The rights that are institutionalized in the legal or civil context insure basic equalities with respect to freedom of the person, speech, assembly, association, and the like. At the same time, however, they institutionalize "equal freedoms" that permit those who enjoy them to engage in actions, the consequences of which are likely to produce differences of status. Thus the freedom of religion, as based in the first amendment to the United States Constitution, legitimizes the choice of a more prestigeful religious affiliation, given that denominations will in fact vary in terms of social prestige. Of course, the same applies to other aspects of the freedom of association. In this respect, however, probably the most important "legal" complex is that of the freedom of contract. The more commercial and financial aspects of contract have of course been highly important, but perhaps particularly important to stratification has been the inclusion here of the contract of employment. With the tendency of the occupational system to move its center of gravity from statuses of proprietorship—e.g., as peasant holder, craftsman or small business man—to that of functionally specific organizations, the immediate basis of the participation of the individual has tended to become increasingly contractual. The relation of freedom of contract to the pattern of equality of opportunity is clear.

The potentials of freedom of contract for facilitating inequality should not, however, be used to minimize the importance of the egalitarian trend of the "rights" complex. Recent legal trends in fields other than civil rights strongly emphasize this.

Similar dual involvements with the problems both of equality and of the legitimation of components of stratification should be seen in the second of

Marshall's citizenship complexes, which he calls political. Historically, the central change came with an egalitarian thrust, namely, the enfranchisement of the mass of citizens through the democratic revolution. Rokkan (1960) in particular has shown how fundamental and universal, within at least the "liberal" world, has been the institutionalization of equalities in this aspect of government. That parallel developments have occurred with respect to a vast welter of private associations does not need to be stressed.

This phenomenon of course raises the question of the other side of the coin. In one respect the development of the democratic franchise, governmental or private, constituted a response to a crisis in the legitimacy of "arbitrary" authority, i.e., that based on grounds other than the explicit consent if not mandate of the governed. It has, however, also given rise to a new basis of the legitimation of inequality, namely in the authority and power of incumbents of elective office relative to that of the larger numbers on whose electoral decisions this grant of power rests.

As noted, this new legitimation of inequality of power extends to the sphere of private associations. At the same time, it is not unrelated to the legitimation of authority in the more bureaucratic aspects of modern formal organization. The most obvious case is that of governmental executive organization where the authority of elective office legitimizes appointive powers. In modern governments this, of course, becomes a very extensive phenomenon indeed.

One special type of case is the business corporation which, historically at least, has been a quasi-democratic association in its top authority, based on the votes of shares of capital rather than numbers of persons participating. Historically, of course, this is in turn a derivative of the rights of proprietorship, which in its earlier phases was neither strictly political nor strictly economic in its functional significance. In the case of the corporation, its economic functions have taken precedence over the political and thereby largely escaped the egalitarian pressures of modern political organization.

To sum up the political aspect of the citizenship complex in Marshall's sense, the focus of equality has been the democratic franchise on the principle of one member, one vote. Most large democratic associations, however, are governed on a representative basis, with elected officers acting on behalf of their constituents. The representative principle is also often combined with that of the separation of powers, as in the cases of the American federal and state constitutions.

Recently there has been a new wave of advocacy of so-called participatory democracy which, in its more extreme form, would go so far as to erase the distinction between basic membership status and elective office—"every member his own officer." A common slogan has been the importance of people coming to "control the decisions which affect their lives." Again the sheer fact of social interdependence makes this an absurdity if carried to the extreme, because if A controls all the decisions which affect his life, he *ipso facto* must control many decisions which affect the lives of others and thus deprive them of the order of control which he claims for himself. Nevertheless, the drive is clearly to extend participation well beyond the traditional limits of representative systems.

The largest scale American example has been the attempt to develop "maximum feasible participation" on the part of the "poor" concerning the administration of the programs associated with the "war on poverty" (cf. Moynihan, 1969a, 1969b). The principal targets in this case have been the welfare and secondarily educational "bureaucracies" which have had a primary responsibility to taxpayers as well as to clients and parents. In the more extreme cases there has been a direct bid of local groups to assume full control of the spending of such funds. Another major example, by no means confined to this country, has been of course the drive of student groups for more participation in academic decision-making, challenging not only the more bureaucratic component of university "administrations"—including their fiduciary boards—but also the professional prerogatives of faculties.

Again these movements are not altogether new. To take only the American case, "populist" movements were very prominent for a considerable time in our history and scored in such fields as the referendum, the recall and the popular election of judges.

It is indeed difficult to assess the limits of such movements; the history of populism would suggest that the limits for stable institutionalization are relatively narrow, though under popular pressure they may go quite far. It is, however, important to bear in mind that this participation movement concerns a complex balance among modes of what, in the analytical sense, is the political control of collective processes, and that there are at least three nonegalitarian modes which are being attacked, namely, the most obviously appropriate target, bureaucratic hierarchy, but also professional control of functions requiring special competence and, finally, the inequalities of power inherent in the institution of elective office, even though the procedures of election are thoroughly democratic. At one level the drive is to widen the scope of affairs organized in terms of the democratic association, but also beyond that, further to "democratize" the democratic association itself by reducing the powers of elected officers relative to those of the average member.

The third of Marshall's components of citizenship governed by egalitarian principles, he calls "social." It has often been said that this has proved necessary to give "substance" to the more "formal" legal and political equalities. It is of course notable that every "industrial" society has adopted more or less of the features of the so-called "welfare state." In terms of content, it comes close to the jurisdiction of the American federal department of "Health, Education and Welfare."

From our point of view there is here, as in the other contexts, a striking duality of reference. The one aspect, focussing on income level, concerns the state of economic welfare in which different sectors of the population find themselves. This includes access to health services and other conditions of welfare. The other aspect brings us back again to the opportunity complex, but with the implication that there will be inevitable differentiation among those who have equivalent opportunities at the start.

It is perhaps correct to say that, in American society at least, there has been a notable shift of concern over the last two generations, from worry about the inequities of the advantages enjoyed by the rich—today, in this context, it is much more inequality of power than of wealth which is the focus—to concern about the other end of the scale, namely the problem of poverty. It is also notable that the weight of evidence indicates that, in a generation, there has been relatively little change in the main pattern of income distribution.[6] Since the general level has been rising, the "poor" are not in any absolute sense "worse off," so that a major problem is raised as to why there has been such a wave of new concern.

As Rainwater (1969) in particular has made clear, the essential answer to the nondisappearance of the problem in the face of increasing general productivity, lies in *relative deprivation,* a view which is of particular relevance in the present context. This is to say that those groups which, for whatever reason, have incomes sufficiently below the normal level of "average" families, are unable, in a variety of ways, to participate fully in normal activities and to utilize normal symbols of self-respect. The evidence indicates that the result tends to be a withdrawal, partly by self-isolation, partly by pressure of other groups, into a "subculture of poverty" which maintains a rather unstable partial integration in the larger society. There has been an increasingly vocal and impressive body of opinion arguing that by far the most effective single remedy for this situation is a massive redistribution of economic resources to the lowest sector of the income scale.

In this connection the emphasis is on the economic factor as such, but the development of the subculture of poverty seems to indicate that the main problem is societal integration and that we are here talking about one major condition of integrating a major sector of the population into the larger community. It seems reasonable, with respect to this integration, to distinguish two analytically separate components, although they overlap and interpenetrate empirically. One may be said to be that of the "style of life," which focuses on what are usually called "consumption" standards, which are not necessarily essential elements of the conditions of developing capacities to exploit opportunities. Much of the area of dress, housing, and

---

[6] S. M. Miller points out that the economic aspect of welfare would take three components into account, namely, income, assets and services. On income distributions, a convenient source is Herman Miller (1964).

furnishings, of food habits and the like belongs in this category. The other concerns the factors of capacity and motivation to take advantage of opportunities for some kind of social mobility.

Economic underpinning is exceedingly important to both, but its provision may probably be relied on to operate more nearly automatically in the former sphere than in the latter. Probably the most important case in point here is education. Whatever may be said about the inferior quality of slum schools, in any drastic sense the "poor" cannot simply be said to have been denied access to educational opportunity. There is of course much argument on various aspects of the problem, but both the findings of the "Coleman report" (1966) and of much recent research in class-linkages in the cognitive aspect of child development seem to indicate that a genuine component of capacity is prominently involved, and that this in turn is a function of the culture of poverty (cf. Bowles, 1963; Coleman *et al.*, 1966; Kagan, 1967). Equal access to education is clearly one of the most important components of the equality of opportunity complex, helping enormously to lift those who can take advantage of it out of economic dependency and to open doors to higher levels of occupational and other success. At the same time it is more than that, not only in the negative sense that the capacities of the deprived are seriously impaired, but also in the sense that levels of education become exceedingly important conditions of the more general participations which symbolize full citizenship. Here what is meant is participation in a sense which includes shares in collective decision-making, but which is more broadly the sense of belonging and "being accepted" in many situations of social interaction. Thus, much as highbrows tend to look down on the mass media and the cultural levels of what they purvey, genuine participation in many aspects of mass media culture is essential to a sense of belonging in the society—a participation which includes politics and more specifically "cultural" concerns.

In several connections I have stressed the importance to modern society of the so-called educational revolution (cf. Parsons and Platt, forthcoming). If this emphasis is well placed, it should follow that the equality-inequality "variable" should have a cultural dimension as well as legal, political, and economic dimensions. In a society where cultural advancement is a process of fundamental importance, it is out of the question that there should be a "flat" equality of cultural level in a large population. Indeed much has been made, often with strongly aristocratic overtones, of the differences between elite and "mass" culture (cf. Ortega y Gasset, 1932; White, 1961). However justified such distinctions may be, it does not follow that there is not an equality problem in this area and that it is not structually similar to those in the political and economic spheres.

One aspect of the problem concerns the extent to which "elite" culture must be ascriptively integrated with diffuse patterns of stratification, as has conspicuously been the case in societies characterized by the strong institutionalization of aristocracy. One major modern trend in this respect has been in the direction of increasing specificity of cultural bases of status, notable perhaps in the field of the intellectual disciplines and the professions. Cultural superiority as a component of the competence essential to an occupational role *is quite different* from the cultural "refinement" of the aristocrat.

If, as seems to be the case, modern society is strongly committed, on value grounds, to the minimization of institutionalized aristocracy, an acute question is raised about the nature and problems of what is sometimes called "general education" (cf. Parsons, 1966). Here there is a problem not only of equality of "levels" but of "commonality" in the sense of transcending specializations. On the side of equality, the modern commitment to mass education clearly implies that there must be a "floor" below which only the "mentally retarded" should be allowed to fall. This floor was first set at simple literacy, but has been steadily rising. Whatever the crudity of the demographic measures of educational level, it is a cardinal fact of the society of our generation that completion of secondary education has become normative for the *whole* of the age cohort. There is a "poverty" problem in the field of education as truly as in that of income, and it is the "drop-outs" who cannot or will not complete secondary education who are becoming the core of the "educational poor."

If cultural standards are to constitute, "across the board," a criterion of position on a scale of stratification, the question of what constitutes a "level" of cultural attainment becomes a critical one. In the lower reaches the problem is relatively simple; virtually no one extols the cultural virtues of illiteracy or inability to understand simple arithmetic. The foundation clearly includes certain basic cognitive skills, and a fund of basic information. At more "advanced" levels problems clearly emerge having to do at the least with differences of competence among the ramified branches of the cognitive universe, and then with ideological and religious differences.

The broad answer is that the factor of "communality" as I have called it is above all a function of the level of generality of cultural orientation, and hence of the capacity to "subsume" differing varieties in the cultural sphere under more general categories. The ecumenical trend in religion is perhaps the most conspicuous example in a socio-cultural field, where points of view previously treated as nearly totally alien to each other have come more or less to be "included" in a single meaningful cultural system. The application of this principle to the sciences is relatively clear. Specialization has, to be sure, proceeded apace, but so has the integration of the corpus of scientific knowledge; indeed this process has begun to bridge the gap between the "natural" and the "behavioral" sciences, perhaps even of science in relation to the humanities.

Another way of putting the point is to say that we have been living in an increasingly pluralistic culture, which is intimately linked to the pluralization of the structure of modern society. In both cases, however, the differentiation which produces pluralization must be matched by corresponding integrative processes and patterns. In another idiom, the universalistic character of the more general cultural patterns has gained a certain ascendancy over the particularism of less generally significant "sectors" of the cultural universe. To me the only sensible way to define "general" education in a sense which permits progressive upgrading is in terms of participation in this process of universalistically defined generalization of the cultural tradition.

THE SYSTEM OF EQUALITY DIMENSIONS

It has thus been possible to identify four principal contexts in which the equality-inequality problem arises, and to give at least reasonable indications why, in a highly differentiated and hence pluralistic modern society, they are to significant degrees independently variable. These are the "legal," political, economic, and social and cultural contexts. They all seem to open the door to opportunity for differential achievement which can be both legitimized and differentially rewarded in various ways. We have also reviewed some of the principal ways in which conditions have been or are being institutionalized, under which such differences are regarded as legitimate.

When the four are looked at as a system, however, an important element of asymmetry appears. This lies in the fact that, while economic, political, and cultural inequalities are legitimized under the general formula of equality of opportunity—and of course other conditions such as "fair competition" and the like—the same is not true in the same way for the legal category. The old constitutional formula about "inalienable" rights seems to be appropriate here. It is significant in particular that the principle of equality in the form of nondiscrimination has been institutionalized for two fundamental "boundary conditions" of human action, both in the formula common to the fifth and fourteenth amendments to the United States Constitution. The first of these concerns the ascriptive qualities of the organism as labelled by the terms "race" and "color." Presumptively other biological fundamentals are so closely related as to fall in the same broad category, namely age and sex. The second concerns the "ultimate" boundary at the cultural end of the cybernetic scale. Here the context is that of religion, and the constitutional word is "creed," but also the provisions about the "establishment" and the "free exercise" of religion in the first amendment are central (cf. Parsons, 1966: 9ff, Freund and Ulich, 1965).

Those considerations suggest, on theoretical grounds, that the "legal" complex has, relative to the other three, pattern-maintenance functions. It has evolved in most modern societies to the point of institutionalizing the principle that there shall be a "base" in the status of citizenship, with respect to which all individual citizens stand as equals, and that these patterns of equality apply in at least three spheres, namely, the citizen's rights of participation *in* government, e.g., through the franchise, his rights *vis-a-vis* government, and, within a considerable range, his rights in contexts of private association. Here the situation is somewhat less obvious, but recent court decisions have made it quite clear that, especially *vis-a-vis* race, but also religion, the freedom to discriminate within private associational contexts is substantially restricted. It seems a fairly safe prediction that these restrictions will tend to increase rather than the reverse.

In my two previous general papers on stratification theory, I have strongly stressed the importance of values as legitimizing differences of ranking. If the present interpretation that in the legal complex we are dealing with a pattern-maintenance function is correct, I should like to suggest that this valuational emphasis applies not only, as is obvious, to the factors of differential ranking, but also to equality—that the evaluative backing of constitutional law in this case constitutes the *specification* of the general value system of the society to the level of the *normative structure of the societal community*. It amounts to saying that the modern societal community shall be "basically" a "company of equals" and hence, so far as empirically possible, legitimate inequalities shall be "won" from a base of equal opportunity and that the rewards which go to differential statuses and achievements shall be justified in terms of functional contribution to the development and welfare of the society (cf. Davis and Moore, 1945). It should be noted that this formula can legitimize some differential opportunity, through the kinship system, for the children of the more favored groups, if they can be held to sufficiently high obligations to contribute. What in effect such a qualification does is to extend the equality of opportunity pattern beyond the span of one generation; indeed it connects with the old aristocratic formula of *noblesse oblige*.[7]

In this connection it is particularly important to be clear about system-references. When I speak of the legal or civil component of the citizenship complex as having pattern-maintenance functions, I do *not* refer to the total

---

[7] Earlier societies, notably in the Western orbit, however, positively institutionalized a pattern of *diffuse* inequality through the institution of aristocracy. This seems to link up with a conception of inherent "substance," i.e., quality in pattern-variable terms. In some respects the "class" division of the Christian church was similar, namely into the "religious" and the "lay" components. The process of "elimination" of this diffuse superiority-inferiority distinction has, significantly, typically taken the form of upgrading of the status of the "common" or "lay" component rather than the reverse. See Parsons, 1968. It is probably correct to regard the persisting stigmatization of groups on grounds of "race" and "poverty" or the combination of the two, as a residuum of this more general historic division.

society but to the *societal community* as the system within and on behalf of which this component has pattern-maintenance functions. The societal community is here conceived as a primary, functionally differentiated *subsystem of a society* (cf. Parsons, 1969a: chap. 2). This is clearly to be distinguished from the pattern-maintenance subsystem of the society as a whole. The latter clearly centers in the system of institutionalized values at the general level and is in that sense especially closely related with the cultural system. The "value-premises" of the rights and obligations here regarded as both egalitarian and inalienable, should be conceived as residing in that more general value system, but the particular relevant "forms" they take, are specifications from these premises on the basis on which that aspect of value-commitments more generally have been analyzed (cf. Parsons, 1969b).

I have just argued that the equality component of the normative structure of modern society comes to focus in the legal or civil complex of citizenship with its presumption of basic equalities of rights—and correlatively of obligations. This complex is normatively grounded in the general societal value system. In a sense underlying the more specific contexts in which the equality-inequality problem arises, which have been reviewed on one level and will be discussed again presently, there are two particularly significant contexts of value-specification which go one step farther than the specification just discussed to the level of the societal community.

The first of these I shall call the *fiduciary* complex. It is grounded in the fact that one basis of inequality lies in the incapacity, for a very wide variety of reasons, of all members of a societal community to take effective responsibility for the protection and furtherance of their own rights and interests, hence there is a necessity for "entrusting" these interests to persons or groups on which such responsibility is focussed.

This principle operates most obviously in those collectivities which have responsibility for the interests of dependent persons, an excellent example being the small child, whose interests are in the first instance entrusted to his parents, but also to various other agencies. In this sense there is a fiduciary component in virtually all differentiated responsibility for societal function. The connection with the legal system is, however, particularly prominent as in the case of the courts taking formal responsibility for the administration of such matters as wardships and guardianships, various kinds of trusts and the like. Indeed we shall note that the courts of law themselves are primarily fiduciary institutions in that small groups of persons are given responsibility for very widespread interests of others. There are, however, two particularly salient and more general cases, the "fiduciary board" as a governing body in organizations, and, in a more diffuse sense, the modern professions.

What I have called the fiduciary complex has an important though complex and often ambiguous relation to the legitimizing functions of government. Indeed, there is an important sense in which the private corporation, in the modern world, has been said to constitute a "delegation" of governmental authority to private groups, as does the institution of private property itself, if we go farther back. Such a line of argument, however, depends on the view that government is the primary matrix from which a main process of differentiation occurs. It seems to me that the appropriate matrix is more the societal community than government and that in the modern phase of societal development government itself has been in process of differentiating from this more diffuse matrix, with the democratic franchise marking one main phase of that differentiation. Thus it seems sounder to regard property and the corporation on the one hand, and government on the other, as two different "branch" developments from the same evolutionary trunk. Both of them involve the institutionalization of authority and power, and hence the elements of inequality inherent in such institutionalization. Both, however, rest on a common basis of legitimation through common values, rather than the former of being legitimized by the latter. Not to understand this fact of differentiatedness may perhaps be called the "Rousseauistic fallacy."

The other component of the "fiduciary" complex which is particularly important to the modern world, and which should be looked at in the present context, is the complex of the professions. Among their basic characteristics is a level of special technical competence that must be acquired through formal training and that necessitates special mechanisms of social control in relation to the recipients of services because of the "competence gap" which makes it unlikely that the "layman" can properly evaluate the quality of such services or the credentials of those who offer them. Professional competence, in this sense, is grounded in the mastery of knowledge of one or a combination of the intellectual disciplines, though of course other factors than knowledge as such are also involved.

What I have called the "competence gap" necessitates a component of inequality in the professional complex, e.g., between physician and patient, lawyer and client, or teacher and student. At the same time, *within* the context of professional organization, in spite of differences in competence, there is a strong tendency to an egalitarian type of associationalism on the principle that a person either is or is not a member of the profession in question, or one of its subdivisions, such as a university faculty or department, and that all such members have a certain equality of status, including the democratic franchise in collective decision-making. This is the most important case where a system of occupational roles is organized on such a basis, which may be called collegial.

It is clear that, though the factor of competence makes for a critical element of inequality—with fiduciary responsibility—it also puts a premium on capacity independent of ascriptively particularistic considerations and hence enhances the general societal stress on equality of opportunity. Indeed, this is particularly important because it operates in the higher levels of the modern occupational system. While classical bureaucratic organization is also in principle governed by equality of opportunity, it is at the same time bound up with an hierarchical pattern of operating organization, much more than in the case of the professions. On the other hand the operation of large modern organizations has become so complex and technical that neither "direct democracy" nor elective office, crucial as the role especially of the latter is, can cover a very large proportion of its functioning, though the latter can form "top" control.

The "educational revolution" has brought the professional complex to an increasingly prominent place in the structure of the society, a prominence by no means confined to the academic world as such nor to the traditional "practicing" professions, but above all permeating both industry and government on a large scale and substantially modifying their patterns of organization, including stratification. It has above all created a new basis of solidarity, cross-cutting the traditional divisions between such spheres as those of "government" and "business." Hence the professional complex, as I am calling it, has the potential not only of a powerful instrumental influence in societal functioning but also as a focus of integrative mechanisms. These can operate above all through a process of balancing the necessary differentiations based on competence and authority, with patterns of equality.

Professions, like many other structurally differentiated groups, also pose problems of control. Since on some level only their members are competent to judge the competence of their fellow members, there is a built-in possibility of monopolistic practices in several contexts such as the restriction of access to membership. In the United States the medical profession, especially through the American Medical Association, has perhaps gone farthest in this direction. This would seem to be one of the inherent hazards to the "public interest" in a modern type of social organization.

Another major point concerns the relations between the "rights" complex of egalitarianism and the "political" complex. In a general institutional context clearly the former takes precedence in that such rights as the democratic franchise must be legally grounded, as we often put it, at constitutional levels. From this point of view the system of courts, and their equivalents in other systems, does not consist only in a "third branch," e.g., of the federal government, but is the fiduciary guardian of the more general legal order within which government itself operates—the institution of judicial review of acts both of the executive and the legislative branches clearly asserts this. This is a special case of the fiduciary principle, which is not, in the usual sense, democratic. Furthermore it is notable that, in most modern societies, these functions are performed by members of an institutionalized professional group which is structurally anchored in many nongovernmental ways in the society and has a long *cultural* tradition of its own which was not created by any act of government, nor of an electorate at any particular time.

The second field of specification referred to above is that of the generalized media of societal interchange, as I have called them. Earlier in the paper I have stressed the importance of the erosion of ascriptive structures and the consequent increase in the mobility of many kinds of resources and the related openness of opportunities. As first became clearly evident in the field of the economic market, the widespread openness of opportunities and extensiveness of markets, as well as high degrees of the division of labor, depended on the development of money as a medium of exchange, and beyond that, as an instrument of credit.

It has proved possible to extend the conception of a generalized medium of interchange beyond the case of money to include political power and what some of us have been calling influence and value-commitments (cf. Parsons, 1969a: chaps. 14–16).

The processes of interchange and the situations in which they occur open up greatly widened possibilities for units in the social system to pursue whatever goals and interests they may be committed to. The media themselves, however, cannot in the same sense be "managed" by unit-interests, but must in some sense become an object of fiduciary responsibility. This has become obvious in the case of money, where the monetary system is a fundamental responsibility of government and certain specialized organs of it. Similar things can be said of the constitutional aspect of the organization of political power, not only that of government, but also as institutionalized in private organizations. Such regulation seems to be necessary because it is the very process of the development of such media, and especially the mobilization of the factors of production and of collective effectiveness, which has opened up new possibilities of inequality and of "exploitation." Thus Marxian doctrine was not fortuitously associated with the maturing of the industrial revolution and its complex relations to the democratic revolution.

It is possible to say comparable things about the relation of value-commitments as a generalized medium to the institutionalization of the culturally interpenetrating pattern-maintenance systems of modern societies. Indeed one source of modern "anti-intellectualism" seems to be a sense of inferiority, and hence of being, if not "exploited"—certainly not in the strictly economic sense—"put upon" by the superiorities of those who have enjoyed superior access to cultural resources. Indeed, the educational revolution has shifted the locus of felt conflict away from the older foci, especially of economic inequality, but also of political power, in the direction of cultural inequality.

If what has just been said about the importance of money, power, and value-commitments is correct, what of the fourth, namely influence as that especially institutionalized with reference to the societal community? My suggestion is that one principal function of influence as a medium, perhaps the most important, is as a mechanism for "handling" the tensions which continually arise in a dynamic society over the balances between the egalitarian and the elitist components of the normative structure of the society and the realistic implementations of this balance. In previous discussions of influence, it has been emphasized that one of the principal functions of the use of influence lay in the "justification" of actions which ego was trying to persuade alter ego to perform; here, justification has been specifically distinguished from legitimation (cf. Parsons, 1969a).

Here it becomes particularly significant that, in normative terms, the pattern-maintenance "base" of the modern societal community is essentially egalitarian. In this perspective, seen in the stratification context, a primary function of influence is to justify functionally necessary forms of *in*equality. At the "pure" social system level, we have argued, these can be reduced to three main types namely, (1) through control of monetary assets, access to generalized economic resources; (2) through political power, access to factors of collective effectiveness; and (3) through value-commitments, access to "cultural resources." The attempt, then is to *"persuade"* the otherwise given holders of such "resources" to make them available for societally justified functional use, *even though* this allocation stands in conflict with some previously established egalitarian "right." In this respect, for example, the equal rights of members of an electorate are "sacrificed" to the cause of effectiveness by the granting of power to elected representatives. Similarly, resources controlled through monetary mechanisms are differentially allocated among claimants. But the burden of proof is shifted to the side of justifying inequalities.

Part II

THE INTERPENETRATION OF SUBSYSTEMS

It is a very important feature of the theoretical scheme we have been using here that at each of the main boundaries of a given primary system or subsystem there is a "zone of interpenetration" between the system of reference and the adjacent system. This conception may be employed here by suggesting that certain crucially important equality patterns, all three of them cases of the more general principle of equality of opportunity, can be located in these zones of interpenetration between the societal community and the other primary functional subsystems of a society.

The first of these, at the boundary *vis-a-vis* the economy, is the "classical" economic conception of the purely competitive market. This has of course been conceived in contrast with monopoly and essentially means that all participants in the operation of such an ideal type of market should have equal opportunities of access, either to the effective demand of consumers of the relevant product, or to the factors of production, or both. When, however, the reference is to pure *competition,* it is made clear that equality of *outcome* of the process is not to be expected. If, however, the competition is "fair," it is expected that differential success will be accounted for mainly by differential efficiency of the competing units, "ultimately" in "satisfying the wants" of consumers or of producing "utility." This then falls under our conception of contribution to the welfare of the societal system. The justification, in the above sense, of "free enterprise" competition thus rests in the assertion that a competitive element in economic production contributes to more efficiency than, for example, a centrally controlled socialist form of organization.[8]

This justification, however, is contingent on keeping monopolistic tendencies under control. Differential success in market operations inevitably produces, for the next stage, differential advantages in competition. If, as is the case for most economic analyses, the firm is taken as the unit entering into the competitive process, it is very unlikely that "pure" competitive equality will prevail realistically over a large share of the market system. If, on the other hand, the step is taken to the socialistic alternative, then the justification problem becomes a matter of the appropriateness of governmental machinery which, we would in general argue, cannot have the primacy of productive efficiency in the economic (but not technological) sense which a market-oriented firm can have.

Turning to the boundary *vis-a-vis* the polity, we conceive the democratic association to be a boundary structure here, which is part integrative, part political in function. The equality of membership rights, anchored especially in the "one member, one vote" principle, is primarily a constituent of the societal community, i.e., the integrative system. Other aspects of the equal rights complex are of course also involved, perhaps above all those associated with freedom of communication, so that the free play of influence can be protected.

Of course, the most conspicuous outcome of the democratic revolution has been the institutionalization of the democratic franchise in the citizenship complex. It should not be forgotten that major developments in this respect have been taking place very recently (viz, the recent U.S. Supreme

---

[8] It may of course be contended that it is not efficiency of production so much as the opportunity of the individual producer to "do his own thing" (in contemporary phrasing) which justifies competition. On this whole complex problem area, see the famous essay of Frank H. Knight (1935).

Court decisions on legislative apportionment) and that the process is probably far from being complete even in democratically "advanced" societies. Second, however, is the exceedingly important development of the same basic set of principles in the organization of many types of private association.

In various discussions of the place of the polity in societal systems, we have argued that its principal value standard is *effectiveness* of collective goal-attainment. There is an obvious tension between the equality principle in the field of participation and the functional imperative of effectiveness (cf. Parsons, 1969: chaps. 13, 14). Effectiveness in turn is a function of concentration of authority and power, not necessarily maximal, but still— where memberships are large and collective functions are both complex and urgent—an appreciable concentration. The most generally evolved institutional solution for reduction—never complete elimination—of this tension is the institution of elective office. Here of course citizens—or members of other associations—exercise their equal rights in contributing to the choice of their elected representatives, but in so doing they establish a special form of *in*equality, namely, as between office-holders and "ordinary" members. My suggestion is, in line with the above discussion, that the justification of this inequality must focus in the importance, to the collectivity of reference, of effectiveness in arriving at collective decisions—i.e., those *binding* on the collectivity—and implementing the decisions arrived at, above all through the mobilization of obligations to contribute to effective collective goal-attainment.

The incumbent of elective office, by virtue of his election, assumes a special share of responsibility, both for contributing to decision-making and for implementation. Especially on the implementation side, "he" is not often in a position to discharge this responsibility by his own action alone. This need for "help" is, in one context, the focus of the development of another major type of organization, namely the "bureaucratic." The ideal type, classically delineated by Weber, is one of an "apparatus" the participants in which are incumbents of full-time occupational roles, remunerated by money salaries, organized collectively in the interest of effective attainment of a goal or "goal-set" which is defined by *other* agencies, what Weber called the "non-bureaucratic top" of the bureaucratic organization. In modern political terms this latter tends to be focussed in elective office—hence the bureaucracy is conceived as responsible to its elected chiefs, and the latter in turn to the electorate.

In terms of the theory of stratification, of course, bureaucracy is a paradigmatic case of inequality established on nonascriptive bases. Here the primary focus of inequality is authority and power, especially the famous concept of "line authority."

The primary value-basis of the justification of inequalities in the outcome of market competition we may say lies in their function as conditions of economic efficiency, which in turn may be interpreted to mean that the more successful units in market competition are presumptively more efficient and hence contribute differentially to the implementation of the societal interest in production or productivity, or both. Such a proposition, of course, is true only under carefully defined conditions, but economic theory has gone rather far in clarifying the nature of these conditions. Similarly, the value-basis of the inequalities of power between ordinary association members and elective officials must, in strictly *political* terms, lie in the contribution of this concentration of power to collective effectiveness. Beyond this the involvement of bureaucratic "apparati" must have a similar justification. Here it is important that the same basic principles of justification apply in both the political and the economic spheres.

As a consequence of the introduction of inequalities to meet functional exigencies, in both cases it follows that certain "rights" meaningfully belonging to the "pure" egalitarian membership status in the societal community have had to be sacrificed. In the political case these would seem to center in rights which are currently often formulated as rights of "participation," or as quoted above, rights to "control the decisions which affect one's life." Our essential reference here is to the fact that the basic issue is that of striking the balance between units and collective rights and hence interests. Where the *functional* context is political, the imperative of collective effectiveness very often overrides interests in unit power and unit control, sometimes involving deciding against a unit interest in a direct conflict, but more often excluding the unit or class of units from participation in ways which avoid a confrontation of conflicting interests.

In the economic case what is sacrificed is not in the political sense power, but some kind or component of "proprietary" rights. In this connection we can call participation in the purely competitive market the case of the "fullest" proprietary rights, corresponding to associational membership participation without "delegation" of any decision-making power to elective officers, to say nothing of bureaucratic apparati—in short the ideal type of "direct democracy." In the economic case we might even say that the equivalent of elective office for the political sphere was the development of the joint-stock corporation, through which owners delegated certain of their proprietary rights to the corporation to administer on their behalf. This distinction between membership and proprietorship seems to be the basis of the justification of the "pseudo-democracy" of the corporation with its enfranchisement of monetary shares rather than members.

In both these functional contexts, the delegation of components of the rights complex is a condition of a process of differentiation by which, through "freeing" certain substructures from ascriptive involvement in the more general "matrix," and allowing or encouraging the development of specialized structures such as elective office, bureaucracy, and corporate proprietorship, far greater functional contributions to the societal system can be made in *these* subsystem terms than would be possible were the original ascriptions retained in force. At the same time, such differentiation heightens tension on the equality-inequality axis. The question arises whether integrative mechanisms have developed or are likely to develop which can sufficiently mitigate this tension.

It is notable that the economic and the political are the two paradigmatic contexts of nontraditional or nonascriptive inequality problems in modern societies. It is important here that *both,* from the perspective of the society as a social system, are subsystems which mediate crucial relations between the society and its environment and, to be technical, its environments which stand lower than it does in the cybernetic hierarchy of the primary subsystems of action in general. In the larger theoretical framework this is formulable as a problem of adaptation. This is to say that, at certain stages of societal evolution, some types of inequality are part of the price paid for high adaptive capacity. Seen in this context it is perhaps not surprising that, under the pressure of the strains produced by processes of evolutionary change, the "sacrifices" of elementary equality which are at some level justified by economic efficiency and political effectiveness, are often held to be at best unnecessary, at worst, immoral, and that there is hence a movement for the restoration or the institution of "true" equality in one or both of these respects.

Indeed, it is striking that the "myth" of a primitive equality in these respects has been exceedingly persistent throughout the history of thought about society, certainly in the Western tradition. The processes of modification of this alleged egalitarian condition are pejoratively labelled as "exploitation" or "predation," underlining the presumption that all such departures are inherently illegitimate.

On the basis of our analytical paradigm, finally, we are obligated to include a third major context of interpenetration, namely between the societal community and the pattern-maintenance system. Here the relevant version of the equality principle seems to be equality of opportunity of access to participation in *cultural* "goods." This is a conception which needs considerable elucidation. One keynote is provided by the anthropological tradition that culture should be regarded as acquired by learning processes by contrast with biological heredity. This implies that it is capable of transmission through some sort of teaching process. Another major reference is to cultural content as modes or versions of human "orientation" organized as symbolic systems of meaning through "codes." This is the basis of an exceedingly important property, namely that the transmission of culture takes place without depriving the agent of the process of control of the "content;" the success of the teacher of a language is not measured by his *loss* of control of the language in favor of his pupil. On the contrary in this sense he relinquishes nothing. He does "spend" time and effort. Contrariwise, the seller of a commodity, if successful, transfers control of the commodity to the purchaser, relinquishing it himself.

It is of course possible, through imposing barriers to communication, to restrict access to cultural content, as by keeping items of information "secret," and indeed the existence of such barriers is *one* basis of cultural inequality. More important, however, is the fact that the "mastery" of cultural content is a process of achievement, success in which requires not only situationally open opportunity, but also effort, ability and, in the most important cases, help. Hence the acquisition of culture in this sense is typically socially organized. An especially important aspect of it is the process which sociologists have come to call "socialization."

We have suggested that it seems justified to add a cultural component of the citizenship complex to Marshall's three. This in turn presumably has several layers and facets. There is a layer of truly common culture in modern societies, of which surely one of the fundamentals is language. Here it is significant both that differentiation by dialect has decreased and the difference between a standard language used by "educated" people and local dialects has decreased. It is also significant that societies with more than one language, like Canada or Belgium, undergo serious difficulties of integration on that account. On quite another level, while "denominational" levels of religion have been considerably pluralized, there does seem to be something like what, for the U.S., Bellah calls the "civic religion," which is common to "all" (cf. Bellah, 1967).

In many connections we have taken the position that strategically the most important component of culture for the social system is patterns of value which define the actor's own situation in crucial respects. Hence in the process of acquisition of culture by individuals, the internalization of value-patterns is a central aspect of socialization. It is because of this central significance of societal values that we have treated value-commitments as the generalized medium of interchange which is anchored in the pattern-maintenance subsystem of a society. The very emergence of such a medium, however, depends on the fact that the value-*system* of a society is highly complex, and not a unitary entity, which as such either is internalized by an individual or a class of them, or is not. There are variations both in "intensity" of commitment, and in selectivity of emphasis among the many different components and levels of a value-system.

In different types of society there may be many different bases of specialization in cultural matters, the base which emphasizes in religion having been particularly important. With the process of societal differentiation, however, such specialization becomes an increasingly important function and comes to be increasingly distinct from command of wealth or power.

At the same time the cultural system itself comes to be more highly differentiated, especially with the emergence, from the matrix of religion, of the arts and the sciences. Finally the institutionalization of values in the structure of the society comes to be more differentiated from their religious base. This process above all leads to the emergence of law as a "secular" cultural structure which is differentiated from direct religious prescriptions. In formal analytical terms, law constitutes, as we have said, the focus of the normative structure of the societal community and articulates, through the mechanism we have called specification, with the moral value component of the cultural system.

Differentiation of cultural concerns from others of functional significance to a society leads to increasing importance of the nature of the capacities on the basis of which the differentiated function can be effectively performed. I suggest that the central role here must be played by *competence* as a capacity to implement the values of cognitive rationality. This is to say that the cultural specialist, as distinguished, let us say from the priest in less differentiated socio-cultural systems, must be superior to nonspecialists above all in his command of the *generalized* cultural structure of his domain and thereby its relevance to more particularized problems. This generalization, and the related systematization, in the first instance has to be cognitively oriented, which is another way of emphasizing the adaptive function with reference to culture (cf. Parsons and Platt, 1968, 1970; Platt and Parsons, forthcoming).

The cognitive is only one of four primary functional categories of a cultural system, the others being expressive-symbolic, moral-evaluational and "constitutive-symbolic." Undoubtedly cognitive primacy as a basis of expert capacity in the cultural sphere is accentuated in societies the values of which lean, as do those of the United States, in the direction of instrumental activism (cf. Parsons and White, 1961). It is also accentuated as a function of high levels of differentiation and hence pluralism of societal structure.

In view of the complexity of these issues, we can here only suggest the consequences of primacies of each of the other three categories. That of the component of constitutive symbolism is, I think, the well-known case of a society which gives structural primacy to its religious orientation. A particularly striking case was that of ancient Egypt, but the case closest to our Western experience is the European Middle Ages—in another cultural tradition the high tide of Hinduism in India also fits this pattern. In the last case the basic axis of stratification became the *ritual* purity of castes and subcastes.

Dominance of the moral-evaluative component of culture seems to be involved with the phenomenon of "legalism," i.e., the establishment of a system of normative rules which, though having strong religious grounding, are relatively autonomous as the main area of implementation of the religious mandate. The classic cases here are postprophetic Judaic and Islamic societies. There is something of this in the earlier phases of ascetic Protestantism, and a persistence of such features in the more "fundamentalist" branches in later phases.

The expressive-symbolic component raises particularly complex problems. It seems to be the most difficult of all to maximize as culturally dominant for a total society because of its particularistic and short-run focus. Probably no society as a whole can be mainly a "work of art." Perhaps the closest approach is a type like that of classical China, which had primarily integrative emphases in its paramount values, but relatively slight activistic stress. Its orientation to stability and the particularistic character of its relational system then seem to have favored strong aesthetic emphases.

The more individualistic type of aesthetic concerns presents another type of problem. In the Western world the aesthetic and cognitive components have, since the time of ancient Greece, been closely linked, perhaps in a kind of "dialectic" relation with each other. There have of course been specially prominent aesthetic movements, such as that of the Renaissance, and of literature and art in the nineteenth century, but they have not gained cultural dominance in total societies.

However these complicated matters may be, we shall assume here that, in our type of society at least, cultural specialization tends to give a particularly prominent place, if not dominance, to the cognitive function. Thus our differentiated cultural system is organized more about *knowledge,* its transmission, acquisition, application, and advancement, than any other single focus (cf. Frye, 1970).

With of course many antecedents, this differentiated culture-dominated system has undergone an immensely accelerated development in what we call the educational revolution, with perhaps the greatest impact being exerted by the advent on the one hand of mass higher education, on the other of the "professional" levels of institutionally organized competence, including that in the advancement of knowledge itself, and the permeation of the whole higher occupational structure by professional components.

There is very much a problem, for modern societies, of the definition and institutionalization of a common base line for cultural level which all full members of the society can and should share. There seems to be evidence that, as suggested, this base line has been rapidly rising, as indicated above all by rising levels of educational attainment. It seems likely that the time will come when the "general education" component of higher education will be universalized and become, however redefined, both a prerogative and a requisite of full citizenship for everyone. There is also the problem of the institutionalization of access not only to the general level of education, but to opportunity for attaining levels both in specific fields and in unspecialized ways, which are well above the general (cf. Porter, 1968; Parsons, 1968a; 1968b; Ben-David, 1963–64).

However these two bases of equality are institutionally worked out, as in the economic and political cases both the differentiation and the upgrading of the culturally primary subsystems of the society lead to increased differentiation in levels of competence and resulting achievement (cf. Parsons and Platt, 1970). Hence the greater the stress on cognitive achievement, through value-commitments and through access to economic and organizational resources, the more it becomes necessary to *justify* the resulting inequalities, and to define the framework within which they, and their consequences, are felt to be justified—e.g., with respect to differential rewards.

As in the other two cases, the culturally "common man" must sacrifice here some of his egalitarian prerogative in recognizing the merits of cultural superiority. It is thus not surprising that there are new currents of what is sometimes called anti-intellectualism, and hence the idealization of a state of affairs where competence above the general level does not count—as well as derogation of the validity of claims to superior competence.

The line of justification of this category of inequalities clearly must rest first on assertions of the functional importance to the society of the institutionalization of the requisite aspects of culture, of its advancement, transmission, and application. The recognition of superiority then must be balanced by what I have referred to above as "fiduciary" responsibility. There must be institutionalized ways of assuring, with tolerable probability, that superior competence will be used in ways which are compatible with societal interests—as in the case of the medical assertion of concern for the "welfare of the patient."

If we are correct that the main center of gravity of the differentiation of that sector of the pattern-maintenance subsystem of modern society in which cultural interests have primacy is the system of higher education, it should not be surprising that the problem of the justification of inequality in matters of cultural competence should be particularly acute at the present time. Furthermore, among the classes of "laymen" in academic matters, students are particularly closely involved through their partial and somewhat equivocal membership in academic collectivities, in such ways that they are subject both to authority and to economic pressures in this relationship. This set of circumstances seems to be important in the background of the present wave of disturbances in the relations of students to universities and colleges.

THE INTEGRATIVE PROCESS

We can now take up the problem of what are the integrative processes by which, on the one hand, these three different kinds of inequality can be, at least in part, reconciled with the egalitarian components of the institutional system; and by which, on the other hand, equality and inequality can be integrated with each other. We must not forget that presumably the major part in this integration is played by institutions which are not alterable on an *ad hoc* basis, but which have evolved over long periods. They, of course, are also continually changing, only in part by conscious decision-making processes.

The more complex and pluralistic a society becomes, however, the more dependent its functioning comes to be on freedom of unit decision and on generalized mechanisms which facilitate and guide those decisions. The four generalized media of societal interchange *all* have, in their respective spheres, integrative functions. Thus it is almost obvious that without money as a medium of exchange the pluralism brought about by the economic division of labor could not be brought into a balance among the various participants in market relations, namely, consumers of myriad commodities and services, producers, employers, members of the labor force, et al. (cf. Parsons, 1969a: chaps. 14–16).

In the area where stratification is a particularly salient phenomenon, I shall however, suggest that the complex of mechanisms which centers on influence as a generalized symbolic medium of interchange is crucial in that its functions are *doubly* integrative. We have defined influence elsewhere as the *generalized* capacity to persuade in the process of social interaction. On the one hand it involves, as such, no situational sanctions such as modes of coercion or inducement. On the other hand, as symbolically generalized, its use is *not* a mobilizing of "intrinsically persuasive" particular arguments; but, in parallel with money, is rather a capacity to persuade independently of intrinsic considerations—in the monetary case the relevant property is "value in exchange," not "value in use" (cf. Parsons, 1969: chap. 15).

We have long contended that the social system, within the general framework of action, is the primary focus of the integration of cultural with "motivational" factors. In the context of action, among the cultural modalities, the normative, the moral values, for obvious reasons takes precedence (vide the "problem of order"). Among the "motivational" components of action which are "subcultural"—i.e., pertain to personality and organic systems—we are assigning precedence to the category of *affect* because of its *inter*personal integrative significance (cf. Schneider, 1968) and at the same time its "access" to the more primordial motivational components, notably the erotic at the organic level.

In analytical terms, however, both moral values and affect are extra-societal categories: each has to be "processed" before it comes to be fully "incorporated" in a social system. In the cultural case, moral values as part of the general "definition of the situation" must be conceived both to be institutionalized, as components of the structure of the social system, and *specified* to the level of norms. Both aspects are clearly involved in the conception of value-commitments as a generalized medium of the social system (cf. Parsons, 1969). Both also are conditions of the operation of influences as medium.

Affect we conceive to be a medium operating at the general level of action, parallel to the "definition of the situation" in the primarily cultural reference (cf. Parsons, forthcoming). To be "transformed" into operative significance at the level of the social system, however, it also must be "institutionalized," or "socialized." This means two primary things. The first is what we call *identification* in the sense of motivational "acceptance"—at levels of "deep" motivational "commitment"—of membership in collective systems, most notably the society itself, which essentially is what we mean by solidarity, when seen from the point of view of function for the collective system, and secondly, internalization of some kind of priority system which structures the manifold of membership expectations for the individual—and somewhat differently for collective units.

Money and power are the obvious generalized foci for the assertion of unit-interest in the outcomes of social participation, and various units, especially persons, may have different levels of "investment" in the maximization of their money and power interests. Influence, as we see it, is a mechanism which *mediates* between these unit interests—with respect to which affective "involvement" is the most important subcultural and subsocial component—and collective interests—with respect to which solidarity presents the most important normative condition, which in turn "reflects" the underlying cultural commitments entering the social system via the institutionalization of values and the specification of these values to the level of norms.[9]

As a generalized medium, we hence conceive influence to operate in the first instance as a mechanism for integrating these two levels, *namely, that of collective solidarity in the implementation of values on the one hand and that of "motivating" units, especially individuals, to participate, including "genuine" acceptance of the obligations of membership, on the other.*

In the nature of the position of cultural components in the system of action, the reference to "justification" must call on more generalized considerations, must tend toward the pattern of universalism. In contrast, the reference to mobilization of "motivation" must invoke considerations special to the nature and situation of the unit of reference, hence more particularistic considerations. Seen in these terms, at the social system level, influence is a way of reconciling these two very fundamental constituents

---

[9] The much discussed problem of the "protection of privacy" has a bearing here. From the perspective of one of an individual's fields of membership participation, e.g., in his family, his "right to privacy" is essentially the claim legitimately to prevent or curb "intrusion" stemming from the expectations generated by participation in *other* membership categories, e.g., in his occupational role.

of social systems. As the history of law amply documents, justification must continually invoke "general principles." On the other hand, "appeal to interest" must invoke considerations more special to the particular characteristics and circumstances of units or classes of them. This process of mediation may be said to define the primary function of influence as a medium.

If the social systems with which we deal were structured as monolithic "confrontations" between units—especially individuals—and "societies"— this formulation would be exhaustive. In fact, however, the most important systems are pluralistically differentiated. This fact introduces the relevance of two other functions of the influence mechanism, namely, contributing to the allocation of loyalties as among plural collective involvements by units, and to the level of responsibility to be assumed by each unit within the structure of each such collectivity.

It should, however, never be forgotten that the specification of societal values to the level of solidarity of the societal collectivity is a step in the direction of particularistic primacy from the more generally universalistic pattern of the value-system, but that at the same time the treatment of the individual societal member in the role of membership, e.g., citizenship for the societal community as a whole, involves a major "universalizing" of *his* orientations. From the point of view of the society, his identifications make him a relatively generalized resource for societal functions, which is capable of allocation among several such functions. At the same time the generalization of affect, socialized through identification, tends to make it motivationally meaningful for him to accept societal guidance in the allocation of his affective interests. At the other end, the specification of values to the societal community qualifies the purer universalism of the more general societal value system and creates a manifold within which a variety of such allocations can in our sense be justified.

It would seem to be the case, however, that the equality principle has its most important focus in the modern type of societal community at these two points. At the point of value-specification, the basic pattern of equality of membership status creates a presumption against the introduction of inequalities which are not positively functional for the system. At the point of affectively anchored interest, on the other hand, there is a presumption against the introduction of inequalities which either impose on the motivated unit the toleration of inequalities in the extra rewards of which he does not share or, contrariwise, imposes on units or classes of them, special status with respect to responsibilities, command of resources, rewards, etc., which are not shared by other members.

It thus follows that the *main* focus of the justification of inequalities should lie in the other two categories. These, it will be remembered, are, first, the differentiation of subcollectivities of the societal community in terms of their functional contributions to the societal community as a whole, and hence the development of differential prestige as a function of memberships in such subcollectivities. Thus obviously government can, for most modern societies, have special kinds of functional significance for the society as a whole. Second, within such functionally differentiated subcollectivities, participating units will have to occupy statuses, individual or collective, which are differentiated on an axis of inequality, e.g., of command of resources, of authority and power, of cultural competence, or some combination.

The most general functions of influence then are first to "combine" and in that sense integrate the considerations of justification of allocations of societal units, the resources they command and the rewards and burdens they receive, among societal functions, and with this to reconcile these justifications with their interests, not only as conceived by the user of influence, but also by the units themselves. Since influence is conceived as a medium of persuasion, this implies the reaching of some kind of consensus between persuader and persuaded with respect to the integration of justification and of interest.[10]

Within this more general framework, then, the functions of influence are secondly to bring about an allocation of subcollectivity organizations and their memberships on the one hand, of statuses and roles within them on the other, which can be said to be compatible with the "collective interest" or the demands of solidarity and at the same time with the interests of units. The same ideal standard of reaching consensus on such allocations applies here. In these areas in particular it will be necessary to justify important

---

[10] The term *justification* has been used several times in the last few paragraphs and with some frequency in other parts of this paper. It is meant here in a technical sense which is above all to be carefully distinguished from the related term legitimation. Both refer to the invoking of grounds of *normative* "authority" for a proposition or for a course of action, past or prospective. They differ in level of the generality of the grounds of normative acceptability. The most familiar example is that of law. In the American system the problem of legitimacy concerns the Constitutional level, in the broadest sense, of the legitimacy of the legal order, its general principles of "Rights" as reviewed above and the powers of government and limitations on those powers. This sense of the concept legitimation is, I think, essentially the same as Weber's usage. Justification, on the other hand, concerns the lower level of generality where the main legitimating framework is assumed. In law it involves the justification of a decision by reference to a more particularized legal doctrine, e.g., decision that publication of a confidential medical record constituted an "invasion of privacy" and that the plaintiff is therefore entitled to damages. The decision in the case is here justified by the prohibition of unwarranted invasions of privacy.

A collective system in which influence operates as a medium must be legitimized as a system, including its normative order as a whole. More particular "allocative" decisions about rights and interests *within* the system, where actual or potential conflict is involved, must be justified. The necessity for the distinction arises out of the more general distinction between pattern-maintenance and integrative functions in social systems.

inequalities which, moreover, rest on *varying* combinations of bases, such as functional importance, competence, levels of authority, etc., and to reconcile these inequalities, both with the interests of the favored, and more difficult, of those who are disadvantaged by the allocative decisions.

If influence is to be treated as a generalized medium of interchange, it must be conceived to operate through a code. We thus conceive the institution of property to be the code through which money as medium operates, and similarly authority to be the code of power. For the code which is central to influence as a medium it seems appropriate to choose a concept which has played a central role in stratification theory, namely *prestige*.

First let us suggest that, though of course it has a quantitative dimension, prestige should not be used only in an hierarchical reference. In this respect it is similar to power—thus we speak of the possession of the franchise as having power. One vote per election is only a little power, but it quite definitely *is* power. Similarly I would suggest that *any* membership status in a solidary collectivity carries prestige and hence influence, no matter how far from carrying special prerogatives not shared by other members. But of course some units, collective or individual, have higher prestige than others.

If membership status is a kind of minimal base-line for the concept of prestige, in line with our treatment of the problem of equality, then two qualifying considerations need to be introduced immediately. First, from the point of view of any given system reference, there may be those who are excluded from membership status, e.g., "aliens" relative to a national society, and they do not share in the prestige of "citizens." Similarly, the "poor" are said to be at least partly excluded (cf. Rainwater, 1969). Second, the structure of such a community is always more or less pluralistic so that different components of prestige will derive from memberships in different subcollectivities within the system—and of course also "intersecting" with it, as in the sense that some honorary societies have foreign members. Hence the prestige of a member unit, again individual or collective, is a function not of one membership status alone, but of some kind of integration of his or its plural membership statuses. In general, the higher the prestige of any of the collectivities of which he or it is a member, the more this membership contributes to his more general level of prestige. Conversely not belonging to given collectivities itself constitutes "membership" in "outgroups" whether the latter are lower in prestige or not.

The amount of influence a unit can command, and hence its level of prestige, is a function in particular of *two* sets of conditions, which need to be clearly distinguished from each other. The first, analogous to the money income of a unit of the economy, is influence deriving from interchange operations through connections of solidarity. Insofar as these operations involve implementations of values shared by others, they can establish what we have called "value-based claims to loyalty." Insofar as they involve assumption of collective responsibilities, especially in leadership capacities, they can also establish claims to reciprocal support; and insofar as they involve actual or prospective valued contributions to societal function, they can generate persuasiveness in assertion of claims to the control of the necessary resources. Here the influence controlled by the unit is an *input* from others.

The other context is that in which such units can in fact "produce" influence in a sense parallel to that in which an authentically productive unit of the economy actually "makes" money, not only in that it enhances its own money income but that it adds to the amount of money circulating in the economic system. Capacity to make influence in this sense is a function of a second set of conditions, namely command of a set of "factors of solidarity" which are analogous to the factors of production in economic theory and of course of the effective use of the factors commanded. In addition to the specification of the general value-pattern to the relevant levels of valuation of solidarity (the equivalent of "land" as an economic factor), these are value-commitments to the relevant forms of association, capacity to invoke policy-decisions binding on the relevant collectivities, and actual control of the necessary generalized resources.

Taken together, these two sets of inputs to the influence system of an acting unit can be expected to produce higher levels for the unit of reference in the relevant prestige-scale in proportion as, first, the functions of the unit in question in the system, regarded as "contributions," are highly valued. These valuations of function, however, break down into two components which it is essential to distinguish. One of these, a), is the function of the valuation of the collective unit of which the unit of reference is a "member." This may be a university of which a given scholar is a member as a faculty participant, or it may be an industry of which a given firm is a member. The other, b), is the function of the valuation of the unit of reference itself. Thus a physicist may be valued more highly than a sociologist though they are members of the same faculty, and a "blue ribbon" firm more highly than a marginal one in the same industry.

Secondly, prestige is a function of the unit's capacity to participate in an extensive "influence-market" and thereby to extend and generalize its access both to influence-income and to factors of influence as these have just been outlined. The conception of extensiveness here is consciously modelled on Adam Smith's conception of the "extent of the market." In our case it refers to the scope or range of interpenetrating solidary collectivities with which a unit has contact, to which it hence enjoys "access" through its own and others' common membership. Thus, even within its differentiated sphere, a modern academic unit is part of a highly pluralistic social system. A professor in a particular discipline, e.g., sociology, in a

modern university, has access not only to his colleagues in his own department, but to certain categories of students, to faculty colleagues in other
disciplines, to colleagues in his own discipline in other institutions, to alumni,
to "outside" groups who have an interest, as "lay" groups, in his contribution, etc. His capacity both to command an "income" of influence, and to
generate it himself is clearly a function of the extensity of this relational
nexus. The familiar distinction between the "local" and the "cosmopolitan"
is relevant here, because only cosmopolitans, with their more extensive
"contacts," can reach certain of the higher levels of prestige.

The third basic factor of prestige is access to instrumentality significant
resources, at a level cybernetically lower than the value-commitments themselves, but definitely including command of influence. This latter point is
directly parallel to the sense in which the "market position" of a firm is a
function of its access to *financial* resources as well as to nonmonetary
factors of production. Thus "funds" of influence may be available for operations analogous to investment in the economic sense.

CONCLUSION

A few crucial points can be made in conclusion which tie up the rather
involved preceding analysis. The first is that though difficult balances must
be held within complex social systems between the imperatives of equality
and those of stratification, both sets of imperatives operate in such a wide
variety of different respects and contexts that there is no guarantee that
they will cohere in a form which is functionally viable for the larger system
unless there are mechanisms which are functionally specialized in the
relevant modes of integration.

There is no simple alternative as between an egalitarian and a stratified
society, or even a question of acceptable "degrees" of stratification in general. Four patterns for the "maximization" of one mode of balance may be
noted. The first, which was more popular a generation and more ago than
now, is based on the strict application of the model of the competitive economic market. The combination of the ideal of equality of opportunity with
the justification of the inequalities generated in the competitive process
seems to provide one basis of reconciling these two opposed imperatives,
with the implication that the successful in the competition of the market
"deserve" not only such rewards as high income, but also the larger share
in control over the processes of the economy that the resulting concentration
brings about.

Interpenetrating with this there are two political models. The one with
egalitarian emphasis is that all integration on the equality-inequality axis
should occur through the pattern of the democratic association, so that the
only inequalities permitted should be the superiorities accorded to incum-

bents of elective office who are held strictly accountable to a fully democratic constituency. This is often held to be the sole basis of a principled
legitimation of inequality which would in turn make possible the justification of more particular forms of inequality.

Largely antithetical with this is the model of the centralization of inequalities by the self-conceived bearers of a higher order of value-commitments; this in turn allegedly justifies the assumption of central control and
all the other primary spheres of inequality—as exemplified in our time by
the fascist and communist dictatorships. There is an important sense in
which this pattern is the obverse of radical democratic associationalism in
that both tend to bring matters to focus on the problem of *control* of collective decisions and resources and thereby to "politicize" the integrative
process. Dictatorship in this sense is generally legitimized in terms of a
pattern I have often called "value-absolutism." The stance is that "the values
to which *we* are committed clearly take precedence, at the value level, over
any others operative in the relevant field, hence we have the legitimate right
to take control and to supress opposition." The content of the values may
be economic, as in the communist case, nationalistic-political as in that of
fascism, or religious, as in that of the early Calvinists; in our terms there
is a basic similarity of pattern.

As against all three of these "models" of integration, the kind of pluralistic society which has become dominant in the modern world is dependent
for its integration on complicated cross-relations among these different
bases of claims to equality and justification of inequality respectively. This
has certain important consequences, of which three may be noted. First,
bases of prestige, in the sense in which we have used that term, must be
functionally diffuse, i.e., a resultant of plural components rather than any
one. Thus in a professional case, competence alone is a limiting case unless
it is combined with a reputation for "integrity" in the sense of concern for
the interests affected by the use of such competence. The access to influence
which results from a position of prestige—higher than average—is thus a
function of *plural* factors in this sense.

Secondly, since we have taken the position that there is a presumption in
favor of equality of status and hence inequalities need to be specifically
justified, the problem of *accountability* has acquired a new salience. This
very old concept has had its most prominent uses in the fields first of "moral"
accountability symbolized above all in terms of accountability to a deity or
to a "moral community" legitimated at the highest level. The democratic
version of accountability to a constituency involves many familiar complica-
tions. That of competitive success in the economic sense attempts to eliminate the problem by suggesting that an automatic mechanism insures that
the successful are also the "deserving."

We suggest that the problem of accountability cannot, in a pluralistic society, be "solved" by any one of these three ways or by any combination of them. Hence, third, we suggest that a fourth focus, which has been discussed at some length above, is necessary, namely, what we have called the *fiduciary* focus. Here the term "responsibility" seems to have a rather special resonance. In this, as in so many contexts, system-references are crucial. For my present purposes, therefore, fiduciary responsibility is to be defined in terms of the social system of reference for most of this discussion, the society. In proportion as such a system is pluralistically differentiated, it becomes less meaningful to focus such responsibility in any one functional context—it is in this sense inherently "diffuse." Thus where government has come to be highly differentiated from the societal community, high governmental office has progressively less of a monopoly of fiduciary responsibility and with it, prestige.

There is here an important kind of relativity. If we take the perspective of any one primary functional context, the fiduciary component must arise from its articulations with others. Thus the socially responsible business man is one who has interests other than those in economic productivity in mind—similarly the socially responsible politician, interests other than those of effective government, to say nothing of his own power. In the academic world, assuming the primacy of cultural commitments, the socially responsible member of the profession is concerned with implementation of the relevant cultural commitments *plus* a concern for their impact on and conditioning by other factors in the society.

There was a sense in which, some centuries ago, a hereditary aristocracy could serve as the focus of fiduciary responsibility at the higher levels. This possibility has clearly been destroyed by the basic conflict of the modern egalitarian complex with the principle of heredity of status. In this structural reference it can perhaps be said that one of the greatest integrative needs of modern society is for a functional equivalent of aristocracy.

In discussing prestige and influence, we have stressed the aspect of "diffuseness." This, of course, is technically most directly evident in the range or scope of the "influence market" as a factor in prestige. Influence is both acquired in part by virtue of highly specific capacities and achievements and dependent for its genesis on such. But there seems also to be an important functional "need" for the more or less visible symbolization of prestige. This is the context often discussed under the heading of style of life or sometimes standard of living. It is often referred to in various contexts in discussions of stratification but in my opinion has not had the careful analytical attention it deserves (cf. Laumann and House, 1970).

The family household has, of course, been the commonest point of reference for such discussions, but I think it should be made particularly clear that *any* unit of a societal system employs expressive symbolism in ways which are significant to its prestige or reputation. This is equally true of "negative" styles of life where, for example, certain of the younger generation use deliberately sloppy clothing as a symbol of protest.

To cite only a few examples of nonfamilial symbolization. A laundry of my acquaintance does not get its wash any cleaner by planting attractive flower beds along the side of the building, but the customers generally "like" it. A publisher generally does not make his physical product as strictly utilitarian, from e.g., the point of view of readability, as possible, but employs book designers to make the product more "attractive." The general principles of "consumption style" hence should be worked out to include all societal units, not just family households.

A second main point needs to be made. The very ready tendency to derogate such symbolism often takes the form immortalized by Veblen in the phrase "conspicuous consumption," with the allegation that people lived in comfortable and tasteful houses, or wore attractive clothes, *in order*, for instrumental motives, to enhance their prestige. This was then held to be a dishonorable motive with no "intrinsic" connection with the "real" functions of the unit. The aspect of the problem which needs to be noted here is that it arises *wherever* generalized media of interchange are involved in human action. Thus it has often been alleged that participants in market systems, in particular businessmen, are motivated "only" by profit, politicians "only" by power, etc. Precisely insofar as influence has become differentiated out as a generalized symbolic medium, therefore, it has become tempting to allege that those who seek and use it are motivated "only" by prestige (cf. Packard, 1959). Of course it is in the nature of such a differentiated system that there is a structurally built-in interest in *both* enhancing command of the medium concerned *and* effectively performing the functions of reference. Thus ideally—though of course often not actually—the more efficient businessman gains higher profits and ideally the politician who prospectively and actually serves the public interest better gains more power. In the academic world ideally, and dare we suggest *sometimes* actually, the man who makes greater "contributions" through good research and teaching gains higher prestige. The nature and extent of the conflict between these two basic interests, i.e., in effective functional performance and in command of a generalized medium, is an *empirical* problem, not one solved by allegations that interest in the medium is "inherently" at the expense of achievement in the function.

TECHNICAL NOTE

For those readers who are concerned to follow the more technical and formal aspects of the theory of social systems as these have been presented in a rather long series of discussions, complete with diagrams, it may be worth while to attempt to fit the dichotomy equality-inequality formally into the more general scheme of paradigms. My starting point was the suggestion of Lipset that equality-inequality might be treated as a pattern variable. This is on the face of it a reasonable suggestion, but the pattern variable scheme, especially in the version presented a few years ago in "Pattern Variables Revisited" has become a rather tightly integrated paradigm, and introduction simply of an additional pair would raise questions about the whole logical structure of the scheme. An alternative, of course, would be to identify, as another pair of terms, this dichotomy with one of those already in the scheme, but this clearly will not work. Here I present, schematically, a third possibility.

I should like to start with reference to Figure 1, the general "format" of a societal, or other action system, interchange paradigm, and then Figure 2, the six sets of four interchange categories between each pair of the four primary functional subsystems for the social system case.

With reference to the format presented in Figure 1, my suggestion is that the dilemma of equality vs. inequality can be used to characterize certain aspects of *both* of the *diagonal* interchange systems, namely L-G on the one hand and I-A on the other. Two important background references are relevant to the rationale of this choice. First, it will be noted that earlier in this paper (footnote 10, p. 50) I have strongly emphasized the importance of

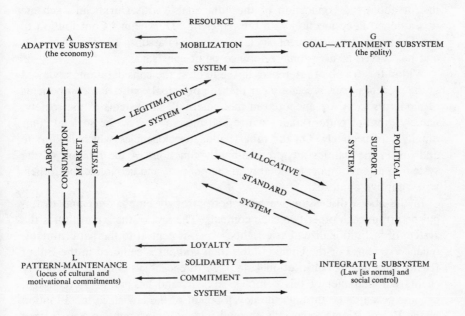

Figure 1. *Format of the Societal Interchange System*

the distinction between *legitimation* and *justification*. In Figure 2 it will be noted that these terms, quite independently of the composition of the present paper, appear, one in each of the two, namely legitimation in the formula "legitimation of authority," treated as a variant of value-commitments as a medium in L-G, and justification in the formula "grounds for justification of claims," treated as a variant of influence as a medium in I-A. The other influence component in the I-A interchange, "standards for allocation of resources" could of course readily be rephrased to include the term justification, as could "moral responsibility for collective interests" in the L-G interchange be rephrased to include the term legitimation. The inclusion of both terms in the analysis of the equality problem on the one hand, the distinction between them on the other, are certainly crucial to the general analysis.

The second background consideration concerns the relevance of these diagonals to Durkheim's famous distinction between mechanical and organic solidarity. The L-G axis concerns the relation between the system's pattern-maintenance base—especially its values—and its capacity for effective collective action in the analytically political sense, which comes very close to the "problem" of mechanical solidarity. The I-A axis, on the other hand, concerns the relation between the system's integrative norms and mechanisms and the problem of allocation of resources, including access to opportunity. The stress here is on pluralistic differentiation and the problems of maintaining solidarity among differentiated units and subsystems. The broad insight about the connection of the "diagonals" with Durkheim's scheme was attained in connection with the paper on "Durkheim's Contribution to the Theory of Integration of Social Systems" (Parsons, 1967b: chap. 1), and has served as a cardinal reference point ever since.

Within this frame of reference, in the light of the considerations reviewed in the present paper, it seems clear that the principal egalitarian components of modern society are anchored in the "internal" subsystems of the society, namely those of pattern maintenance and integration (or the societal community), respectively. On the other hand, the exigencies which legitimate and justify inequalities are predominantly functions of the relation of the system to its environments, notably in the political and economic, but otherwise adaptive contexts.

In the above discussion we have both strongly emphasized and distinguished from each other two such contexts. The first of these constitutes the system of institutionalized basic rights, which is central to the pattern-maintenance system. For the United States their content is centered in the Bill of Rights, thus having constitutional status for the legal system. The essentially egalitarian character of this complex is clear, and has, as we have noted, become accentuated through the development of the law since the adoption of the Bill of Rights, especially through judicial interpretation and further institutional amendments, but also through legislation and executive action.

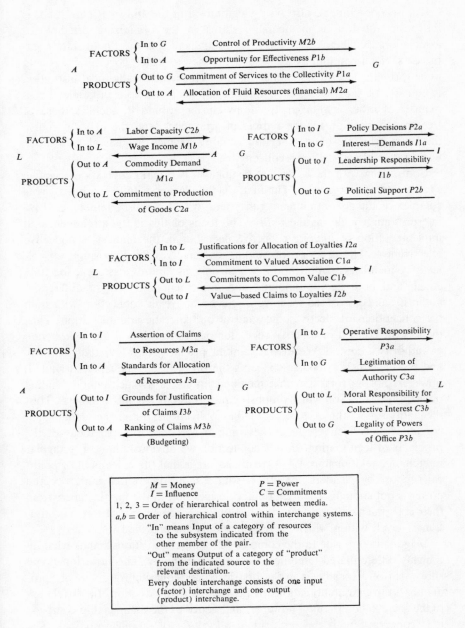

Figure 2. *The Categories of Societal Interchange**

*See Parsons, 1969b, "On the Concept of Political Power," Technical Note.

The second context, also partly legitimized in the Bill of Rights itself, is the basic equality of membership status as the organizing principle of associational collectivities. The most fundamental is the "politically organized" societal community as the constituency to which government is held to be formally accountable under the law. The symbolically focal institution is equality of the franchise on the one member-one vote principle; but a number of other egalitarian freedoms cluster around it, such as those of free speech, petition for the redress of grievances, and the like. Of course the basic principle of membership equality extends in general to a much wider range of associational collectivities.

Contrasting with these, we can distinguish two main contexts of positive sanctioning of inequalities. The first, diagonally opposite to the basic rights complex, is the goal-attainment subsystem, which it will be remembered we interpret analytically as the *polity*. The focus of this is the attainment and implementation of *binding* collective decisions in the interest of collective effectiveness. The criterion of bindingness involves the imposition on collectivity members of obligations which only in limiting cases can be fully equal; and both decision-making and implementation require differential authority and power, as we have discussed above in connection with both the conceptions of elective office and of bureaucratic administration. This, then, is the context in which Weber's famous conception of the *legitimation* of authority is central. Weber was thinking primarily of *differential* authority and power, which of course concerns the problem of inequality. It should, however, not be forgotten that membership status as such entails binding obligations, some of which impose equal burdens on all members. Thus inequality is not "the essence" of binding obligations, but is one fundamental condition of collective effectiveness and hence one principal focus of the problems of legitimation. In this connection we obviously have a triangular interchange relationship. What we are saying is that the enjoyment of political support by "leaders" or others who assume differential authority and power is not enough. Their legitimacy derives not, in the first instance, from their constituencies, but from the institutional framework, at the "constitutional" level, within which such differentials are provided for.

Diagonally opposite to the complex of membership status stands what, in a highly differentiated reference, we call the *economy*. This, as a functional subsystem of a society, is in the first instance the structural locus of "production" through combinations of the factors of production. In its relation to the societal community, however, and hence to the membership complex, it is concerned with the problem of *allocation* of mobile resources. The *standards* which regulate the allocative processes, as distinguished from the concrete processes of allocation themselves, derive in the first instance from the nature of the societal community as an association of members. Here, as we put it, on the background of the egalitarian base of membership rights, unequal allocations require *justification* in the above technical sense of that term, a process which is in some respects at least similar to that of adjudication in its legal meaning. This is to say claims have to be evaluated and implicit or explicit "judgments" rendered.

A certain focus falls on the economic aspect of allocation, that is of fluid resources which are at the disposal of one unit or class of them relative to others. This aspect of the allocative problem, however, becomes bound up with two others in particular. One concerns the allocation of capacities to utilize resources, once available. The base line in this connection has been the distribution of the genetically given components of achievement capacity. On "top of" this, however, come the factors which enter into the development of capacities—or their extinction or diminution—all along the path of the life course. Here, of course, particularly important are "socializing" influences starting with the family of orientation and the more "formal" aspects of education. Of course, fluid resource allocation constitutes one major factor in the development of capacities in these respects, hence operates again and again at different stages, e.g., through the allocation of societal resources to educational functions.

The second aspect of the allocative problem concerns what is often called the "opportunity complex." One factor here concerns the possession by units of fluid resources adequate to take advantage of available opportunities. The other, however, is less fluid, what may be called the "structure of opportunities." Thus the manifold of "places" in good institutions of higher education is not, at any given time, a simple function of the capacity of some agency to pay for them in the short run.

The upshot of this combination of capacities, resources, and opportunity structures, however, becomes the primary focus, in the structure of a modern society, of patterns of inequality in the distribution of valued achievements, whether of individuals or of collective units. The thesis is that such inequalities need to be *justified* in terms of their functional contributions to the social system.

The specific manifold of the distribution of authority and power in a complex society, including, but not confined to, the dimension of inequality in it with respect to both public and private power, requires, if it is not to be unduly disruptive of societal order, legitimation in terms of *generalized* mediation. I hence suggest that legitimation of such distribution constitutes one of the most important functions of value-commitments considered as a medium of interchange. In this context such commitments are *specified* (cf. Parsons, 1969b) to the functions of collective effectiveness—remembering the pluralistic structure of collectivities—and to various levels in the interpenetrating hierarchies of authority and power. Legitimation as a function entails denial of its positive version in cases which are judged to be incompatible with the integrity of the value-commitments in question. Value-commitments, however, at the same time have functions in other connections than the legitimation of authority, notably, that of commitment to participation in contexts of valued association and that of participation through "commitments to labor" in the instrumental functions of the society. The relationships just reviewed are schematically set forth in Figure 3.

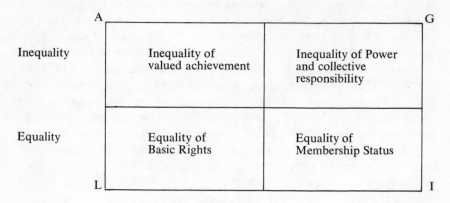

Figure 3

When the relationships are set forth in this way the question is urgently posed of why I have stressed the two diagonal relationships, why not all six equally? There certainly are important relations, for example, between equality of membership status and inequalities of power and authority—a theme discussed above in connection with the institution of elective office in democratic systems. Similar things can be said about the other three interchange relations between primary subsystems.

My general rationale for selecting the diagonals, in addition to the considerations advanced above with respect to the distinction between negative and positive sanctions and between mechanical and organic solidarity, concerns a formal consideration which was prominent for a time in considering the general interchange paradigm, but which was not even included in the version which appeared in the Technical Note to the paper on Power (Parsons, 1969b, Figure 3) which is reproduced here as Figure 2. This is that the distinctions between the three pairs of interchange sets—namely, in the figures, horizontal, vertical, and diagonal respectively—had functional significance. Specifically, the horizontal interchanges had mainly adaptive significance, the vertical ones, goal-attaining, and the diagonals, integrative significance.

This is not the place to go fully into the rationale for this set as a whole. For the horizontal let me suggest only by illustration that the A-G interchange is the primary locus of the famous means-end relation. That fluid resources are means to goal-attainment goes without saying, but the relation is reciprocal, namely through the fact that political effectiveness (political in the analytical sense) is an essential means to efficient economic production. Hence the importance of the firm as political entity. In the vertical context, for households attainment of an adequate standard of living is certainly a major goal, but so for the economy is the securing of adequate labor capacity as a factor of production.

It seems clear that, on the basis of the considerations reviewed in the present paper, the problem of equality and inequality is, as Lipset has often emphasized, of particularly clear integrative significance. This becomes evident in the first instance because, probably increasingly as ascriptive inequalities have lessened in significance, inequalities which are neither legitimized nor justified, in the technical senses in which we have used these terms, are likely to be especially disruptive of the social systems in which they actually or allegedly occur. The ubiquity with which aggrieved groups use such terms as "oppression" and "exploitation" surely strongly suggests this.

One of the virtues of working with a formal paradigm is that the existence of "empty cells" or other formal components to which no special significance is attributed, raises questions which keep nagging for answers. If the equality-inequality problem is to be especially related to the internal-external axis of the social system paradigm, the question naturally arises of whether another dilemma of comparable integrative significance should be related to the other, the instrumental-consummatory axis, again with special reference to its relation to the diagonal interchanges. Precisely in the course of working out the formal position of the equality-inequality problem as just presented, it gradually became clear that there was indeed another such dilemma which could be treated in a comparable way, namely the very old and much discussed one of freedom vs. constraint (for the latter, I deliberately select the term used by Durkheim).

That there has been a major dilemma in this area is probably obvious, as is the fact that it has taken rather definite theoretical shapes at least since Rousseau (cf. Weinstein and Platt, 1969). Starting then with the assumption that these terms refer to genuine dilemmas of the human condition and that there is a certain coherence among their various meanings, it at least makes sense to try to fit them into a system paradigm. If, then, the instrumental-consummatory axis is chosen as a place to try the fit, the first question is, which of the two concepts in the paradigm fits which of the "horns" of the dilemma? It will be remembered that initially it was by no means obvious in common sense terms that equality has, as we have put it, its "anchorage" in the *internal* subsystems of the social system.

My suggestion here is that the key conception would be the relation of the freedom-constraint dilemma to the *temporal* axis of action systems, including the social system. If this is done, then it seems clear that the ongoing process of action is in one aspect always a matter of the foreclosing of previously open alternatives. To be sure a process of expenditure of funds may be balanced by an equal flow of income, but the *particular* funds commanded in the T_1 initial period, when they have been spent, are no longer available in T_2.

This seems to mean that, from the point of view of action, moving forward in time always means the sacrifice of some freedoms and the corresponding acceptance of some new constraints. This basic relation is of course balanced by what in some sense is a "feed-back" phenomenon, namely that all along the temporal course of action processes, man-imposed constraints have to be "set up" (the ways in which this occurs are of course highly problematical) so that acting units or systems are never concretely as "free" as they "theoretically" might be, and, conversely, remaining freedoms have to be protected at later stages. To use a familiar illustration, much has rightly been made of the genetic plasticity of the human child—he presumably has the potential for example, of learning *any* language as his "native" tongue, but he cannot learn them all. Because he is socialized in a particular speech-community, his initial "freedom" is "constrained" by the linguistic institutions of that country. In principle the same things can be said of all other institutions, none of us is free to opt for *any* of the alternatives which have in some sense been intrinsically open to lines of human social, personal, or cultural development; we are always constrained by what is sometimes called the "history" of the particular action systems in which we are involved. This does not mean that they cannot change or be changed, but it does mean that processes of change must *start* from the state of affairs which exists at the time in that system, and in an abstract sense that is always "constraining."

Since we are here dealing with the analysis of social systems, we assume that concretely there is *never* either absolute freedom or absolute constraint, but that what we are presenting is a paradigm of components of both, in a sense in which *all* concrete states of affairs are combinatorial resultants. Under this assumption we therefore identify freedom with the instrumental side of the paradigm, constraint with the consummatory.

As in the case of equality-inequality, and in many other connections, it is likely to be necessary to carry analytical "breakdown" at least to the point of subdividing each of the main categories into two, on the basis of their relation to the other main axis of the system, the internal-external. For reasons of historical comprehensibility, it is probably better to begin with the constraint side. Here a striking fact is that the external-internal axis links very directly with Durkheim's last two of three meanings of the very crucial concept of constraint (French *contraint,* which fortunately presents no problem of translation). The first, constraint by the objective existence of situational "reality" need not concern us here. The second, however, was constraint by the imposition of sanctions through human decision—the criminal law, and the exposure to legal penalties being for Durkheim clearly the paradigmatic case. This clearly fits in our general "political" context. It seems appropriate to designate it as "constraint by collective decisions and sanctions," assuming that the *authority* of the individual decider or imposer of sanctions is collective in origin.

Durkheim's third mode of constraint, our second, he called "constraint by moral authority." The moral authority of collectivities was thus felt to operate through the internalization of their normative orders in the personalities of their members. The sense in which such a member was not "free" to act in violation of these norms came to be that he accepted their legitimacy or justification and that violation would expose him to "internal" sanctions—if an individual is the actor of reference, guilt or shame. Durkheim conceived this type of constraint as definitely bound to solidary collectivities, so I have phrased it as "constraint by moral authority in a community."

The "freedom" side of the dichotomy again can be seen to involve two subtypes. One is the mode of freedom which is relatively independent of immediate normative controls in terms of the values of the social system. This connects with economic considerations and long-standing ideas about the "rational pursuit of self-interest"—the self of reference of course may be a business firm, rather than an individual. Hence an appropriate designation seems to be "freedom to pursue unit interest."

The other subtype concerns freedoms with respect to involvement in the normative obligations and commitments which are institutionalized in the system. In my paper on the "Concept of Value-Commitments" (Parsons, 1968b), I have stressed the importance of the combination of integrity of commitment to a value-pattern at high levels of generality, and freedom of the unit, individual or collective, to *allocate* his more specified commitments among functions, levels of specification and along the line collectivities and types of contribution. We may hence speak of "freedom of units to allocate commitments." This suggested ordering of the freedom-constraint dilemma is formalized in Figure 4.

Considerations very similar to those discussed in relation to the equality-inequality dilemma serve to justify the emphasis on the diagonal relationships in Figure 4. I suggest that the L-G axis in this respect constitutes a kind of superordinate locus of "social control" in the relevant respects, in that, if the system is to be a *social* system, the unit freedom to allocate commitments at will must be constrained by concern for *collective* goals and interests. Furthermore, the "hard-nosed" suggestion is made, that if collective interests are to be sufficiently protected, it is not possible to rely *only* on moral authority, however fundamental that may be—and I personally think it is—but that *collectively binding* decisions, with the appropriate (including negative) sanctions are also functionally necessary.

These "hard" necessities of the L-G syndrome do not, however, exclude an equal importance being accorded to the other diagonal relation, namely between freedom to pursue unit interests on the one hand and constraint by moral authority on the other. In terms of the dual conceptions of the "division of labor," that of economic differentiation of function associated especially with the name of Adam Smith, and that of differentiation of the societal community (or pluralism) associated with that of Durkheim, this is on the one hand a sphere of especially increased "autonomy" on the part of units. *At the same time,* it is essential to recognize that such autonomy cannot be generalized in a social system without the complementary set of constraints which are "ideally" those of moral rather than coercively political authority.

A Freedom	Constraint G
Freedom to pursue unit interests	Constraint by collective decisions and sanctions
Freedom of units to allocate commitments	Constraint by moral authority in community
L	I

Figure 4

Finally, when the *two* dilemma components are systematically related, in the above way, the question must arise of what the nature of the *resultant* patterns may be. The origin of such resultants is in the nature of the case clearly complex. It involves a "balancing" not only of equality and inequality and of freedom and constraint, but of both in relation to each other and in relation to the other exigencies of a social system.

I suggest that there is indeed a pattern of distinction among such resultants and that this pattern makes it possible to "locate" in terms of analytical "paradigming" certain syndromes which for a long time have appeared to be very important, but the exact theoretical status of which has not hitherto been clear. An important principle of this last paradigm to be presented is that, presumably because of the importance of feed-back considerations, each category involves a component of its "dialectical" opposite. Thus in the cell in which "justified or legitimized inequalities" have been located, a "secondary" principle of equality appears, and in the cells in which constraints constitute the keynote, special institutionalized freedoms appear. The same holds *mutatis mutandis* for the obverse relations. These resultants are presented in Figure 5.

A	Freedom	Constraint	G
Inequality	Equality of opportunity for achievement	Equal Protection of the Laws	
Equality	Fiduciary Responsibility (moral authority)	Institutionalized Individualism (class prestige)	
L			I

Figure 5. *Resultant Patterns of the Balancing of Legitimized and Justified Equalities and Inequalities* and *Freedoms and Constraints*

Perhaps the least problematical is the A-Cell. In a modern society the justification of inequalities of achievement, and of course of the rewards which are in some sense inseparable from them as *social* phenomena, is dependent on equality of *opportunity* to attempt the kind of achievement in question. Here of course it is fundamental, first that the reference is to *unit* achievements and second that units are "free" to attempt such achievements, but not "forced" to do so. Finally, it is inherent in this syndrome that there should be a competitive aspect of the relational system.

The G-Cell combines inequality and constraint. In a society such as our own, where both equality and freedom are not only highly valued but in certain respects "insisted upon," this is empirically perhaps the most problematical case. Theoretically, however, the *legitimation* of the inequalities and the constraints in question demands that there should be "balancing" guarantees of equality and protections of freedom. My suggestion is that the great Constitutional principle of *equal protection of the laws* comes very close to formulating these conditions. It may be interpreted to mean that, on the one hand binding collective action shall not infringe the "basic rights" of units of the social system, and that units of the requisite categories are basically equal in these rights—notably, of course, individuals. On the other hand, such action shall not unnecessarily abridge freedoms—which are part of "basic rights"—either at the level of pursuit of interests, or that of allocation of commitments.

The I-Cell resultant seems to present a combinatorial synthesis of the two variables in that, on the one hand, it asserts the basic importance of equality of membership status, but at the same time makes allowance for the inequalities which will result from achievement motives protected by equality of opportunity. On the other hand, this implies acceptance of the constraints by moral authority implied in membership in a community—which is pluralistically differentiated—which rests for its integration on the institutionalization of basically moral values. This is the syndrome which I, and a number of associates, have for some years been calling that of "institutionalized individualism," a concept of which the immediate intellectual ancestor was clearly Durkheim. It is indeed the spelling out of the conception of organic solidarity to a special conception of a balance, at the integrative core of social systems, between freedom and constraint on the one hand, equality and inequality on the other.

There seems to be a special set of implications of this balance for the theory of social stratification. First I would suggest that the more organic solidarity, the more the legitimacy of political inequalities is likely to be challenged, in the first instance in favor of equality of membership status. The repercussions of this may well strengthen claims to equality of opportunity, but may also activate claims to freedoms in the area of basic rights.

However these complex dynamic relations may work out in particular cases, this seems to be the focal center of social stratification, under modern conditions especially, but probably more broadly. In the body of the paper, I have used the concept of prestige as the primary institutional code of influence systems, corresponding to authority in the political context and property in the economic. Prestige is in the first instance an aspect of diffuse status, going beyond the specificity of particular capacities, achievements or powers or, for that matter, particular specified value-commitments. Inequality of prestige is in the first instance a function of the relation of cases to the institutionalized standards of justification, interrelated as these are with standards of legitimation. Institutionalized stratification then is a scale of relative prestige among units in the structure of the social system of reference. Such a scale is of course possible only if there are institutional mechanisms which render qualitatively diverse components comparable. This is, in general, precisely what the generalized media of interchange, as used by actors of course, in fact do. In this sense all of them perform integrative functions, but influence is the integrative medium in a double sense, in that it develops a higher order integration of the integrations already accomplished by the other three. Only when this has worked out according to the standard we have called "consensus" (Parsons, 1969c), can we speak of an acceptable *generalized* prestige status of a societal unit.

Because of the trend of modern societies toward a high level of the institutionalization of freedoms, such a prestige scale must, so far as the location of particular units or classes of them is concerned, be highly fluid.

The L-Cell in Figure 5, finally, provides a theoretically meaningful location for another major concern of the body of this paper, namely the *fiduciary* complex. Here, in a sense parallel to that in which equality of membership status is balanced in the resultant syndrome by inequalities of prestige among units, so equality of basic rights is balanced by inequalities of responsibility, though all members bear some fiduciary responsibility. The inequality component has been illustrated by the professional case. By virtue of his special competence, which in the nature of the case cannot be equally shared by "laymen" relative to his profession, notably of course his clients, but also others, the professional bears a special responsibility for the legitimate and justified use of that competence. In particular, we have made *integrity* a criterion, on a par with competence itself, of institutionalized professional status. This means integrity of commitment to the relevant values which are in principle shared by professional and laity in the case of the sphere of competence. In the academic world, for example, a crucial value is what we call cognitive rationality, which, however, must be fitted into a broader and more general value system. The academic professional has a special responsibility, by virtue of his competence both for the implementation of this specified value, and for its "fit" in the broader value system from which it constitutes a specification.

These interpretations of the suggested content of Figure 5 perhaps show why, in a social system, accountability *only* to the wishes of a democratic constituency, *or* to the discipline of the market, *or* to formally enforceable law, cannot suffice for the institutionalization of responsibility in the functioning of social systems generally. There must also be a sphere in which the responsibility is not to any identifiable specific social agency or category of them but to the actor's own "conscience" in the sense of his commitment to the values he accepts and to their implementation. His action will of course be evaluated by others, hence the immense importance of value-consensus for the stability of a social system.

I have suggested that the stability of fiduciary responsibility is to be to a very high degree a function of the actor's capacity to command moral authority, the more so the more stratified in the relevant respects such assumptions of responsibility become.

REFERENCES

Bell, Daniel (ed.)
1968   Towards the Year 2000: Work in Progress. Boston: Houghton Mifflin. P. 19.
Bellah, R. N.
1967   "Civil religion in America." Daedalus (Winter): 1–21.

Ben-David, J.
1963–64 "Professions in the class system of present day societies: a trend report and bibliography." Current Sociology 12:247–330.

Bowles, F.
1963 Access to Higher Education. New York: Columbia University Press.

Coleman, J., *et al.*
1966 Equality of Educational Opportunity. Washington, D.C.: U.S. Office of Education.

Davis, K., and W. E. Moore
1945 "Some principles of stratification." American Sociological Review 10, No. 2: 242–249.

Freund, F., and Ulich
1965 Religion in the Public School. Cambridge, Mass.: Harvard University Press.

Frye, Northrop
1970 "The critical path: an essay on the social context of literary criticism." Daedalus (Spring).

Jencks, C., and D. Riesman
1968 The Academic Revolution. Garden City, New York: Doubleday.

Kagan, J. (ed.)
1967 Creativity and Learning. Boston: Houghton Mifflin.

Knight, F. H.
1935 "The ethics of competition." in Ethics of Competition. New York: Harper.

Laumann, Edward O., and James S. House
1970 "Living room styles and social attributes: the patterning of material artifacts in a modern urban community." Sociology and Social Research 54 (April) (in press).

Lipset, Seymour M.
1960 Political Man. Garden City, N.Y.: Doubleday.
1963 The First New Nation. New York: Basic Books.
1966 "Value patterns, class and the democratic polity." Pp. 161–171, in R. Bendix and S. Lipset (eds.), Class, Status and Power. New York: The Free Press.

Marshall, T. H.
1965 Class, Citizenship and Social Development. Garden City, New York: Anchor Books.

Mayhew, Leon
1968 "Ascription in modern societies." Sociological Inquiry (Spring): 105–120.

Merton, Robert
1968 "The Matthew Effect in science." Science 159, No. 3810 (January): 56–63.

Miller, Herman
1964 Rich Man, Poor Man. New York: Signet Books.

Moynihan, Daniel P.
1969a On Understanding Poverty. New York: Basic Books.
1969b Maximum Feasible Misunderstanding. New York: The Free Press.

Ortega y Gassett, J.
1932 The Revolt of the Masses. New York: Norton.

Packard, V.
1959 The Status Seekers. New York: David McKay.

Parsons, Talcott
1954 Essays in Sociological Theory. New York: The Free Press.

1959   "The school class as a social system." Harvard Educational Review 29, No. 4 (Fall): 297–318.
1965   "Full citizenship for the Negro American? a sociological problem." Daedalus (Fall): 1009–1054.
1966a Societies: Evolutionary and Comparative Perspectives. Englewood Cliffs, N.J.: Prentice-Hall.
1966b "Youth behavior and values." in E. Landy and A. Kroll (eds.), Needs and Influencing Forces. Cambridge, Mass.: Harvard Graduate School of Education.
1967a "Pattern variables revisited." in Sociological Theory and Modern Society. New York: The Free Press.
1967b "Durkheim's contribution to the theory of integration of social systems." Sociological Theory and Modern Society. New York: The Free Press.
1968a "Professions." in David Sills (ed.), The International Encyclopedia of the Social Sciences. New York: Macmillan Company and The Free Press. 12:536–547.
1968b "The academic system: a sociologist's view." The Public Interest 13 (Fall): 173–197.
1968c "The problem of polarization on the axis of color." in John H. Franklin (ed.), Color and Race. Boston, Mass.: Houghton Mifflin.
1969a Politics and Social Structure. New York: The Free Press.
1969b "On the concept of influence"; "On the concept of political power"; "On the concept of value commitments." in Politics and Social Structure. New York: The Free Press.
       forthcoming "Some problems of general theory in sociology." in J. McKinney and E. Tiryakian (eds.), Theoretical Sociology: Perspectives and Developments. New York: Appleton-Century-Crofts.

Parsons, Talcott, R. Freed Bales, and Edward Shils
1953   Working Papers in the Theory of Action. New York: The Free Press.

Parsons, T., and G. M. Platt
1968   "Considerations on the American academic system." Minerva VI, No. 4 (Summer): 497–523.
       forthcoming "Decision-making in the academic system: influence and power exchange." in Sheldon Messinger and Carlos Kruytbosch (eds.), The State of the University: Authority and Change. Beverly Hills, California: Sage Publications.
       forthcoming "Higher education, changing socialization, and contemporary student dissent." in Matilda Riley, et al. (eds.), Aging and Society. New York: The Russell Sage Foundation.

Parsons, T., and W. White
1961   "The link between character and society." in Lipset and L. Lowenthal (eds.), Culture and Social Character. New York: The Free Press.

Porter, J.
1968   "The future of upward mobility." American Sociological Review 33, No. 1: 5–19.

Rainwater, Lee
1969   "The problem of lower-class culture and poverty war strategy." in Moynihan (ed.), On Understanding Poverty. New York: Basic Books.

Rokkan, Stein
1960   "Citizen participation in political life." International Social Science Journal 12.

Schneider, D.
1968   American Kinship: A Cultural Approach. Englewood Cliffs, New Jersey: Prentice-Hall.

Spady, W.
1967   "Educational mobility and access: growth and paradoxes." American Journal of Sociology 73, No. 3 (November): 273–286.

Weber, Max
1946   "Politics as a vocation." in H. Gerth and C. Wright Mills (eds.), Essays in Sociology. New York: Oxford University Press.

Weinstein, F., and G. M. Platt
1969   The Wish to Be Free. Berkeley: University of California Press.

White, Winston
1961   Beyond Conformity. New York: The Free Press.

Willey, R. J.
1969   "Taking the post office out of politics." The Public Interest 15:57–71.

The Emergence and Stabilization of Stratification in Simple and Complex Social Systems

JAMES C. KIMBERLY
Emory University

Work on the emergence and stabilization of stratification in small groups is reviewed. The work on emergence points to three basic conditions underlying the development of stratification in small groups and raises the question as to what mechanism substitutes for some of these conditions in larger systems. Several theories are shown to offer possible solutions. The work on stabilization raises questions as to the nature of the social-psychological processes involved. The relevance of various reinforcement and cognitive consistency theories is considered. Finally, a number of theories concerning the ways stability may be achieved in small groups and larger systems are considered.

In this paper we shall consider how stratification emerges and stabilizes in simple and complex social systems. A considerable amount of work has been done on these processes in simple systems. One of the main purposes of this paper will be to attempt to develop some of the implications of this work for complex systems.

A simple system is defined as one in which contact among members is primarily of a face-to-face character. A complex system is defined as one in which contact is primarily of an indirect character. In complex systems, contact is primarily through intermediaries or mass media. In terms of concrete systems, small groups are simple systems, and organizations, communities, and societies are complex systems.[1]

In simple systems, members have much knowledge about one another and the system. They also tend to agree about the system. In complex systems, the reverse is true. Members have little knowledge about one another and the system. They also tend to disagree about the system.

For our purposes, the aspects of individuals about which degree of knowledge is important are skills and motivations. The aspects of systems about which degree of knowledge and agreement are important are goals and norms, positions, performances relative to positions, and criteria for evaluating positions and performances. These will be discussed in greater detail later in the paper.

---

[1] For similar distinctions see Homans's discussion of the institutional and subinstitutional (1961: chap. 18) and Blau's treatment of value consensus as a medium of social transactions (1964: chap. 10).

Because of the large amount of work considered in the paper, the focus is necessarily conceptual and theoretical. However, every effort has been made to indicate locations of reviews and discussions of empirical work.

THE EMERGENCE OF STRATIFICATION: ATTEMPTS TO FORMULATE FUNDAMENTAL EXPLANATIONS

In this section we shall present first some attempts to explain the emergence of stratification in small groups. Then we shall consider the question of how the explanations advanced for such groups may operate in larger systems such as organizations, communities, and societies.

Explanations at the level of the small group. An early attempt to formulate a fundamental explanation of stratification in small groups appears in Homans's *The Human Group* (1950:121–127, 138–149). In this work Homans treats stratification as a consequence of conformity to group norms. Specifically, he holds that the greater a member's conformity to norms, the higher his rank. In his more recent *Social Behavior* (1961:chap. 8), Homans puts this proposition into exchange terms. Specifically, he holds that persons give social approval (the general base of rank) for conformity.

In *Social Behavior* Homans goes further, however, than just putting his conformity-rank proposition into exchange terms. In *The Human Group* he was primarily concerned with norms which are applicable to all members of a group (see the discussion of the norms of the bank-wiring room, 1950:79). In *Social Behavior* he recognizes that conformity to such norms is generally within the skill of all members of the group and, therefore, not very valuable. It is only when conformity is to norms which are within the skill of only one or a few members that it becomes valuable enough to bring about a high degree of social approval and esteem (social approval of the group as a whole and the general base of status)[2] (1961:145–149). Thus, Homans suggests that it is conformity to norms which do not apply to all members of the group that brings about stratification. As he puts it, conformity must be both valuable and scarce (in terms of the number of persons who can supply it) before it results in high status (1961:162–163).[3]

This later treatment by Homans points to the need for a more precise conceptualization of the normative structure of systems. The author has suggested in several works (Kimberly, 1966:214–216; 1967:172–174; in

---

[2] Throughout this paper the term status is used in the sense of evaluation or prestige. In order to articulate certain sections of the paper with the work of specific authors, the terms social approval, esteem, and respect are used synonymously with status.

[3] For a discussion of empirical studies which bear on this explanation, see Homans (1961:153–162).

press:section entitled, "Basic Concepts") that it is important to distinguish between norms which apply to all members of a system and norms which apply to only some. It is argued that the former define activities which require no more skill than that possessed by the least able member of the system. Thus, the degree to which members conform to these norms is held to reflect differences in motivation to participate in the system. It is also argued that the latter define activities which require various amounts of skill. Thus, the degree to which members conform to these norms is held to reflect differences in skill or motivation, or both.

In relating the normative structure to individual members of the system, the author (Kimberly, in press, section entitled, "Basic Concepts") views norms which do not apply to all members of the system as grouped into sets which apply to different individuals (cf. Bates, 1956:314). The term "position" is used to refer to such sets.

Homans completes his account of the emergence of stratification in *Social Behavior* (1961:chap. 14) with a treatment of the emergence of authority, which he defines as the amount of influence which one exerts relative to others. Authority differences are seen as paralleling status differences. They emerge, according to Homans, because the social approval given for a valuable and scarce activity is not exchange *in kind* and, hence, can never be sufficient payment for the activity. The granting of compliance completes the debt to the high status person (1961:297–298).[4]

A second early attempt to formulate a fundamental explanation of stratification appears in Bales's *Interaction Process Analysis* (1950:chap. 5). In this work Bales views stratification as a consequence of increasing difficulty in the group's adapting to the demands of the environment. He holds that as functional problems (instrumental, adaptive, integrative, or expressive) become more pressing, strains are created toward the definition of more specific positions. These are defined in terms of particular persons who are given responsibility for solving specific problems. This, in turn, leads to the emergence of a status structure based on the felt importance of the different positions. It also leads to the emergence of differentiated resource and reward structures and a differentiated and centralized control (authority) structure, all of which are also based on the felt importance of the different positions.

This account of the emergence of stratification is somewhat similar to that of Homans. The idea that problems become more pressing or difficult to solve and, hence, certain positions more important, corresponds to Homans's concept of the value aspect of an activity. In Bales's terms, the felt importance of a position increases as the problem toward which it is

---

[4] For a review of empirical studies which demonstrate the relationship of esteem and authority, see Homans (1961:288–293).

directed becomes more difficult to solve. This might be called *the demand aspect of stratification*. The idea that positions develop around particular persons who are given responsibility for solving specific problems corresponds to Homans's concept of scarcity. The implication is that only certain persons are capable of solving certain problems. This might be referred to as the *supply aspect of stratification*.

Thibaut and Kelley in *The Social Psychology of Groups* (1959:chap. 7) offer an explanation of stratification that is in some ways like Homans's and Bales's, but in other ways quite different. These authors begin with power, not status. They view power as resulting from the fact that persons are dependent on one another. Some are more dependent than others because persons have differential abilities to affect one another's outcomes. Outcomes are defined as rewards and costs incurred in behavioral sequences performed during interaction. Behavioral sequences are viewed as sets of specific motor and verbal acts that exhibit various degrees of sequential organization directed toward attainment of various end states (1959:10–13). In assigning values for dependence on outcomes, Thibaut and Kelley assume that outcomes presently being obtained are better than those available in other relationships. Otherwise, the interactions in which the outcomes are received would not occur. Put another way, various individuals' best available alternatives define the zero points on their scales of dependence on outcomes (1959:100–101). Within this framework, power differentials are defined simply in terms of net differences in their abilities to affect the values of other individuals' outcomes.

The concept of dependence is clearly implicit in the accounts of stratification presented by Homans and Bales. In Homans's work, it appears in terms of the scarcity of persons to perform valuable activities. In Bales's work, it appears in terms of the idea that only certain persons can fill certain positions which are essential to the solution of problems facing the system. What Thibaut and Kelley have done is to define· dependence somewhat more precisely by viewing scarcity in terms of persons' best available alternatives.

Thibaut and Kelley's treatment of status is, however, quite different from those of Homans and Bales. Basically, they hold that status emerges when persons with similar realms or ranges of power compare outcomes. Persons with the best outcomes have the highest status and vice versa (1959:chap. 12). This idea has important implications for the stabilization of stratification and will be considered in greater detail later in the paper.

Emerson (1962) treats power in much the way Thibaut and Kelly do. He holds that dependence and power exist whenever one person aspires to a goal which is facilitated by the actions of another. Emerson focuses on power differentials. He argues that persons attempt to equalize power differences, and he defines a number of ways in which this may be accomplished. Only one of these relates directly to stratification. This is a process in which status is exchanged for power.

According to Emerson, the giving of approval or status to another whose power is greater than one's own reduces the power difference which existed prior to the granting of status. This occurs because granting status makes the recipient dependent on the giver for status, and this increases the power of the grantor. Because power differences are reduced by increasing status differences, the power and status structures of systems do not parallel one another. This idea also has important implications for the stabilization of stratification and will be considered in greater detail later in the paper.

In *Exchange and Power in Social Life* (1964:chap. 5), Blau pulls together many of the ideas of the previous theorists. He also modifies and suggests alternatives to certain of their ideas. Like Thibaut and Kelley and Emerson, he sees dependence as the base of power. Like Homans, he sees both status and power as rewards for valuable and scarce services. However, he differs from Homans in that he holds that the regular rendering of services makes the recipient more dependent over time because he comes to expect them. Thus, failure to render them becomes a punishment (1964: 115–118). In this way he introduces expectation processes into the demand aspects of stratification. This is clearly a move in the direction of putting demand into a more normative context. From this perspective the need for services is not simply a function of difficulty of goal attainment. Rather, it is a function of this plus what past successes in goal attainment have provided in the way of rewards. It is not simply a question of goal attainment, but goal attainment at a given level (cf. Thibaut and Kelley's concept of comparison level, 1959:21–23).

With regard to the question of why power emerges from the process in which status is exchanged for service, Blau suggests an alternative to the explanation offered by Homans. As indicated earlier, Homans holds that compliance results because the low status person cannot return to the high status person rewards in kind, that is, valuable and scarce services. Blau holds that compliance results because social approval (referred to by Blau as respect) depreciates over time. This occurs because the giving of it increasingly marks the giver as inferior (1964:126–129). Thus, he suggests something similar to a satiation process but with the decrement in value coming not from gratification of the recipient but from the reduction of the status of the grantor.[5]

In a recent paper the author (Kimberly, in press: section entitled, "Dimensions of Stratification") has formulated a general conceptualization

---

[5] Satiation generally (viewed in terms of the marginal utility of services) is dealt with by Blau in terms of gratification of the recipient. He uses this concept, however, to account for the leveling off of exchange, not the emergence of power (see 1964: 90–91).

and explanation of stratification in simple systems which incorporates a number of the ideas considered above. Positions and performances are viewed as structural bases of status. Since positions consist of norms which do not apply to everyone in the system, they are viewed as defining the division of labor. The individual attributes of skill and motivation are viewed as additional bases of status. It is held that position, performance, skill, and motivation as a set are evaluated in terms of the availability of persons able to fill the set (cf. Emerson, 1962:40).

Norms which apply to everyone in a system are not viewed as a structural base of status. However, it is held that the degree of conformity to such norms is a base of status. This latter base is viewed as the one base on which all members of the system can be equal.

Power as well as status is viewed as related to these bases. It is argued that it is created potentially by the dependencies which are created by the division of labor. It is further argued that it becomes actualized because the incumbents of some positions are more easily replaced than others. An easily replaced incumbent is held to have little power even though other incumbents depend upon him to carry out certain essential activities. The converse, of course, is held to be true of incumbents who can be replaced only with great difficulty.

Economic rewards are viewed as rewards for performance in a position. Thus, it is held that their allocation parallels the evaluation of positions and performances (Kimberly, in press: section entitled, "Processes of Rank Equilibration").

The author's treatment of stratification involves certain basic assumptions which should be spelled out here. First, all of the processes involved in the emergence of status, power, and economic reward hierarchies in a system do not occur unless there is commitment on the part of system members to the system goal. Without this, positions, performances, and the attributes of skill and motivation would not be of significance to system members, and evaluation, compliance, and differential allocation of economic rewards would not occur. This view is similar to Parsons's view that stratification is the ranking of units in a system in accordance with the standards of a common value system (1953:93–94). It is also similar to Cartwright's and Zander's conception of group goals as sources of evaluation (1960:366–367).

Second, in order for the processes involved in the emergence of stratification to occur, system members must have knowledge of the bases of stratification (positions, performances, skills, motivation, and conformity). In the absence of such knowledge, evaluations and willingness to grant compliance and economic rewards would tend to vary from member to member.

Third and finally, in order for the processes in question to occur, there must be consensus on the criteria to be used in evaluating the bases of stratification. A lack of such consensus would produce the same type of variation a lack of knowledge produces.

Explanations at the level of larger systems. In small groups the unit of analysis is the individual or the individual in a position. A basic question in considering larger systems is whether or not a similar unit of analysis can be employed. Studies of occupational stratification (see, for example, the summary papers of Hodge and his colleagues, 1966a, 1966b) have generally viewed stratification in terms of individuals in positions. Community studies, on the other hand, have generally viewed it in terms of social classes conceived as groups of people who interact selectively on the basis of shared status characteristics (see Gordon, 1958, chaps. 3–5, for a review of community studies).[6]

In our view, the unit of analysis in larger systems should be something larger than the individual in a position. It is not necessary that this be a social class in the full sense of that term as defined above. It might be, for example, departments in an organization, neighborhoods in a community, or regions in a society. It might also be occupational strata which cut across such units. The basic criteria would appear to be: (1) some consensus about the bases of stratification, and (2) some sense of differences among units coupled with some sense of similarity within units with regard to these bases.

The Davis-Moore theory of stratification (1966:47–53) takes as the unit of analysis the individual in a position. However, it lends itself readily to analyses employing strata as the unit of analysis. Basically, this theory holds that a position is evaluated and rewarded in terms of two criteria: availability of persons to fill the position and functional importance. When the number of persons who are able and willing to fill the position decreases, its evaluation and rewards increase, given constancy of functional importance. The functional importance of a position is defined in terms of its uniqueness and the extent to which other positions are dependent on it. The uniqueness criterion refers to the degree to which there are no other positions which can fulfill the activities the position entails. The dependence criterion apparently refers to the degree to which the activities of the position involve control or coordination (or both) of other positions (see Davis and Moore, 1966:n. 48).

The author (Kimberly, 1966:216–217; 1967:173) has criticized the concept of functional importance. The criticism involves a detailed analysis of the criteria of uniqueness and dependence. With regard to the former criterion, it is pointed out that when a system's activities are divided among positions in such a way that no two positions entail the same activities, every

---

[6] For attempts to bring the occupational and social class perspectives together, see Laumann (1966) and Eisenstadt (1968).

position in the system is unique. However, this does not mean that positions are equal in difficulty and, consequently, equal with regard to the availability of persons to fill them. Thus, the criterion of uniqueness may be simply another way of talking about scarcity of personnel.

With regard to the latter criterion, it is pointed out that when a system's activities are divided among positions in the way just described, every position in the system is dependent upon every other. This analysis is carried out in terms of productive positions, but it would seem to be capable of being extended to include control and coordination positions.[7] In terms of the analysis, such positions would be considered simply as involving additional things that must be done if the goal of the system is to be achieved. If all of the positions in the system are necessary to goal attainment, differential evaluation and rewards would not be based on dependence, but on how easily people in the various positions can be replaced (cf. Kimberly, in press: section entitled, "Dimensions of Stratification"). Thus, the criterion of dependence also may be simply another way of talking about scarcity of personnel.[8]

In summary, the Davis-Moore theory of stratification stripped of the concept of functional importance appears to be primarily a demand-supply model (cf. Simpson, 1956) very similar to the models advanced by Homans and Blau. However, the Davis-Moore theory is supposed to account for societal stratification whereas the other two theories are not. Homans is explicit about the fact that his model does not apply to larger systems (1961:152), and Blau makes a specific attempt to modify his basic model so as to make it apply to larger systems (1964:chap. 10). We shall consider Blau's modification later in this section.

The basic problem in using the Davis-Moore theory to account for stratification in larger systems is that it assumes knowledge concerning the difficulty of positions and availability of persons qualified for them as well as consensus on criteria for assessing difficulty and qualifications. The author (Kimberly, in press:section entitled "Effects of Increasing System Ranks on Stratification of System Members") has pointed out that in larger systems there is apt to be less of these kinds of knowledge and consensus. A number of theorists have presented possible solutions to the problem this poses.[9]

---

[7] For a recent attempt to formulate relations between certain features of supervisory positions and interdependence of activities within a system, see Stinchcombe and Harris (1969:13–23).

[8] For experimental and quasi-experimental studies bearing on possible modifications of the Davis-Moore theory, see Miller and Hamblin (1963) and Burnstein, Moulton, and Liberty (1963).

[9] For some suggestions concerning ways in which the Davis-Moore theory might be empirically tested, see Stinchcombe (1963).

Parsons (1953:108–109) points out that there are serious limitations to the mechanism of direct evaluation. One limitation is the level of competence necessary for adequate judgment. Essentially this is the question of how the judgment of those who are competent to make evaluations in given instances is brought to bear and generalized throughout the system.[10] Another limitation is that there simply may not exist sufficient knowledge to establish clear and definitive criteria of evaluation. A third limitation is that the phenomena being evaluated may not be comparable. This concerns the problem of establishing an underlying scale of evaluation.

Parsons advances a number of ideas concerning how these problems are solved. One is that possessions, because of the way they are consumed, symbolize status differences. This is, of course, why "style of life" is so important in stratification analyses (1953:105). In modern societies, possessions are allocated primarily through the mechanism of money. Parsons sees the public communication system in modern societies as a second mechanism whereby symbols of status are allocated. It is "reputation" that is distributed in this process (1953:109).

Blau (1964:chap. 10) offers a somewhat different solution to the problem of knowledge concerning positions and consensus on criteria of evaluation in larger systems. He views common values of various types as media which expand the compass of social interaction through both space and time. Crucial to the analysis of values in relation to stratification is Parsons and Shils's distinction between particularism and universalism (1951:82). The differentiating criterion is whether or not standards governing interaction are dependent or independent of the relationships between actors' status characteristics. Universalistic standards are independent of such characteristics. They are media of social exchange and stratification.

According to Blau, exchange in large systems is indirect in the sense that it occurs between the collectivity and the individual rather than between individuals. In organizations, for example, members are rewarded for contributions by the organization rather than by other members, even though it may be these other members who are most benefited by the contributions of the members in question (1964:255–263). The crucial problem of such exchange is that of a generally valid standard for comparing different contributions. For such a standard to exist in a large system, there must be universal agreement on a standard of value in terms of which diverse contributions can be compared. Universalistic values serve as such standards (1964:268–270).[11]

---

[10] This problem is the focus of a book on organizations in modern societies. See Thompson (1961).

[11] Parsons, of course, also deals with the role of common values in stratification (1953:97–103). However, this is at the level of functional substructures. The problem of knowledge occurs for him at the level of positions (1953:108–109).

A third solution to the problem of knowledge and consensus in larger systems is the theory of status characteristics and expectation states developed by Berger *et al.* (1966). This theory was formulated to account for the repeated finding that the external status characteristics of the members of a task group determine the distribution of power and prestige within the group. For example, studies of jury deliberations have shown that sex and occupational status are associated with choices of jury foremen, initiation of interaction, and influence.[12] External status characteristics are defined as having states which are differentially evaluated. They are associated with other specific traits, for example, mathematical and verbal ability, and other general traits, for example, general ability and morality. Because of the latter property, they are referred to as diffuse status characteristics.

According to these theorists, diffuse status characteristics are activated in situations in which: (1) persons are required to act together to complete a task at which they desire to succeed; (2) a specific status characteristic is believed to be instrumental to such success; but (3) persons do not know which state of the specific characteristic to assign to one another; and (4) they see only one social basis, the diffuse status characteristic, with regard to which they differ. Given such conditions, there is pressure on the persons to assign states of the specific characteristic in accordance with the possession of states of the diffuse characteristic. In the jury example mentioned above, ability as a foreman (specific characteristic) was assigned in accordance with occupational status (diffuse characteristic). The social-psychological base of this theory is, of course, balance theory (Heider, 1946; 1958, chap. 7). In the absence of knowledge to the contrary, assignment of states of the specific status characteristic in any manner other than in accordance with the diffuse status characteristic would create an imbalanced cognitive structure.

Although this theory was developed in the context of small groups, we think it is more applicable to large than to small systems. Our reason for thinking this is, of course, that it involves the condition that knowledge of the distribution of specific status characteristics among persons must be lacking before diffuse status characteristics are activated. A lack of knowledge of the distribution of specific status characteristics is much more likely to exist in large than in small systems.

In the present state of knowledge, it is difficult to assess these possible solutions to the problem of knowledge and consensus in larger systems. Parsons's ideas suggest that a lack of knowledge may lead to emphasis upon the economic reward dimension because it is a major base of "style

---

12 For a summary of empirical studies relevant to the theory, see Berger *et al.* (1966:30–31). For recent experimental support of the theory, see Moore (1968, 1969).

of life" which symbolizes status. How power enters into this process is not completely clear. Parsons suggests that it is involved in that it is a source of control of possessions which can then be used for symbolizing status (1953:109). These ideas lead directly to the question of types of relations among dimensions of stratification. This problem is considered in the next section.

Blau's ideas give us some conception of the kind of values that permit the stratification of larger systems. This raises questions as to the conditions under which such values, namely, universalistic ones, will be stressed and as to the consequences this will have for the stratification structure. As we shall see in the next section, stress on universalistic values appears to lead to certain kinds of relations among the dimensions of stratification while stress on the opposite, namely, particularistic values, appears to lead to certain other kinds of relations among the dimensions.

The theory formulated by Berger *et al.* suggests that individuals tend to develop generalized identities which are operative in each new group or system they enter. Eisenstadt (1968: especially 68–70), working at the level of societal analysis, has recently advanced a very similar point of view. This raises questions as to what characteristics tend to coalesce into such identities and as to why, once formed, they are taken as indicative of generalized ability or skill (see the discussion of diffuse status characteristics by Berger *et al.,* 1966:31–34, especially, 33).

In concluding this section, we should note that we have considered only a limited number of treatments of stratification in larger systems. These were selected because they seem to provide suggestions as to how the theories of emergence of stratification at the level of small groups can be extended to larger systems. The failure to discuss a given theory of stratification in larger systems in no way reflects on the importance of that theory. It simply reflects the fact that we have found it difficult to relate it in any fairly specific way to small group research.[13] The linking of such theories and small group research should be a focus of future research.

STABILITY OF THE STRATIFICATION STRUCTURE: ATTEMPTS TO FORMULATE FUNDAMENTAL EXPLANATIONS

In this section we shall follow the same procedure as in the previous one. We shall first present some attempts to explain the stability of the stratifica-

---

[13] Lenski's theory of power and privilege (1966) is perhaps the most notable example. This theory deals with such variables as level of technology; demographic, political, and productive patterns of organization; level of productivity and size of economic surplus; military participation ratio; degree of constitutionalism; and nature of the societal distributive system.

tion structure in small groups. Then we shall consider the question of how the explanations advanced for such groups may operate in larger systems.

Explanations at the level of the small group. Chronologically, attempts to account for the stability of the stratification structure in small groups have followed rather than preceded attempts to account for this type of stability in larger systems. Thus, we shall be considering explanations in an order reverse to that in which they were developed.

In a recent work, Adams (1965) reviews the research relevant to the problem of just distribution of various kinds of rewards. Since all three of the stratification dimensions considered above—status, power, and economic rewards—are from one perspective hierarchies of rewards, this work is of basic relevance to the problem at hand. If status, power, or economic rewards are not justly allocated among the units—be they individuals, groups, or strata—making up a system, we can expect the stratification structure to be unstable in the sense that there will be constant attempts to change the amount of status, power, or economic rewards that one or more units receive.[14] Stability, then, as we shall use the term, refers to the tendency for each of the units of a system to receive, over an extended period of time, constant amounts of status, power, and economic rewards.[15]

Adams traces the social psychology of just distribution of rewards to the work on relative deprivation. He argues—and correctly, we think—that a review of the experimental literature in this area (1965:268–272) leads to the following conclusions.[16] First, the dissatisfaction associated with relative deprivation results from felt injustice, rather than directly from relative deprivation. Second, what is just is based upon strong expectations. Third, a comparative process is inherent in development of expectations and the perception of injustice. Fourth, and finally, felt injustice is a response to a discrepancy between what is perceived to be and what is perceived should be.

Thibaut and Kelley (1959:21–23) present a concept which is similar to these conclusions. This is the concept of comparison level, which they

---

[14] It should be pointed out that it is the amount of status, power, or economic rewards a unit receives relative to what other units receive, not the absolute amount it receives, that is important. This derives from the fact that ranks on the dimensions of stratification are significant primarily in terms of comparison with other units.

It should also be noted that instability may be either intradimensional or interdimensional. If the former, it involves an unjust distribution of a *specific type* of status, power, or economic rewards. If the latter, it involves an unjust distribution of *overall* status, power, or economic rewards.

[15] This assumes, of course, that the units do not change in ways that will affect what they consider to be just amounts of status, power, and economic rewards.

[16] For another review of empirical studies of relative deprivation and a discussion of their relation to just distribution of rewards, see Pettigrew (1967:261–273).

define as the standard against which an individual evaluates the attractiveness of a given relationship. Attractiveness is a function of how close the outcomes, that is, the rewards and costs, of the relationship are to what the individual feels he deserves. The comparison level is based on all outcomes known to the individual. It is viewed as some modal or average value of such outcomes, each of which is weighted by its salience.

The author (Kimberly, 1962:23–29; 1966:217–220; 1967:176–177) has used this concept in formulating a social psychology of status inconsistency. In terms of the conceptualization of the structure of stratification presented earlier (see pp. 77–79, above), it is argued that an individual's comparison level is determined by his skill. Because of this, placing a person in a position which requires either more or less skill than he has affects rewards and costs in specific ways. If a low skill person is placed in a difficult position, rewards for position (evaluation of position) increase. Rewards for performance (evaluation of performance) decrease because the person cannot perform at the level expected. Costs, defined as experienced difficulty in performing in the position, increase because the person's skill is less than that required by the position. Thus, low skill-difficult position inconsistency results in a situation in which some rewards are increased, other rewards are decreased (which probably maintains overall rewards), and costs are increased. The result is that the overall outcome, that is, rewards minus costs, is less than it would be if the person were in a position which required the amount of skill he has.

If a high skill person is placed in an easy position, rewards for position decrease. Rewards for performance will not change because the person can perform at the level expected. (This assumes that performance is evaluated relative to what is expected for each position.) Costs decrease because the person's skill is more than that required by the position. Thus, high skill-easy position inconsistency results in a situation in which some rewards are decreased, other rewards are unchanged (which lowers overall rewards), and costs are decreased.

At first glance, high skill-easy position inconsistency would not appear to be stressful. Rewards have decreased but so have costs. However, following an idea advanced by Thibaut and Kelley (1959:89–90), the author is able to show that this type of inconsistency also should be stressful. The idea is that low skill persons emphasize costs while high skill persons emphasize rewards.[17] Thus, in the situation in question, the decrease in rewards tends to outweigh the decrease in costs. (Thibaut and Kelley's idea, of course, simply makes low skill-difficult position inconsistency even more stressful. In that situation overall rewards are maintained and costs are in-

---

[17] For a review of empirical studies which tend to support this idea, see Thibaut and Kelley (1959:90–95).

creased, while the person having low skill weights costs more heavily than rewards.)

Homans's concept of distributive justice (1961:chap. 12) is in certain ways similar to Thibaut's and Kelley's concept of comparison level. He, like these authors, thinks in terms of outcomes consisting of rewards and costs. His concept of investment corresponds to their concept of comparison level. An investment is a background characteristic such as age, seniority, or skill. The most general statement of the concept of distributive justice is that a person in an exchange relation with another will expect the profits (rewards minus costs) of each to be proportional to their investments (1961:244).

The author (Kimberly, 1967:177) has pointed out that this concept is also adaptable to inconsistencies between skill and position, but that it must be qualified in terms of the weighting processes described above before it consistently predicts that such inconsistencies are stressful.

Adams's theory of inequity (1965:276–296) differs from the models of both Thibaut and Kelley and Homans in that it involves an adaptation of dissonance theory (Festinger 1957; Brehm and Cohen 1962) rather than reinforcement principles. Adams uses the term "inputs" to refer essentially to what Homans means by investments. His definition is perhaps somewhat more restrictive in that he refers to inputs as contributions to exchange. Both Adams and Homans employ the term "outcomes," Adams using positive and negative to mean essentially what Homans means by rewards and costs. Adams, like Homans, also holds that the definition of fair or just exchange involves a comparison with another. According to Adams, inequity exists when a person perceives that the ratio of his outcomes to inputs and the ratio of other's outcomes to inputs are unequal. After defining inequity, Adams formulates a number of propositions concerning ways in which inequity can be reduced. Some of these will be discussed later in this section when we consider certain modes of achieving stability in the stratification structure.

These various formulations of the social-psychological processes underlying tendencies toward stability of the stratification structure employ theories which are representative of the two major perspectives in current social psychology: reinforcement and cognitive consistency theories. The work of Thibaut and Kelley and Homans and the author's adaptation of these falls within the first perspective. Adams's work attempts to integrate both perspectives.

There are other theorists who have dealt with the social psychology of the stability of the stratification structure. We have postponed consideration of their work to this point because they have been concerned primarily with specific ways in which all of the various types of social-psychological theory apply to the problem of the stability of the stratification structure.

The author (Kimberly, 1966:217–218; 1967:176–177) has suggested that cognitive consistency theories may not be generally applicable to the problem with which he deals, namely, inconsistency of skill and position. It is argued that balance theory, which holds at the most general level that the affect characterizing the individual's responses to the parts of an entity should be of like sign, may not apply because when position is ascribed, skill and position may not be seen as parts of the same entity. When positions are achieved, skill is seen as the cause of holding the position. When they are not, this relationship is destroyed.

The author also contends that a similar problem exists with regard to dissonance theory. Work on this theory (Brehm and Cohen, 1962) has shown that for the theory to apply there must be commitment to a cognition (in the sense that the act to which it refers cannot be undone) which is inconsistent with one or more other cognitions. Commitment occurs through engaging in behavior or choice. Once one has committed himself, any cognitions inconsistent with that commitment are dissonant. This work has also shown that the more volition the person feels he had in making the commitment, the greater the dissonance it generates (1962:chap. 11). When position is ascribed, it seems likely that often there may be little or no commitment. The individual may not behave as expected in the position. An elaboration of this argument is that volition also should be low in the case of ascription.

Sampson (1963) and Geschwender (1967) have advanced conceptions which involve a somewhat different approach to the problem in question. Sampson suggests that ranks which are objectively inconsistent have effects (in the sense of producing dissonance and attempts to resolve it) only when they are associated with inconsistent expectations for behavior. This is related to Homans's distinction between justice and status congruence (1961:248–251). The latter refers to whether or not the stimuli a man presents to others all rank above the corresponding stimuli of another. (They could, of course, also be equal to or rank below the stimuli of the other.) Status congruence and justice, of course, go together. However, Homans feels that congruence produces new forms of behavior in addition to those produced by justice. Inconsistent stimuli may cast doubt on the level of a person's status. For example, if responsibility and pay are inconsistent, which is to be used in deciding overall status? In addition, there are costs for others who have to relate to him. It is difficult for them to coordinate their behavior with his, and, consequently, they tend to avoid him (1961:251–255).

In a similar fashion Geschwender (1967) argues that it is inconsistency of expectations that makes rank inconsistency stressful. Like Sampson, he relates such inconsistency to inconsistent expectations (and the dissonance they produce (1967:161–163). Like the author, he suggests that status inconsistency can be related to Homans's concept of distributive justice by viewing certain ranks as investments and certain other ranks as rewards. (The author, it will be remembered, treats skill as investment and position and performance as rewards.) Geschwender views education and ethnicity as investments and occupation and income as rewards. Because of his choice of ranks, his conceptualization is specifically related to larger systems. Additional aspects of his work will be considered later in the paper when we consider the stability of the stratification structure in larger systems.

The work of the authors who emphasize the role of expectations in rank consistency is, in our view, one way of approaching the problem of relevance bonds among cognitions. The author's assessment of the relevance of balance and dissonance theories (see p. 87), can be reassessed from this perspective. Implicit in the author's analysis is the idea that skill is viewed as a cause of performance, which, in turn, is viewed as the basis for holding a position. Involved are a specific set of relevance bonds connecting the three phenomena. Also implicit in the author's analysis is the idea that in an ascriptive structure, these bonds are violated because positions are assigned irrespective of skill. The expectation models just discussed suggest that perhaps these bonds rather than being simply violated are related in different ways in ascriptive systems. They also suggest that in an ascriptive structure, additional ranks may be introduced and some of the three ranks dropped out of the expectation structure or, at least, related in more variable ways to one another. For example, in an ascriptive structure, it may be that certain specific ethnic or religious attributes are required for a position while entire ranges, or at least very wide ranges, of skill and performance are acceptable for it. A major area of future research then would appear to be the formulation of the kinds of expectation structures which are characteristic of different types of social structures.[18] The expectation approach should be, we think, very fruitful if employed in this way.[19] A danger in this approach, however, is that behavior predicted to ensue as a consequence of expectation inconsistency may be simply taken as support for the approach. This would be to commit an error similar to that of assuming that behavior predicted to ensue as a consequence of objectively defined rank inconsistency—that is, rank

---

[18] Kimberly and Crosbie (1967) have conducted a small group experiment in which they used variations in rewards to "override" and to intensify the causal relations among skill, performance, and position. Rewards were varied so that structures approximating extreme ascriptive- and achievement-oriented structures were created.

For a theoretical discussion of the relationship between status and power in ascriptive- and achievement-oriented systems, see Parsons (1966:250–255).

[19] For a recent review of experimental research carried out in terms of the expectation approach, see Sampson (1969).

inconsistency defined by the researcher—is support for a given social-psychological interpretation of rank inconsistency (cf. Doreian and Stockman, 1969). In both cases, independent evidence of the person's awareness of the type of inconsistency involved is required.

Thus far, we have discussed primarily the social-psychological processes that may underlie the tendency of stratification structures to move toward and remain in a state of stability. Now we shall consider modes of rank equilibration, that is, ways in which an unstable stratification structure may move toward stability. First, we shall consider the problem of intradimensional stability. To our knowledge, the only work which has been done explicitly at this level of analysis is the author's work on equilibration of types of status. We are not aware of work on equilibration of types of power or economic rewards.[20] This, however, would appear to be a fruitful area for future research. Second, we shall consider the problem of interdimensional stability. Most of the work that has been done is in this area.

The author (Kimberly, 1966:221–223; 1967:174–176) defines two modes of equilibrating skill and position status. One is a commonly recognized mode, namely, position mobility. It is noted, however, that status aspiration and the type of inconsistency determine whether or not this mode is acceptable to the individual. If status aspiration is high and the type of inconsistency is low skill-difficult position, it is predicted that mobility, which would be downward, will not occur. In lieu of this, it is predicted that an attempt to *despecialize* the system will be made. This involves *decreasing differences* in the difficulty of positions. The specific mechanism involved is reallocation of expectations for activity (norms) among positions. This mode of equilibration *decreases* the *average* difficulty of *difficult* positions. Consequently, it will reduce, at least somewhat, the stress to which the low skill-difficult position inconsistent is subjected. It will not, however, make his position lower than that of anyone else in the system.

If status aspiration is high and the type of inconsistency is high skill-easy position, the author predicts that mobility, which would be upward, will occur. If this is blocked, it is predicted that an attempt to *specialize* the system will be made. This involves *increasing differences* in the difficulty of positions. The mechanism is the same: reallocation of expectations (norms) among positions. This mode of equilibration *decreases* the *average* difficulty of *easy* positions. Consequently, it will increase the stress to which the high skill-easy position inconsistent is subjected. The purpose of this is to dramatize the inconsistency so that pressures will develop in the sys-

---

[20] The problem of interrelations among types of power is touched upon by Collins and Raven (1969:168–184).

tem to reduce it. It should do this because it makes the inconsistency even greater.[21]

Let us consider now the problem of interdimensional stability. In the previous section, we noted that the theorists considered there hold different views of the way ranks on the different dimensions of stratification are related to one another.[22] Homans, Bales, and Blau view status, power, and, while not emphasizing them, economic rewards, as being aligned, although they differ concerning the way this comes about. Homans sees high power as accruing to a high status person because status is not sufficient reward for valuable and rare services. Economic rewards are aligned with status and power through the justice process. Bales apparently sees the three kinds of ranks as being aligned primarily because status is a reward for solving important problems, and power and economic resources facilitate this. Blau sees status and power as being aligned because the repeated giving of status depreciates it, primarily through reduction of the status of the grantor. In this formulation, as in Homans's, power or compliance is granted in order to repay fully the high status person for valuable and scarce services.[23]

The author (Kimberly, in press: section entitled "Processes of Rank Equilibration") takes a similar position but advances different reasons. It is argued that status and power are aligned except when variations in demand for services or supply of competent persons (or both) cause temporary imbalances.[24] The rationale is that both status and power are based on the same set of factors, namely, position (assessed in terms of difficulty), performance, skill, and motivation. As in Homans's formulation, economic rewards are seen as being aligned through a justice process. However, it is noted that all of these processes are conditional upon knowledge of the

---

[21] For evidence that persons do "protest" inconsistency by making their situation worse, see Patchen (1961: 142–144, 152–155).

For a small group experiment dealing with equilibration of types of status very similar to what Kimberly calls skill and position, see Burstein and Zajonc (1965).

[22] The section that follows (pp. 90–91) draws heavily upon ideas developed in collaboration with Lynne G. Zucker of Stanford University. Zucker and the author are currently writing a paper (tentatively entitled "Relations Between Status and Power: Toward an Integration of Contemporary Conceptions") on this problem.

[23] Blau does not view *overall* status, power, and economic rewards as tending toward complete alignment. In his work on social integration (1960, 1964: chap. 2), he holds that once major stratification structures have developed, secondary ones on which low status persons rank higher than high status persons may be developed in an effort to promote cohesion within the system (1960, 1964: 33–50, especially 43–50). This is very similar to a classic view of cohesion advanced by Simmel (Wolff, 1950: 283–291). Jones, Gergen, and Jones (1963) have conducted an elaborate small group experiment which, on the whole, supports Blau's idea.

[24] For an empirical study relating to such imbalances, see Hodge (1962). For an elaboration of supply-demand effects in terms of the elasticity of supply and demand, see Blau (1964: chap. 7).

bases of stratification and agreement on criteria of evaluation of these bases. In the absence of such knowledge and consensus, it is held that the three ranks are aligned, but it is postulated that alignment occurs through an altogether different process. We shall consider this process when we discuss equilibration processes in larger systems.

Thibaut and Kelley and Emerson appear to view status and power as being nonaligned. Thibaut and Kelley see status as emerging from the comparison of outcomes. Since, according to these authors, only persons of similar power make such comparisons, the range for status should be greater than that for power. Thibaut and Kelley (1959:229–233) also hold, along with Emerson (1962:39–40), that the giving of status makes the high status person dependent on the low status person. Thus, power *differences* should decrease as status differences increase.[25]

It may be possible to reconcile the conflicting views of the relation of status and power by developing Blau's idea (described briefly in footnote 23, above) that after major stratification dimensions develop, secondary ones emerge on which low status persons are higher than high status persons. This is viewed as a mechanism for integration of the group. We suggest that the views of Homans, Bales, Blau (his major position), and the author can be reconciled with those of Thibaut and Kelley and Emerson by developing the conception of secondary stratification dimensions. We hypothesize that such dimensions involve structures which are "local" in character and, thus, based on particularistic rather than universalistic values. The major stratification dimensions are based on the latter type of values, as Blau indicates. We further hypothesize that the kind of process described by Thibaut and Kelley and Emerson occurs only when a low power person grants a high power person status on a secondary stratification dimension. Our rationale is that status granted on a major dimension cannot reduce power because such status, being based on universalistic values, can be obtained from other systems. An example of the process thus defined would be a senior professional relinquishing some of the power based on his professional reputation in a relationship with a junior because the junior offers him approval which is based on certain of his attributes which are idiosyncratic or, at least, not relevant to the professional stratification structure.[26]

Explanations that may apply to both small groups and larger systems.

---

[25] Thibaut and Kelley do say at one point that status and power tend to be aligned (1959: 232), but they qualify this with the propositions outlined here. On the whole, it seems fair to say that their basic view, though not fully explicit, is that status and power tend *not* to be aligned.

[26] This suggests a wholly new way of viewing the literature on locals and cosmopolitans (Merton, 1957:387–420). Zucker and the author are developing this idea in the paper referred to in footnote 22, above.

A number of other theorists have defined modes of rank equilibration that may apply to both small groups and larger systems. Their treatments do not always relate clearly to the three dimensions of stratification we have been considering but are presented because of their general significance for the problem of the stability of the stratification structure.

Malewski (1966) accepts the idea that it is conflicting expectations which make rank inconsistency stressful. He defines the following modes of rank equilibration: mobility; avoidance of persons who react to lower, inconsistent ranks; and rejection of the system of evaluation which is (we would say "is seen as") responsible for the inconsistency of his ranks.

Malewski sees mobility as involving the raising of lower ranks to the level of the highest rank. This assumes aspiration for high ranks. In our view, it is important to treat aspiration as analytically separate. This permits the possibility that equilibration may be effected through downward mobility in systems in which there is low aspiration for high ranks. The avoidance mode is self-explanatory. Rejection of the system of evaluation is used by Malewski to refer to shifts in political affiliation, political attitudes, and voting behavior. Such shifts are viewed as involving acceptance of political positions which offer some hope of elevating lower ranks.[27]

Adams (1965:283–296) defines a number of modes of reducing inequity which can be applied to the problem of reducing rank inconsistency. Basically, these involve the individual increasing or decreasing his inputs or outcomes, distorting these factors cognitively, withdrawing from the situation, and changing the object of comparison. Some examples of altering inputs would be increasing or decreasing productivity or the quality of work. Examples of altering outcomes would be increasing or lowering pay or authority. Distortion is self-explanatory. It should be noted, however, that use of this mode is limited by conditions which make it impossible to avoid information concerning inputs and outcomes. This particular mode, because it requires limited information, is probably more common in larger systems. Withdrawal is self-explanatory. Use of this mode would depend, of course, on the alternatives available in other systems. Changing the object of comparison is limited to situations in which self and other stand in an exchange relationship with a third party such as occurs in the case of an employer and two workers. If (relative to the other) one such worker experiences inequity, he can reduce it by finding and comparing himself with another whose ratio of inputs and outcomes are equal to his own. An example would be a worker who has a high school education and who makes $5,000 a year. If he compares with a worker in a different job who also

---

[27] For reviews of empirical studies relevant to the relationship between rank inconsistency and political behavior, see Lipset and Zetterberg (1966) and Anderson and Zelditch (1964).

has a high school education but who makes $10,000 a year, he experiences strong inequity. By shifting his comparison to a worker in a different job who has a junior college education and makes, say $7,500 a year, he could achieve equity. (This example involves the assumption that a junior college education is viewed as half again as valuable as a high school education.)[28]

Zelditch and Anderson (1966) have presented a theory of rank balance which is designed to encompass ranks of all kinds. They define the social-psychological process underlying the tendency toward stability of the stratification structure in terms of a balance (Heider, 1946; 1958:chap. 7) rather than a dissonance or reinforcement model (1966:248–249). A rank is defined as any value on any criterion. An individual's ranks are balanced if they are all above, all equal to, or all below those of other individuals in the same system. The stratification structure is balanced if the ranks of all individuals within it are balanced (1966:246–248).

These authors define a number of modes of equilibration which fall within the scope of Adams's idea of changing the object of comparison. These are referred to as forms of withdrawal. Isolation involves simply ceasing to compare one's ranks with those of others. Insulation involves shifting to a comparison with others among whom one's own inconsistent ranks are not significant ranks. Role differentiation involves restricting comparison to statuses (as opposed to the more general comparison of actors) which do not involve inconsistent ranks (1966:255–256, 259).

Like Malewski, Zelditch and Anderson treat mobility as a basic means of rank equilibration. They distinguish between ranks which are viewed as causally related and those which are not. If ranks are not causally related, the lower rank will be elevated. If ranks are causally related, the dependent rank will be changed in the direction of the independent rank (1966:260; cf. Kimberly, 1966:223; 1967:171–172). Expectations concerning mobility are viewed as affecting the intensity of reactions to rank inconsistency. If mobility is anticipated, reactions are less negative (cf. Goffman, 1957). Three forms of mobility are distinguished: individual, stratum, and mobility of a status or collectivity. The first type is self-explanatory. Stratum mobility involves movement of a large number of actors from one rank to another. Mobility of a status (position in our terms) or collectivity is defined as a reevaluation of the status or collectivity.

This more differentiated conception of mobility makes it possible for Zelditch and Anderson to formulate mobility processes which occur only in larger systems. One of these is that an inconsistent stratum which is blocked has greater tendencies to organize (in the sense of a social move-

---

[28] Adams reviews a number of empirical studies which are relevant to the modes of equilibration he defines. See 1965:283–296.

ment) than blocked individuals. Another is that the more members of stratum that expect to be mobile and to rise out of that stratum, the less the tendency of the stratum to organize. (1966:261–263).

Another major mode of equilibration considered by Zelditch and Anderson is redefinition of the system of stratification. Two kinds of redefinitions are identified. A left-wing protest involves an attempt to decrease the importance of an old, established rank which is seen as blocking mobility, and an attempt to increase the importance of a new rank with respect to which the equilibrating unit has been rising recently. A right-wing protest involves an attempt to increase the importance of an old, established rank of the equilibrating unit and an attempt to decrease the importance of a new rank which is seen as replacing it (1966:263–264).

Galtung (1966) deals with rank consistency and equilibration as a part of the broader problem of social integration. He focuses on the relationships among three factors: crisscross, rank equivalence, and equality. Crisscross refers to the degree to which there are individuals in a social system who can serve as bridges between completely disparate conflict groups. This is approached from the point of view of links. If two status sets, that is, groups of statuses (positions, in our terms) have a status in common, there is a link. For example, a Negro and a white medical doctor would be linked by the status of doctor. Rank equivalence or consistency refers to the degree to which individuals have statuses of equal rank in their status set. For example, being white and a medical doctor in many places has higher equivalence than being Negro and a medical doctor. Equality refers to the degree to which individuals are similar with regard to total rank. For example, in many places a white medical doctor has higher total rank than a Negro medical doctor (1966:145–148).

Because of the focus of this paper, we shall not explore in detail the relationships Galtung defines among these three aspects of social structure. Briefly, they are as follows. In the case of rank equivalence and equality, the relationship can be summed up by saying that what is lost on one is gained on the other. In the case of the other two relations, the matter is more complex. One can obtain crisscross only at the cost of rank equivalence and equality. However, the relationship is parabolic. Rank equivalence or equality can be greatly increased without a correspondingly large loss in crisscross (1966:148–158).

Like many of the theorists previously discussed, Galtung sees mobility on lower ranks as a mode of equilibration. He specifically relates this to aspiration for maximum total rank (1966:158–160).

On the basis of this formulation, Galtung develops a number of basic propositions concerning interpersonal conflict. We shall mention only those that are most closely related to the focus of this paper. Viewing interaction between two individuals in terms of their status sets, he defines rank congruency in terms of degree to which differences between each of the individuals' ranks are the same. Note that in congruent sets, one individual many rank overall above, at the same level, or below the other individual. What is important in congruency is that the *differences* between individuals' ranks be the same. In terms of this definition, Galtung predicts that the lower the rank congruency, the less associative the relationship (1966: 160–168).

The whole scheme is next enriched by introducing the concepts of ascribed and achieved statuses. This is used to specify individuals' reactions to a lack of rank equivalence or consistency. When inconsistency involves a high ascribed and a low achieved rank, Galtung predicts intrapunitivity, psychological stress, isolation, and attempts to elevate the achieved rank. When the inconsistency involves a low ascribed and a high achieved rank, he predicts extrapunitivity, political radicalism, and attempts to form protest groups (1966:168–171).

Finally, Galtung extends this analysis so as to include disequilibration of the system of which the individual is a member. He argues that in societies with little in the way of resources but much in the way of achievement—what he calls ascribed low-achieved high societies—individuals who have achieved less than their ascribed characteristics imply they should, have their tendencies toward self-blame greatly intensified. Conversely, he argues that in societies with much in the way of resources but little in the way of achievement—what he calls ascribed high-achieved low societies—individuals who have achieved more than their ascribed characteristics imply they should, have their tendencies toward political resolution of their problem greatly intensified. Indeed, as he puts it, disequilibration of this kind is probably among the recipes for revolution (1966:172–177).

Explanations at the level of larger systems. Geschwender, whose work (1967) was discussed partially earlier, postulates that equilibration attempts move from simple to complex modes. He defines individual mobility as the easiest. Next in difficulty is striking out against individuals and categories of individuals, that is, prejudice and discrimination. The most complex mode is an attempt to alter society. Withdrawal or social isolation and suicide are also seen as ways of coping with rank inconsistency.

Geschwender develops a very complex set of possibilities by relating types of rank inconsistency to these modes of equilibration (1967:163–168). We shall present only those involving inconsistencies between ranks which he views as investment and reward ranks. Persons with two types of inconsistency are referred to as underrewarded inconsistents. These are high ethnicity and low occupation and income, and high education and low occupation and income. The psychological reaction to these types of inconsistency is anger. Persons with the former type of inconsistency can be upwardly mobile on their lower ranks if their education is sufficient. If it is not, prejudice and discrimination are likely. If this fails, they are likely to join a racist social movement. Persons with the latter type of inconsistency can be mobile on their lower ranks if age permits. If it does not, prejudice and discrimination are likely. If this fails, they are likely to join an extremist social movement.

Persons with two additional types of inconsistency are referred to as overrewarded inconsistents. These are low ethnicity and high occupation and income and low education and high occupation and income. The psychological reaction to these forms of inconsistency is guilt. Persons with either of these types of inconsistency are unlikely to be mobile on their lower ranks. Ethnicity and education are difficult to change. Persons with both types of inconsistency may develop prejudice. If this fails, they may advocate moderate liberal reforms within the society (1967: 168–171).

The author (Kimberly, in press: section entitled "Effects of Increasing System Ranks on the Stratification of System Members") has dealt with the equilibration of ranks of systems. A system is defined as a set of positions which are directed toward a common goal. Systems are viewed as having status, power, and economic reward ranks. These are considered to be arrived at by averaging the status, power, and economic reward ranks of the positions within the system. It is argued that there is a considerable reduction in knowledge of the bases of stratification and consensus concerning criteria of evaluation of them as one moves from the individual to the system level. In the absence of such knowledge and consensus, it is hypothesized that persons assess status, power, and economic rewards in terms of whichever of these ranks is the clearest in the sense of being best known or having the greatest amount of agreement with regard to criteria of evaluation (or both). For example, if economic resources are clearest in this sense, there will be a tendency for persons to attribute status and power ranks which are commensurate with the economic resource rank.

CONCLUSIONS

The work on the emergence of stratification poses a number of important problems. First, there is the question as to the basic conditions making for stratification. The work reviewed suggests the following: (1) commitment of system members to the system goal, (2) wide-spread knowledge of the bases of stratification, and (3) consensus on criteria of evaluation of these bases. The work of a number of authors is addressed in various ways to the fact that the conditions of knowledge and consensus may not obtain in larger systems and to the question of what mechanism may substitute for these conditions in larger systems. Some authors suggest that the substitute mechanism involves something like a generalized identity which diffuses throughout a large number of systems. Others suggest it involves something like a symbolizing process in which rank on one dimension of stratification is taken as indicative of rank on another. Actually, these two views are not basically different. The former simply focuses on a larger number and more varied set of characteristics than the latter, which restricts itself to ranks on the dimensions of stratification. Yet another view is that consensus does exist in larger systems but that it is of a different sort from that obtaining in the small group, namely, that it consists of universalistic values that in some way help resolve the problem of knowledge.

Second, given the basic conditions described above, there is the question as to what are the specific mechanisms which account for the emergence of status, power, and economic reward hierarchies. It seems fair to say that with perhaps one exception all of the authors considered conceive of the mechanism to be something like a supply-demand process in which commitment to the system goal and, hence, to the positions directed toward it, constitute the demand features and the availability of persons able to fill the positions constitute the supply features.

Third, there is the question as to whether the emergence of one dimension of stratification in some way affects the emergence of one or more of the others. Most of the authors considered appear to assume that status, power, and economic rewards are based on the same factors and, hence, that units will tend to have equal ranks on the three dimensions. A few of the authors postulate that the emergence of power differences leads to the emergence of status differences which, in turn, leads to a leveling of power differences. We think that the conflict between these two points of view can be reconciled by introducing the idea that status is based partly on the universalistic factors of position, performance, skill, and motivation and partly on idiosyncratic attributes of the person. We think that it is the latter base of status, not the former, which erodes the high status person's power. Thus, if the high status person avoids accepting such status, the leveling of power differences cannot occur.

The work on the stability of the stratification structure also poses a number of important problems. First, there is the question of how current social-psychological theories relate to tendencies toward stabilization. It seems clear that some type of general reinforcement model is required to account for the effects of rank inconsistency (for empirical evidence on this point, see Moore, 1969). The relation of cognitive consistency models to tendencies toward stabilization is less clear. The most important problem at present would appear to be specification of the ways ranks are related to one another in achievement- and ascription-oriented systems. Once this is done, it should be possible to integrate the more traditional theories of cognitive consistency (balance and dissonance models) with the newer theory of expectancy consistency. At the present time, it appears that both reinforcement and consistency models are required to explain tendencies toward stabilization. Perhaps in the future it will be possible to integrate these two kinds of theory.

Second, there is the question of what means can be used to achieve stability. Rank mobility is clearly one means. Less well defined are means which involve changing the social system in certain ways. We think that these take the form of reallocating responsibilities among positions in ways that reduce or remove inconsistencies. When done on a system-wide basis, such reallocations constitute basic changes in the degree of specialization of the system (see pp. 89–90). Since social movements may be designed to effect such changes, this idea is compatible with predictions that participation in various kinds of social movements is a response to rank inconsistency.

Third, there is the question of how the mechanism which substitutes in larger systems for certain of the basic conditions of stratification, namely, knowledge of the bases of stratification and consensus on criteria of evaluation of them, affects the various means of achieving stability. Are tendencies toward mobility and changing the social system moderated by processes which involve attributing unknown structural bases of stratification or attributes on the basis of known ones? How does consensus on universalistic values direct persons to certain indicators of structural bases of stratification or attributes so that knowledge is less of a problem? Additional questions could be posed but these appear to be the more important ones.

REFERENCES

Adams, J. Stacy
1965   "Inequity in social exchange." Pp. 267–299 in Leonard Berkowitz (ed.), Advances in Experimental Social Psychology, Vol. 2. New York: Academic Press.

Anderson, Bo, and Morris Zelditch, Jr.
1964   "Rank equilibration and political behavior." Archives Europeenne de Sociologie V:112–125.

Bales, Robert F.
1950   Interaction Process Analysis. Cambridge: Addison-Wesley.

Bates, Frederich L.
1956   "Position, role, and status: a reformulation of concepts." Social Forces 34 (May): 313–321.

Berger, Joseph, et al.
1966   "Status characteristics and expectation states." Pp. 29–46 in Joseph Berger, Morris Zelditch, Jr., and Bo Anderson (eds.), Sociological Theories in Progress, Vol. I. New York: Houghton Mifflin.

Blau, Peter M.
1960   "A theory of social integration." American Journal of Sociology 65 (May): 545–556.
1964   Exchange and Power in Social Life. New York: Wiley.

Brehm, Jack W., and Arthur R. Cohen
1962 Explorations in Cognitive Dissonance. New York: Wiley.

Burnstein, Eugene, Robert Moulton, and Paul Liberty
1963 "Prestige vs excellence as determinants of role attractiveness." American Sociological Review 28 (April): 212–219.

Burnstein, Eugene, and Robert B. Zajonc
1965 "The effect of group success on the reduction of status incongruence in task-oriented groups." Sociometry 28 (December): 349–362.

Cartwright, Dorwin, and Alvin Zander
1960 "Individual motives and group goals: introduction." Pp. 345–369 in Dorwin Cartwright and Alvin Zander (eds.), Group Dynamics. Evanston: Row, Peterson.

Collins, Barry E., and Bertram H. Raven
1969 "Group structure: attraction, coalitions, communication, and power." Pp. 102–204 in Gardner Lindzey and Elliot Aronson (eds.), The Handbook of Social Psychology, Vol. IV. Reading: Addison-Wesley.

Davis, Kingsley, and Wilbert E. Moore
1966 "Some principles of stratification." Pp. 47–53 in Reinhard Bendix and Seymour M. Lipset (eds.), Class, Status, and Power. New York: Free Press.

Doreian, Patrick, and Norman Stockman
1969 "A critique of the multidimensional approach to stratification." Sociological Review 17 (March): 47–65.

Eisenstadt, S. N.
1968 "Prestige, participation and strata formation." Pp. 62–103 in J. A. Jackson (ed.), Social Stratification. Cambridge: University Press.

Emerson, Richard M.
1962 "Power-dependence relations." American Sociological Review 27 (February): 31–41.

Festinger, L.
1957 A Theory of Cognitive Dissonance. Evanston: Row, Peterson.

Galtung, Johan
1966 "Rank and social integration: a multidimensional approach." Pp. 145–198 in Joseph Berger, Morris Zelditch, Jr., and Bo Anderson (eds.), Sociological Theories in Progress, Vol. I. New York: Houghton Mifflin.

Geschwender, James A.
1967 "Continuities in theories of status consistency and cognitive dissonance." Social Forces 46 (December): 160–171.

Goffman, Irwin W.
1957 "Status consistency and preference for change in power distribution." American Sociological Review 22 (June): 275–281.

Gordon, Milton M.
1958 Social Class in American Sociology. Durham, N.C.: Duke University Press.

Heider, Fritz
1946 "Attitudes and cognitive organization." Journal of Psychology 21 (January): 107–112.
1958 The Psychology of Interpersonal Relations. New York: Wiley.

Hodge, Robert W.
1962 "The status consistency of occupational groups." American Sociological Review 27 (June): 336–343.

Hodge, Robert W., et al.
1966a "Occupational prestige in the United States: 1925–1963." Pp. 322–334 in Reinhard Bendix and Seymour M. Lipset (eds.), Class, Status, and Power. New York: Free Press.

1966b "A comparative study of occupational prestige." Pp. 309–321 in Reinhard Bendix and Seymour M. Lipset (eds.), Class, Status, and Power. New York: Free Press.

Homans, George C.
1950 The Human Group. New York: Harcourt, Brace and World.
1961 Social Behavior. New York: Harcourt, Brace and World.

Jones, Edward E., Kenneth J. Gergen, and Robert G. Jones
1963 "Tactics of ingratiation among leaders and subordinates in a status hierarchy." Psychological Monographs 77 (No. 3): Whole No. 566.

Kimberly, James C.
1962 An Experimental Test of a Theory of Status Equilibration. Unpublished Ph.D. dissertation, Duke University.
1966 "A theory of status equilibration." Pp. 213–226 in Joseph Berger, Morris Zelditch, Jr., and Bo Anderson (eds.), Sociological Theories in Progress, Vol. I. New York: Houghton Mifflin.
1967 "Status inconsistency: a reformulation of a theoretical problem." Human Relations 20 (No. 2): 171–179.

In press: "Relations among status, power, and economic rewards in simple and complex social systems." In Joseph Berger, Morris Zelditch, Jr., and Bo Anderson (eds.), Sociological Theories in Progress, Vol. II. New York: Houghton Mifflin.

Kimberly, James C., and Paul V. Crosbie
1967 "An experimental test of a reward-cost formulation of status inconsistency." Journal of Experimental Social Psychology 3 (October): 399–415.

Laumann, Edward O.
1966 Prestige and Association in an Urban Community. Indianapolis: Bobbs-Merrill.

Lenski, Gerhard
1966 Power and Privilege. New York: McGraw-Hill.

Lipset, Seymour M., and Hans L. Zetterberg
1966 "A theory of social mobility." Pp. 561–573 in Reinhard Bendix and Seymour M. Lipset (eds.), Class, Status, and Power. New York: Free Press.

Malewski, Andrzej
1966 "The degree of status incongruence and its effects." Pp. 303–308 in Reinhard Bendix and Seymour M. Lipset (eds.), Class, Status, and Power. New York: Free Press.

Merton, Robert K.
1957 Social Theory and Social Structure. Glencoe: Free Press.

Miller, L. Keith, and Robert L. Hamblin
1963 "Interdependence, differential rewarding, and productivity." American Sociological Review 28 (October): 768–778.

Moore, James C., Jr.
1968 "Status and influence in small group interactions." Sociometry 31 (March): 47–63.
1969 "Social status and social influence: process considerations." Sociometry 32 (June): 145–158.

Parsons, Talcott
1953 "A revised analytical approach to the theory of social stratification." Pp. 92–128 in Reinhard Bendix and Seymour M. Lipset (eds.), Class, Status, and Power. Glencoe: Free Press.
1966 "On the concept of political power." Pp. 240–265 in Reinhard Bendix and Seymour M. Lipset (eds.), Class, Status, and Power. New York: Free Press.

Parsons, Talcott, and Edward A. Shils (eds.)
1951 Toward a General Theory of Action. Cambridge: Harvard University Press.

Patchen, Martin
1961 "A conceptual framework and some empirical data regarding comparisons of social rewards." Sociometry 24 (June): 136–156.

Pettigrew, Thomas F.
1967 "Social evaluation theory: convergences and applications." Pp. 241–311 in David Levine (ed.), Nebraska Symposium on Motivation. Lincoln: University of Nebraska Press.

Sampson, Edward E.
1963 "Status congruence and cognitive consistency." Sociometry 26 (June): 146–162.
1969 "Studies of status congruence." Pp. 225–270 in Leonard Berkowitz (ed.), Advances in Experimental Social Psychology, Vol. 4. New York: Academic Press.

Simpson, R. L.
1956 "A modification of the functional theory of social stratification." Social Forces (December) 35: 132–137.

Stinchcombe, Arthur L.
1963 "Some empirical consequences of the Davis-Moore theory of stratification." American Sociological Review 28 (October): 805–808.

Stinchcombe, Arthur L., and T. Robert Harris
1969 "Interdependence and inequality: a specification of the Davis-Moore theory." Sociometry 32 (March): 13–23.

Thibaut, John W., and Harold H. Kelley
1961 The Social Psychology of Groups. New York: Wiley.

Thompson, Victor A.
1961 Modern Organization. New York: Knopf.

Wolff, Kurt H. (ed.)
1950 The Sociology of Georg Simmel. Glencoe: Free Press.

Zelditch, Morris, Jr., and Bo Anderson
1966 "On the balance of a set of ranks." Pp. 244–268 in Joseph Berger, Morris Zelditch, Jr., and Bo Anderson (eds.), Sociological Theories in Progress, Vol. I. New York: Houghton Mifflin.

Educational Stratification in the United States*

ROBERT M. HAUSER
University of Wisconsin

Recent research on education in the stratification system of the United States is reviewed in light of the demands for data and interpretation which would be generated by a set of national accounts for educational stratification. A descriptive scheme for locating school variables and educational outcomes in the stratification process is proposed. The basic characteristics of the present system of educational stratification in the United States are outlined. Some of the difficulties of measuring changes in the stratification process are illustrated. Methods and results of large-scale surveys of educational stratification are reviewed. Our limited capacity to produce detailed interpretations of the process of stratification which can be generalized to population cohorts is a major obstacle to improved knowledge and policy in the area of educational stratification.

Schools are the primary agencies of social selection for children and youth in the United States. It is likely that they are also the most important site of socialization outside the family. If there is a distinct youth or peer subculture, whether it supports or subverts the official organization of the school, it is manifestly tied to the school. The dependence of the selective and socializing aspects of schooling on social origins and the effects of schooling on adult social and economic achievement are the subject matter of educational stratification.

Educational stratification is defined by reference to a set of variables, a social setting, and a stage of the life cycle. Consequently, social, psychological, and biological mechanisms must all be taken into account in describing the role of education in the stratification process. Educational stratification exists as an area of interest within the more general study of the achievement process because of the generally recognized importance of educational institutions in the stratification systems of industrial societies (Cooley, 1909; Sorokin, 1927: 171, 189; Barber, 1957: 392; Dahrendorf, 1959: 359; Lipset and Bendix, 1959: 227; Lenski, 1966: 389–390; Blau and Duncan,

*The research reported here was supported by grants from the National Institute of Health, U.S. Public Health Service (M-6275) and the Social and Rehabilitation Service, U.S. Department of Health, Education, and Welfare (CRD-314). The author wishes to thank the following persons for their thorough criticism of an earlier draft of this paper: Otis Dudley Duncan, David L. Featherman, Avery M. Guest, William Spady, and Hal H. Winsborough. William H. Sewell and Vimal P. Shah kindly supplied some of their unpublished data.

1967: chap. 5). There is also a political argument for a special interest in educational stratification. Of the several social arenas where the stratification process takes place—in the family, the peer group, the school, the labor market—the school is the most accessible to demands for public accountability and change. In principle, school practices affecting stratification can be manipulated by direct administrative action and by resource control (Center for Policy Studies, 1968; Janowitz, 1969). As fragmented and localized as the educational system is, the family and the labor market are even more atomized and less easily subject to public control.

Stimulated by a continuously high level of public interest in the supply of skilled manpower and in the relationships among poverty, race, and education, a great deal of small and large scale research on educational stratification was produced in the past decade. In spite of this large volume of effort, it is doubtful that there has been much movement toward consensus or consolidation with regard to choice of concepts or orientations toward data, let alone powerful explanatory schemes or detailed empirical findings. For example, assessments of the extent of educational opportunity in the United States run the gamut from Kenneth Clark's (1968: 101) statement that "American public schools have become significant instruments in the blocking of economic mobility and in the intensification of class distinctions," to Beverly Duncan's (1967: 371) observation that "the relation of schooling to social background is sufficiently loose that a boy's attainment is not strictly determined or even sharply limited by the circumstances of the family into which he is born." To cite a more extreme example, it is apparent from the published reactions (*Harvard Educational Review*, Spring 1969 and Summer 1969) to Arthur Jensen's essay on IQ and race (1969) that there are ideological barriers to empirical research on this aspect of educational stratification which are respected by many academicians.

I think that it is only possible to produce an integrated description of the process of educational stratification by adopting a social accounting approach. While such a perspective yields no special insights into mechanisms of interindividual differentiation, it is a powerful aid to the interpretation of such mechanisms at the societal level. An accounting framework continually directs attention to the problems of representing populations accurately and of interpreting changes over time correctly. Minimally, a social accounting scheme for educational stratification presupposes (1) knowledge of which indicator variables are relevant to educational opportunity; (2) knowledge of (a) the causes, (b) the consequences and (c) the interrelations among the relevant indicators; (3) practical and valid methods for measuring the indicators; and (4) periodic and comparable measurements of the indicator variables on appropriate populations and subpopulations (Cohen, 1967; O. D. Duncan, 1967; Coleman, 1969). In this essay I have attempted to illustrate the value of an accounting approach by using it to outline the system of educational stratification in the United States and to assess recent research on educational stratification.

The appropriate unit of analysis for the study of educational stratification is the birth cohort, a group of persons born in a single year or a short span of adjacent years. The identification of individuals with cohorts provides a mutually exclusive and exhaustive categorization of the members of a society. Cohort analyses permit explicit treatment of the two meanings of age at a point in time: position in the life-cycle and position in history. Age-specific inter-cohort comparisons are the raw material of the study of societal change. Social change proceeds largely via the succession of cohorts, and the cohort is the modal social milieu for its members as they pass through the educational system (Ryder, 1965). There are, of course, educationally relevant aggregates which are neither composed of, nor exhaustive of, the membership of a single cohort, if the latter is defined by year of birth. Such is the case, for example, with the aggregate of pupils enrolled in the sixth grade in a given year or with the aggregate of persons leaving school during a given year. However, the societal import of research findings on such subpopulations is determinate only when those findings tell something about the distribution, causes, or consequences of educational outcomes in a birth cohort. Subpopulations for which detailed educational data are accessible rarely can be aggregated to represent birth cohorts, and this poses a major obstacle to valid generalization about the details of the stratification process.

VARIABLES IN THE SCHOOLING PROCESS

Stratification is a process, not a state. The relationships between social origins and performances in the educational system develop over a period of years, as do those between educational performances and adult achievements. The primary task in the study of educational stratification is the identification and interpretation of mechanisms linking social origins, performances in the educational system, and adult achievements. As a research operation, this takes the form of a search for intervening variables which can be identified with socialization or selection processes within the school and which function to link social origins and destinations. These remarks suggest that the life-cycle is an appropriate framework for examining variables in the schooling process.

Some of the salient linkages can be observed in Figure 1, which depicts several classes of school variables and educational outcomes together with antecedent and consequent variables. The columns are in a temporal order running from left to right, but the arrangement is not intended to foreclose the possibility of causal relationships among the variables within each column. The referent of each of the concepts in Figure 1 is the experience of the individual student as he passes through the system, not the structure of educational institutions in cross section. That is, the composition of educational resources and practices at a point in time need not be identical to the cumulative exposure of any student or cohort of students. The importance of this distinction is underscored by the inclusion of geographic mobility among the background variables. To my knowledge no educational researcher has dealt with the probability that most students are exposed to a heterogeneous mix of curricula, school facilities, and teaching practices over a ten to twenty year period as a result of intraschool and interschool mobility within and between grade levels. In school studies the fact of student mobility tends to be treated as a source of data loss rather than a social fact with some relevance for outcomes of the educational process. Even cross-sectional distributions of educational practices among institutions need not correspond to their distributions among students. This was recognized in many tabulations of school characteristics in the Coleman-Campbell Report (1966), which used the individual student as the unit of aggregation.

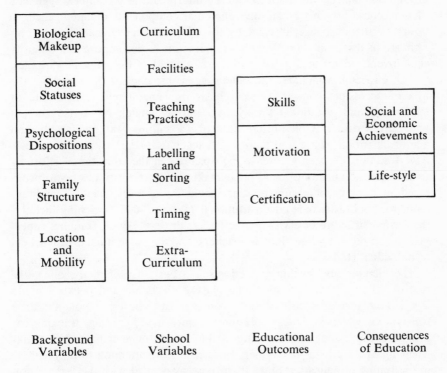

| Background Variables | School Variables | Educational Outcomes | Consequences of Education |

Figure 1. *Educational Variables in the Stratification Process*

It is obvious from Figure 1 that specification of the role of schooling in effecting relationships between social origins and destinations involves numerous causal linkages in both directions. This fact has sometimes been ignored. For example, O. D. Duncan (1969: 104–105) notes that Sibley's (1942) forecast of the future of occupational mobility anticipated a possible attenuation of the effects of social origins on educational attainment (which did not occur) and ignored a possible increase in the effect of education on occupational achievement (which probably did occur). In general, school studies are prone to postulate linkages between school variables and adult achievement without documenting them. For that reason the importance of socioeconomic differentials in school facilities or academic performance are often overinterpreted.

Whatever the merits of the distinctions among biological, psychological, and sociological levels of explanation, all three classes of phenomena are germane to the explanation of success in school. They undoubtedly have a mixture of unique and overlapping effects on educational outcomes whose decomposition is essential to an understanding of mechanisms of stratification. For example, the gross relationship between socioeconomic background and college attendance might be interpreted as a complex aggregate of differences in genetic and environmental components of intelligence, in desire to attend college, in capacity to pay for higher education, and outright status discrimination by colleges. An effort to decompose and quantify such diverse effects must begin with measurement of the relevant variables.

The curriculum includes the official academic content of schooling, the mix of accessible courses, the emphasis on general and transferable or specialized and vocational knowledge, and the match of course content with future demands on present students. Facilities—the availability and age of classroom space and equipment, teaching materials, and the like—have traditionally been granted a high priority in the educational effort by educational administrators and policymakers. This priority has been recognized in one recent argument that inequality of per capita expenditure among school districts is unconstitutional (Wise, 1969). Teaching includes the formal structure of classroom activities; the experience, training, supervision, and other qualifications of teachers; and the commitments of teachers to individual students.

The labeling and sorting of students is a basic aspect of the allocative role of schools. Such activities take place both within and between grade levels. They include decisions made from standardized tests (though not the trait values which such tests presume to measure); grading, tracking, or programming; failing or promoting; and accepting or rejecting aspiring matriculants. Educational researchers have paid little attention to differentials in the timing of education other than those associated with the termination of schooling by high school dropouts and non-college entrants. Timing factors of some importance include the age at school entry, grade acceleration or retardation, and temporary nonenrollment associated with delinquency, marriage, childbearing, jobholding, or military service (Eckland, 1964; B. Duncan, 1968; Masters, 1969; Conlisk, 1969).

The division between school variables and educational outcomes separates what schooling does to a student from what he gets out of it. While assessments of skill, motivation, and formal qualification are abundant throughout the educational process, the values of those traits at the time of school-leaving take on special importance. For each individual the ultimate values of those traits are presumably of greater consequence for his later history than earlier values. Because age and grade at school-leaving are highly variable, the distribution of those ultimate values in a cohort is aggregated from age-grade specific distributions in several years.

This list is neither detailed nor very well culled. For example, teacher discrimination (Rosenthal and Jacobsen, 1968) has little demonstrated importance (Hauser, 1969). Similarly, the findings of the Coleman-Campbell Report (1966: 292–302) suggest that unequal expenditures by school districts are not a major source of inequality in educational outcomes. The importance of other school variables will be considered below.

A distributive definition of educational stratification implies that some educationally relevant social facts are treated only indirectly, while others are ignored. For example, the political control of schools is not treated explicitly, nor are educational processes or structures in different localities, regions or societies compared. My expectation is that the effects of political or other organizational variations in the schooling process will be manifest, insofar as they are relevant, in the form of variations in the parameters of models of individual educational achievement. The construction of such models is a prior task, and one of its outcomes may be the location of key variables for comparative study. Before turning to details of the educational process, it seems advisable to outline the larger process, that is, the connections between social origin statuses, educational outcomes and adult social and economic achievements.

EDUCATIONAL ATTAINMENT AND STRATIFICATION

The basic facts about educational stratification include measurements of the central tendency and dispersion of distributions of educational outcomes and the correlations of those outcomes with antecedent and consequent aspects of social structure. We should like to know whether and to what degree these measurements vary from time to time, from place to place, and over special subpopulations, such as those defined by race, sex, ethnicity, or religion.

If correlation with socioeconomic background alone were the grounds for choice, we should have to examine data sets for numerous educational outcomes. Charters (1963: 740) observes:

> Social class position predicts grades, achievement, and intelligence test scores, retentions at grade level, course failures, truancy, suspensions from school, high school drop-outs, plans for college attendance, and total amount of formal schooling. It predicts academic honors and awards in the public school, elective school offices, extent of participation in extracurricular activities and in social affairs sponsored by the school, to say nothing of a variety of indicators of 'success' in the informal structure of the student society. Where differences in prestige value exist in high school clubs and activities, in high school curricula, or in types of advanced training institutions, the social class composition of the membership will vary accordingly.

For many of these indicators it would not only be difficult to assemble a body of data meeting the above description for a single nationally representative cohort, it would also be impossible to make valid comparisons over time or space.

Educational attainment (years of regular schooling completed) is the educational outcome about which most is known and which may be most useful in studying stratification. Educational attainment can be ascertained with satisfactory accuracy from self-reports (Siegel and Hodge, 1967), and it is relatively easy to measure for large and representative samples of the population. For mature individuals it is a remarkably valid indicator of the quality of education because of the close connection between academic performance and continuation in school (O. D. Duncan, 1968b). Intertemporal comparisons of educational attainment can be made from cross-sectional data classified by age because, as Beverly Duncan (1968: 602) has noted, "schooling measured in years of school attendance or grades completed is cumulative and irreversible for the cohort as for the individual."

Table 1 displays basic data on the stratification of educational attainment for white and nonwhite males in the United States. The data were obtained in a March 1962, supplement to the Current Population Survey, "Occupational Changes in a Generation." The usefulness of the data in making Negro-white comparisons is limited to some degree by the small number of Negroes picked up in the sample and by the use of a White-Other split rather than a Negro-Other split in tabulation. Fortunately, the federal government has recently adopted a Negro-Other split for future tabulations by color. When the OCG survey is replicated (hopefully in 1972), we may hope that Negroes will be oversampled.

The age breaks in Table 1 permit comparison of the educational attainments of cohorts completing school since about the end of World War I. For whites and for nonwhites the mean number of years of schooling has been increasing, and the standard deviation of years of schooling has been decreasing. Thus, in an absolute sense the amount of opportunity for educa-

Table 1

INDICATORS OF EDUCATIONAL STRATIFICATION
FOR RECENT COHORTS OF U. S. NATIVE MALES, BY COLOR, 1962

	White Age in 1962			Nonwhite Age in 1962		
	27–36	37–46	47–61	27–36	37–46	47–61
Educational Attainment:						
Mean	11.9	11.2	10.1	9.8	8.1	6.6
Standard Deviation	3.2	3.4	3.6	3.2	4.1	4.0
Regression Coefficients in Raw Form:						
Education of Family Head	.192	.195	.217	.220	.199	.329
Occupation of Family Head	.040	.041	.047	.034	.055	.051
Intact Family	.671	.626	1.203	.763	.718	.435
Number of Siblings	−.225	−.223	−.222	−.043	−.246	−.168
Regression Coefficients in Standard Form:						
Education of Family Head	.215	.224	.234	.245	.185	.314
Occupation of Family Head	.267	.270	.270	.157	.167	.155
Intact Family	.073	.069	.122	.105	.083	.052
Number of Siblings	−.198	−.195	−.184	−.044	−.191	−.129
Coefficient of Determination	.267	.281	.283	.136	.137	.167

SOURCE: O. D. Duncan, "Discrimination Against Negroes," *The Annals* (May, 1967), p. 100; B. Duncan, *Family Factors and School Dropout: 1920–1960*, Cooperative Research Project No. 2258, United States Office of Education (Ann Arbor: University of Michigan, 1965), p. 43.

tion has been increasing, and the amount of inequality of education has been decreasing.

The remainder of Table 1 displays the results for each cohort of a regression analysis of educational attainment on the education and occupation of the family head (at the time the respondent was about age 16), the presence of both parents in the home, and the number of siblings in the family of orientation. Regression coefficients in raw form express the net effect on the dependent variable of a one unit change in the predetermined variable. For example, net of the other three background variables, living in an intact family was worth an extra 1.2 years in school to white men aged 47 to 61 in 1962. Regression coefficients in standard form express net effects of unit standard deviation changes in the predetermined variables in terms of standard deviation changes in the dependent variable. They permit comparison of the net effects of predetermined variables with differing metrics. For example, the effects of head's occupation are larger than those of head's education in each of the cohorts of white males.

TRENDS

Inter-cohort comparisons of the coefficients suggest that the effects of family background variables on educational attainment have been quite stable. The coefficients of determination, which express the proportions of variance for which the background variables account, are no more than moderately large. If social origins explain about fifteen to thirty percent of the variance in educational attainment, then factors completely unrelated to social origins must account for the remaining seventy to eighty-five percent of the variance. The effects of family background on educational attainment may have decreased slightly for both whites and nonwhites. Regardless of color, in every cohort it has been advantageous for a young man to come from a family with few children, with both parents present, and with a family head of high educational and occupational status. The only systematic trends in the net effects of the background variables are apparent increases for nonwhites and decreases for whites in the influence of intact family. This finding is congruent with the view that Negro family structure is a crucial barrier to reduction of social and economic inequality between the races (U.S. Department of Labor, 1965), but the importance of intact family itself should not be overstated (B. Duncan and O. D. Duncan, 1969). One important finding about trend which can not be discerned from Table 1 is that little of the gain in educational attainment over time need be attributed to improvement in the social origins of successive birth cohorts (B. Duncan, 1967: 372).

The regression coefficients may be interpreted as indexes of inequality of educational opportunity within (but not between) the white and nonwhite populations. That is, the relationship between social origins and educational achievements can only be weak in a society in which chances for schooling do not depend on circumstances of birth. The converse is not true because genetic inheritance alone would produce a positive intergenerational correlation if opportunities were equalized in both the generation of fathers and that of the sons. Moreover, it is not clear that we want to define opportunity so broadly (Coleman, 1968b) as to include all sources of differentials in educational achievement (B. Duncan, 1967). At some point opportunity ends and achievement begins. Thus, if we are willing to believe that attenuation in measurement of the variables is not large (Siegel and Hodge, 1967), the measures of effect in Table 1 must be read as overestimates of the extent of inequality of opportunity. Of course other socioeconomic background characteristics affect a man's educational achievement, but (contrary to common belief) each additional background variable makes a smaller marginal contribution to the predictability of success in the educational system (Lutterman, 1968; Blau and Duncan, 1967: 199–205).

COLOR DIFFERENTIALS

Comparison of the data for whites and nonwhites indicates that the racial gap in educational attainment has been declining in both absolute and relative terms. The greater dispersion of educational attainment among non-whites is disappearing, and in general there is a lesser dependence of educational attainment on family background among nonwhites than among whites. This perverse kind of equality of opportunity within the nonwhite population may make it more difficult to reduce color differentials in educational attainment (O. D. Duncan, 1968c). That is, blacks do not enjoy as great a payoff in education as do whites for any given increment in socioeconomic background conditions.

To what extent is the racial gap in educational attainment a consequence of the inferior social origins of blacks? Duncan (1967) has shown that statistical controls for educational attainment and occupational status of the family head, intact family, and number of siblings account for about half the differential in educational attainment in each cohort. Over time the residual effects of color have decreased absolutely and relatively to the total white-nonwhite differential.

CONSEQUENCES OF EDUCATION

Educational attainment is a powerful intervening variable in the stratification process. Socioeconomic origins (race excepted) have rather small effects on adult socioeconomic achievements beyond those implicit in their influence on educational attainment and its influence on later achievements (Duncan and Hodge, 1963; Blau and Duncan, 1967: chap. 5; O. D. Duncan, 1968a; Featherman, 1969). As Paul Siegel phrased it in a recent conversation, everything that happens to a boy before his sixteenth birthday influences everything that happens after that by way of his education. Still, in view of the large role of chance in determining educational attainment, we may reformulate Barber's hypothesis (1957: 395): education is primarily a mechanism providing for social mobility; only secondarily is it a mechanism whereby social class positions are stabilized across the generations.

Seemingly disparate conclusions about the trends in educational stratification follow from arrangements of the same data which restrict attention to the impact of social origins on specific transition points in the process of schooling. Spady (1967), for example, used the OCG data to examine trends in actual and conditional probabilities of completing high school, entering college and completing college, by father's education, for four cohorts of United States males. He concluded that the effect of father's education on a son's chances for secondary education had declined, while its influence on the son's chances for higher education had increased. For sons of fathers with little education, the conditional probabilities of entering college (for high school graduates) and of finishing college (for college entrants) had declined. Such results may be of some import in discussions which focus directly on absolute levels of educational attainment, but they need not mean that the degree of stratification has changed. Results like those reported by Spady follow directly from changes over time in mean attainment levels in the absence of changes in the regression of son's education on father's education. Confusion of trends in the impact of social origins on access to higher education with trends in educational stratification *per se* is also evident in the Jencks and Riesman (1968: chap. 3) discussion of stratification in higher education.

EDUCATIONAL ATTAINMENT AND EDUCATIONAL QUALITY

Is educational attainment worth this much attention? It has been argued that years of schooling is a crude indicator of the quantity of education—of a level of social certification—but not necessarily of competence (Cohen, 1967). The argument apparently calls for more direct measurement of educational quality. Its popularity may be greatest among those who believe that the educational system is the source of racial differentials in social and educational achievement. However, the available evidence suggests that educational attainment is a rather good indicator of educational quality. We already know that educational attainment accounts for most of the influence of social background on adult achievements; refinements of intervening variables can not add to the importance of education in that respect. To the degree that academic performance is a condition of continuation in school, years of schooling becomes a valid performance measure. Duncan (1968b) has argued that intelligence has small effects on occupational achievement and income beyond those implicit in its relationship with educational attainment. The correlations between Armed Forces Qualification Test scores and educational attainment are virtually the same for white and Negro men, and the regression of AFQT scores on attainment is four-fifths as steep for Negro as for white men. This suggests that blacks are not markedly less able than whites to transform years of schooling into competence.

The existence of grade-specific differentials in academic performance by color or by socioeconomic origin is not a sufficient demonstration of the quality argument. Killingsworth's (1969: 229–231) discussion of sources of Negro-white economic differentials exemplifies the error. He cites the twelfth grade color differential in verbal aptitude reported in the Coleman-Campbell Report (3.3 years in the metropolitan northeast) as an explanation for the high unemployment rates of Negroes with only a high school education. The problem is that academic achievement differentials for students enrolled at a given grade level can not be equated with achievement differentials among students who completed their schooling at that grade level. For whites and blacks low performance increases the likelihood that the given grade level will be the highest completed. In the absence of good panel data, tests of the educational quality hypothesis require measurements at maturity of both certification and competence, as well as indicators of relevant socioeconomic variables. The popularity of the quality education argument is sustained by the operational difficulty of obtaining valid direct measurements of personal competence for representative samples of adults.

DISPOSITIONAL VARIABLES

Whatever the merits of years of schooling as an indicator of educational quality, we know more about it than any other indicator of the role of education in the stratification system. Dispositional variables are a case in point; these are nonacademic outcomes of socialization which are at least partially effected by schooling. Included are concepts as varied as achievement motivation, self-concept, sense of control over the environment, achievement values or orientations, ambitions, aspirations, and plans. Variables based on such concepts have been credited with impressive explanatory power. For example, Rosen (1959) argued

> that many racial and ethnic groups were not, and are not now, alike in their orientation toward achievement, particularly as it is expressed in their striving for status through social mobility, and that this difference in orientation has been an important factor contributing to the dissimilarities in their social mobility rates.

While Rosen's argument is congruent with a long tradition of sociological interpretation, it has yet to be validated in a large and representative sample. Morgan and his associates (1962: 359–370) found that need-achievement did not account for socioeconomic differentials in educational attainment in a national sample of adults. Featherman's (1969) intensive analysis of data from the Princeton Fertility Surveys suggests that work-related values and orientations are of little value in the explanation of socioeconomic achievement differentials among religio-ethnic groups. In general, the importance of dispositional variables in explaining differential social and economic achievement is not well established (Katz and Gurin, 1969: 360–368).

TRENDS IN ASPIRATIONS

Levels of educational and occupational aspiration have probably been investigated more thoroughly in representative samples than other dispositional variables. In part this may be attributed to the ease with which aspirations can be ascertained from children in school, but they have also shown impressive explanatory power. For example, the educational aspirations of high school seniors are moderately powerful predictors of college attendance and account for a substantial share of the effects of ability and socioeconomic background on college graduation (Sewell and Shah, 1967). In view of these facts a description of the national trend in aspiration levels would be an appropriate addition to our set of accounts for educational stratification.

Expressions of professional opinion about the trend of motivation have not been absent from the sociological literature. The pessimistic views of Havighurst (1947) and Hertzler (1952) about the trend of social mobility in the United States were partly based on presumptions of a decline in motivation to get ahead in life. Despite the continuation of secular upward shifts in the education, occupation, and income distributions, a similar sentiment was expressed recently by Porter (1968: 16–17):

> By contrast, the most advanced industrial societies with great possibilities for economic growth are threatened by inadequate levels of mobility aspirations. In the period of post-modernity, even for the middle class the educational demands may well be excessive.

While there have been six relevant national surveys during the period 1939 to 1965, it is difficult to draw any conclusions about trend.

The available data are presented in condensed form in Table 2. Only the 1939 Roper survey was based on as few as one thousand cases. The table shows no continuous trend, but there are so many sources of noncomparability that even the conclusion of no trend cannot be advanced wholeheartedly:

1. Reported aspiration levels are sensitive to minor variations in question wording. No two questions in the series were alike. In the autumn, 1965 survey, 65 percent of the seniors reported that they definitely or probably would attend college in the fall of 1966, while only 58 percent said that they ever wanted to have some college training.
2. Aspiration levels vary with the time of year. In October, 1959, forty-seven percent of high school seniors planned to attend college the following fall, but 53 percent of those who graduated from high school in the spring of 1960 had reported having college plans the preceding October. This shift by attrition in a single cohort is probably accompanied by individual changes in aspiration during the school year.
3. The target populations vary among the surveys. The 1939 data were ascertained from a household survey of non-college youth under 20 years old. It included youth who had been out of school for years as well

as youth enrolled in school. The other surveys were aimed at currently enrolled youth, but one excluded youth in private schools, who have higher aspirations than those in public schools.

4. Aspiration levels may shift with changes in the place where the respondent is contacted because of changes in population coverage or in response sets. The two fall 1965 surveys asked almost identical questions of students in the same cohort, but one survey was conducted at school and the other in a household survey. The surveys produced estimates of 65 percent and 57 percent with definite or probable plans to attend college in the fall of 1966.

Table 2

TRENDS IN EDUCATIONAL ASPIRATIONS

Survey Date	Population	Percentage Aspiring to College
1939	Persons under 20 years old not in college	54%
Winter Quarter 1955	Public high school seniors	58%
October 1959	High school seniors	47% *
October 1959	1960 high school graduates	53% *
Spring 1960	High school seniors	66%
Autumn 1965	High school seniors (at school)	58–65%
October 1965	High school seniors (at home)	57%

SOURCES: Jaffe and Adams, 1964; Educational Testing Service, 1957; Cowhig and Nam, 1961; Flanagan and others, 1964; Coleman, Campbell, and others, 1966; Johnson and Zappolo, 1969.

*Percentages of students with plans to attend college in the fall of 1960.

Finally, as school retention has improved, successive senior high school classes have become less highly selected for high aspiration levels. Even if we had perfectly comparable measurements obtained at the same time of the year for successive senior classes, and these measurements showed a steady decline in aspiration levels, we could not be certain that aspirations were falling in successive birth cohorts.

If we cannot say anything about gross trends in aspiration levels, what can we say about trends in socioeconomic or color differentials in aspirations? Or in more sophisticated measures of motivation? Or in academic achievement? If we can not say much about trends in levels and differentials in aspirations, what can we say about variables which have been less thoroughly researched? The capacity of social scientists to field large and repeated surveys on educational matters carries with it an obligation to standardize practices with regard to population coverage, measurement techniques, and publication of basic tabulations.

THE EQUAL OPPORTUNITY SURVEY AND PROJECT TALENT

During the past decade there were two massive national studies of youth in school. Project Talent was initiated in 1960 with a two-day testing program for some 440,000 students in grades nine through twelve in 1,350 schools (Flanagan and others, 1962a, 1962b, 1964). Data were also collected for all fifteen-year-olds (Shaycoft and others, 1963), and numerous resurveys of the sample have carried out or are scheduled for the period through 1984 (Flanagan and others, 1966; Shaycoft, 1967; Folger, Astin, and Bayer, 1969). In 1965 the Equality of Educational Opportunity (EEO) survey of some 600,000 students in grades one, three, six, nine, and twelve (Coleman, Campbell, and others, 1966) was carried out in accord with the mandate of the Civil Rights Act of 1964 that a survey be made "concerning the lack of availability of equal educational opportunities for individuals by reason of race, color, religion, or national origin in public educational institutions at all levels in the United States" (Coleman, Campbell, and others, 1966: iii). The elementary and secondary school survey was supplemented by studies of the degree of racial segregation in colleges and universities, of potential teachers, of nonenrollment, and of the effects of school integration, and by case studies of school desegregation.

The EEO survey focused directly on some aspects of educational stratification from the viewpoint of the student as consumer by right of educational services. Project Talent was based on the complementary view of the student as potential supplier of skilled manpower. From one perspective the student who performs poorly is a victim of unequal opportunity; from the other he is talent wastage. The EEO survey was designed primarily to measure the extent and consequences of racial segregation in the schools. Achievement and aptitude tests were given, but there was an extensive effort to gather data on the school and home environments of students. (One wonders why the EEO mental tests were not selected from the "benchmark" tests created for Project Talent.) Project Talent's efforts were directed primarily toward the measurement of psychological traits: aptitudes, achievements, and interests. In the initial two-day testing program less than eighty minutes were devoted to the collection of basic social background data (Flanagan and others, 1962a: 225), and the Student Information Blank was designed to make insufficient time a major source of item nonresponse. Extensive and early efforts were made to assess the reliability of the mental test scores and to construct composites thereof (Flanagan and others, 1962a; Flanagan and others, 1964: chap. 3, Appendix B), but a simple composite socioeconomic status variable was not produced until 1966 (Flanagan and others,

1966: Appendix E). A question on the proportion of students who were Negroes was included in a questionnaire administered to principals, but the initial round of Project Talent did not ascertain race for individuals.

No doubt these differing emphases on psychological and social measurement reflect changes in national priorities and racial etiquette as much as the substantive and analytic interests of designers of the two studies. Still, it is an embarrassment that these two large studies with so much potential overlap could have been carried out within a five-year period with virtually no comparability in measurement. In view of the national political situation and the recalcitrance of school officials, the future of national school surveys is already in doubt, but certainly no future study of this genre should be undertaken without adequate provision for comparison with the Project Talent and EEO surveys.

SCHOOL EFFECTS

The EEO survey documented the nearly complete racial segregation which exists in the nation's public schools, and it also established the existence of substantial grade-level-specific racial and ethnic differentials in academic performance. Other parts of the survey yielded no obvious conclusions about the sources of the academic performance differentials. Contrary to expectation, the survey produced no evidence of massive inequality in the distribution of school resources. Moreover, on a gross basis, the school attended contributed no more than ten to twenty percent of the variance in the performance of whites and Negroes at any grade level. Despite this evidence, but presumably because of the accessibility of schools as administrative units, the major analytic effort in the survey report (Coleman, Campbell, and others, 1966: 290–334) was a methodologically controversial attempt to account for the variation in student performance levels among schools (Bowles and Levin, 1968a, 1968b; Bowles, 1968; Coleman, 1968a; Cain and Watts, 1968).

The major argument of the EEO analysis was that the composition of the student body, most notably with respect to socioeconomic status, and to a lesser degree, with respect to race (U.S. Civil Rights Commission, 1967; Pettigrew, 1968), was the most significant factor influencing the school differentials in performance which remained after individual background factors had been taken into account. The economist-critics of the Coleman-Campbell Report argued that the effects of school facilities and teaching quality had been slighted in the EEO analysis, but another defect may be more important. The EEO report's operationalization of the influence of association with fellow students by gross aggregate measures of student body composition is simply artifactual. On one hand, it ignores the effects of differential association which occur within any school (Rhodes, Reiss, and Duncan, 1965; Duncan, Haller, and Portes, 1968); and, on the other hand, it overestimates the ability of differential association to account for school differences (Hauser, 1969; Hauser, 1970). The school context argument has remained resilient in the face of methodological arguments (Pettigrew, 1969) and essentially negative empirical findings (Wilson, 1967) by its own leading proponents. If the analysis of school effects in the EEO survey was open to criticism, it was at least more ambitious than the corresponding cross-sectional effort in Project Talent (Flanagan and others, 1962b), which consisted largely of uninterpreted masses of interschool correlations and which did not attempt to cope with the methodological difficulties of multilevel analysis.

Leaving to one side the interpretation of school differences, the EEO finding that school differences were small is undoubtedly correct. None of the studies of school effects leaves any reason to doubt the validity of this finding (Hauser, 1968). Moreover, we can reduce gross school effects to the point of substantive (if not statistical) insignificance by recourse to the moderately powerful sociological theories of individual achievement which are presently available (Sewell and Armer, 1966; Hauser, 1969). One Project Talent monograph (Shaycoft, 1967) provides instructive data on this point. In 1963 Shaycoft retested nearly ten thousand high school seniors who had taken the Project Talent battery as ninth graders in 1960. Shaycoft's data are not from a probability sample. For example, schools were selected in order to vary as widely as possible (Shaycoft, 1967: 2–2), but this makes the data more useful for the present purpose. In a reanalysis of some of Shaycoft's published data (Table 6–1a and Table 7–2d) on six mental test scores, I found that school attended added from 3.7 percent to 5.8 percent to the variance explained in twelfth grade scores when ninth grade scores (uncorrected for reliability) were controlled statistically.

Another longitudinal assessment of the effect of the high school is presented in a report (Folger, Astin, and Bayer, 1969: Table 5.4) on the five-year Project Talent follow-up of 1960 high school graduates. Again, the data are suspect, but zero order correlations of .268 for males and .217 for females were found between the proportion of students in the high school class who attended college and the college attendance of the respondent. These imply that 7.2 percent of the variance in boys' college attendance and 4.7 percent of that for girls occurs between high schools. When thirty-three other nonschool variables were controlled in a multiple regression analysis, the residual effects of the high school on college attendance were reduced to negligible values.

However small school effects may be on a gross or net basis, there is good reason to doubt the much-quoted conclusion of the Coleman-Campbell Report (1966: 325):

that schools bring little influence to bear on a child's achievement that is independent of his background and general social context; and that this very lack of an independent effect means that the inequalities imposed on children by their home, neighborhood, and peer environment are carried along to become the inequalities with which they confront adult life at the end of school. For equality of educational opportunity through the schools must imply a strong effect of schools that is independent of the child's immediate social environment, and that strong independent effect is not present in American schools.

In fact most variation in achievement occurred within schools, not from school to school, and most within-school variation in achievement was independent of individual social backgrounds, attitudes, and environmental factors (Coleman, Campbell, and others, 1966: 298–325). This large component of unexplained interindividual variation coexists with a moderate homogeneity of home backgrounds and peer environments within schools (race excepted). It may be interpreted as a contribution of schooling itself, if not "the school attended," to a component of the inequalities with which students confront adult life which is independent of social origins. When schooling is viewed as a long-term process of interindividual differentiation, the relevance to the stratification process of cross-sectional interschool differences in academic achievement is no longer obvious.

PROBLEMS IN PANEL STUDIES

One of the disappointing things about the EEO survey was the failure to identify individual students for later restudy (Sewell, 1967; B. Duncan, 1968). It means that we have lost a rare opportunity to study the long-term influence of grade-level academic performance and school factors. On the other hand, the experience of some of the Project Talent panels leaves little room for optimism about the utility of large-scale panel studies for social accounting purposes.

For example, we have already noted Shaycoft's use of a purposive sample of schools in her longitudinal study of academic achievement. In addition large numbers of students were lost as a result of deliberate exclusion of schools in very large cities; nonparticipation of selected schools; use of a backward rather than a forward record matching procedure; and exclusion of school dropouts. My rough estimate is that Shaycoft's 1963 panel included a nonrandom fifty-five percent of the still-enrolled members of the cohort and forty-four percent of the total cohort.

Only about fifteen percent of the Project Talent panel of 1960 high school seniors was represented in the analysis of 1965 data by Folger, Astin, and Bayer (1969: Appendix B). Only about a third of the cohort sample of 100,000 responded to a four-page mailed questionnaire, and the investigators eliminated all case records for which any of the nearly forty variables of interest had not been ascertained. Some 11,000 of the 1965 respondents had failed to report 1959 income in the 1960 survey. Folger, Astin, and Bayer concluded rightly that their data were not representative of univariate distributions in the initial cohort, but they also argued that they could estimate "the interrelationships and the interaction of these variables as they operate to influence subsequent educational attainment." Further, they stated that "the homogeneity of the sample does, however, tend to yield lower correlation coefficients than would be expected in the general population and . . . tend to reflect conservative estimates of the impact of the various factors on educational attainment." I am skeptical of the claim that a non-random fifteen percent sample of any size permits generalization to anything beyond the size of zero order relationships, if that. Surely, we do not need fifteen or thirty thousand questionnaires to predict the sign of the relationship between some social or psychological background variable and college attendance.

The problem is neither to avoid overestimating the influence of background variables nor to establish the direction of their effects with absolute certainty, but to estimate and interpret the effects correctly. If conclusions as to the sign of relationships were all that mattered, small but intensive personal interview follow-ups would suffice, and they would not yield biased estimates of univariate or multivariate statistics. Satisfactory response rates can be achieved from mail questionnaires in large-scale panel studies provided the questionnaire is short, interesting, and easy to answer, and provided there is a serious effort to locate nonrespondents (Sewell and Shah, 1967). Care in questionnaire design and a balance of efforts to reduce sampling and nonsampling error are required to produce data worth analyzing. Neither huge samples, nor repeated measurements, nor multivariate analyses are worth the loss of generality entailed in response rates below fifty percent. For educational studies the implication is that careful measurement in moderately large samples will yield the greatest payoff.

MEASUREMENT AND MODEL CONSTRUCTION

The difficulties of interpreting complex social processes which extend over scores of years are not solved merely by accurate representation of the populations of interest or by standardization of measurement techniques. Some concepts can not be represented by any directly observable indicator (Blalock, 1967; Costner, 1969), and substantive conclusions may rest on the value of a high-order effect measure. The construction of cogent and self-consistent theories requires methods which permit simultaneous examination of all aspects of a proposed interpretation. For these reasons, and because stratification variables are often measured on interval scales and in unambiguous temporal order, causal models promise to be of great value in research on educational stratification. There are already numerous examples of the use of causal models in stratification research (for example, Blau and Duncan, 1967; Sewell and Shah, 1967; O. D. Duncan, 1968a, 1968b; Duncan, Haller, and Portes, 1968; Sewell, Haller, and Portes, 1969; Hauser, 1969), and the list is growing rapidly.

The kind of results which can be obtained from a modelling approach are illustrated by the path diagram in Figure 2 (Duncan, 1966). The diagram represents a portion of the model of educational attainment and early occupational achievement recently proposed by Sewell, Haller, and Portes (1969). The numerical results pertain to a cohort of 850 farm boys who were graduated from Wisconsin high schools in 1957. No direct comparison may be made between the results in Figure 2 and the published findings of Sewell, Haller, and Portes because of several differences in the data set and in methods used to obtain a numerical solution.

In a path diagram causal assumptions are symbolized by unidirectional arrows pointing in the direction of postulated causal influence. The curved two-headed arrow between X_6 and X_5 symbolizes the fact that this model does not attempt to analyze their intercorrelation. All relationships among variables are assumed to be linear and additive. Further, each variable to which direct causal paths run from one or more measured variables is assumed to be completely determined by the effects of those variables and an error variable. The error variables, whose effects are symbolized in Figure 2 by unlabeled arrows on the edges of the diagram, represent the combined effects of causal factors not included in the diagram, random measurement errors, and violations of the assumptions of additivity and linearity.

The model is intended to interpret the relationships between mental ability (X_6) and socioeconomic status (X_5), shown on the left-hand side of the diagram, and ultimate educational attainment (X_1), shown on the right-hand side of the diagram. Three intervening variables are introduced in an effort to explain the influence of the two predetermined variables (X_5 and X_6) on educational attainment. They are high school rank (X_4), significant others' influence (X_3), and college plans (X_2). Each of the intervening variables is influenced by ability and socioeconomic status and in turn influences educational attainment. Further, high school rank influences the perceived expectations or actions of the significant others and college plans, and significant others' influence affects college plans. Finally, we assume that ability and socioeconomic status may influence educational attainment directly, as well as indirectly through the intervening variables.

From a methodological point of view, the most interesting aspect of Figure 2 is the measurement of socioeconomic status and significant others' influence. As depicted in the diagram, each of those variables was not measured by a single observed indicator. There are four indicators of socioeco-

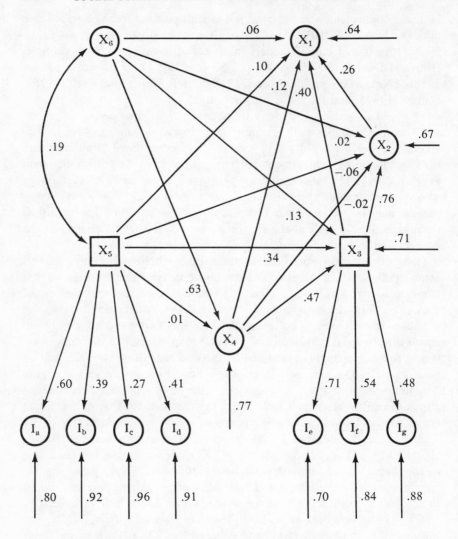

Figure 2. *Educational Attainment of Wisconsin Farm Boys*

[Item identifications are: X_1 = Educational attainment in 1964; X_2 = Educational aspiration; X_3 = Perceptions of significant others; X_4 = High school rank; X_5 = Socioeconomic status; X_6 = Mental ability; I_a = Father's education; I_b = Mother's education; I_c = Father's occupation; I_d = Average parental income; I_e = Parental encouragement; I_f = Teacher's encouragement; and I_g = Friends' college plans.]

nomic status (I_a = father's education, I_b = mother's education, I_c = father's occupation, and I_d = average annual parental income, 1957–1961) and three indicators of the perceived influence of significant others (I_e = parental encouragement, I_f = teacher's encouragement, and I_g = friends' college plans). In both models, following the logic of Costner's exposition (1969), the indicators are reflections of the variables which they represent. That is, we assume that the indicators are related to one another and to other variables in the main model only by virtue of their determination by socioeconomic status (for I_a, I_b, I_c, and I_d) or by perceived expectations or actions of significant others (for I_e, I_f, and I_g). The technical details of the solution of the model are not of interest here. One salient point is that the coefficients in the main model and those of the measurement model are interdependent. We could not assume that the I-variables are better or worse indicators of the concepts which they represent without changing coefficients in the main model, and vice versa.

From a theoretical point of view, the model in Figure 2 is not especially complicated. Simply stated, it argues that the effects of ability and socioeconomic background on educational attainment are mediated by levels of aspiration, social-psychological supports, and academic performance, yet it is not clear that those ideas could be represented adequately by any less complicated scheme. Aside from the analytic complexity of the model, it is pertinent in the present context to mention that the data for Figure 2 were merged from five sources over a seven-year period: (1) a spring 1957 school-administered questionnaire (I_a, I_b, I_e, I_f, I_g, X_2); (2) school records (X_4); (3) the Wisconsin State Testing Service (X_6); (4) the Wisconsin State Department of Revenue (I_c, I_d); and (5) a 1964 postcard questionnaire (X_1).

The coefficients on the paths are regression coefficients in standard form. They express the net effect on a dependent variable in standard deviation units of a unit standard deviation change in a predetermined variable. The correlations among the variables may be reproduced and the patterns of indirect effects interpreted by adding up the products of the coefficients along each distinct path leading from one variable of interest to another. The only restrictions in constructing compound paths are that no line segment can be used more than once in any compound path, and only one change of direction can be made in tracing along a compound path. In the present context no extensive decomposition of the model in Figure 2 seems necessary. The direct effects shown on the diagram suggest that social-psychological supports play a crucial role in mediating the effects of socioeconomic background and ability on educational attainment. Significant others' influence accounts for nearly all of the effects of ability, socioeconomic status, and high school rank on college plans, and it has an effect on attainment which is substantially greater than that of college plans. The model is not entirely successful in accounting for the influence of socioeconomic background and ability on educational attainment; each of the predetermined variables retains a modest direct influence on attainment.

Of course, one may disagree with the choice of variables employed in

Figure 2, with some aspects of the causal ordering, or with the measurement assumptions. Changes in any or all of these aspects of the model may modify substantive conclusions. For example, I am not convinced that the model in Figure 2 is entirely defensible. The value of model construction does not lie in the results of any single effort, but in the potential for criticism, reconsideration, replication, and cumulation of analytic findings which it creates.

CONCLUSION

Retrospective cohort data suggest that schools function to a significant degree as channels of upward and downward mobility, while studies of currently enrolled youth often emphasize the role of schools in maintaining status across generations. This conflict of interpretation is partly a consequence of the failure of most school studies to measure the effects as well as the causes of educational variables. It also arises from the difficulty of reconciling data for individuals in school with the progress of birth cohorts through the schools. Detailed educational histories for actual birth cohorts are required before we can render descriptively accurate accounts of the role of educational institutions in the stratification process.

Recent research on educational stratification has not produced much movement toward a merger of cohort and institutional approaches. It seems unlikely that we shall be able to generate interpretable time series for major variables extending very far into the past, and some opportunities for longitudinal analyses in large and representative cohorts have been neglected or mishandled. Still, there are a few longitudinal studies of representative samples in progress, and the growing use of explicit causal models promises to improve the quality of analysis and interpretation. At least we may hope for increased recognition of the limitations of alternative data sources.

This essay has emphasized data and methods, rather than theory and policy. The emphasis is deliberate. There is no dearth of ideas about what happens in educational stratification, nor about what should be done to change the parameters of the stratification process in the United States. On the contrary, there are probably too many ideas in circulation and too few workable mechanisms for discarding those which are not useful. There is a large gap between our willingness to talk about the system of stratification and our capacity to describe analytically how it actually works and how it might be changed. No disproportionate effort need be devoted to matters of method as we try to close this gap. What is required is a disciplined capacity to apply what we already know about conducting social research to the vast backlog of theoretical notions which affect our thinking about the stratification process.

REFERENCES

Barber, Bernard
1957   Social Stratification: A Comparative Analysis of Structure and Process. New York: Harcourt, Brace.

Blalock, Hubert M., Jr.
1967   "The measurement problem: a gap between the languages of theory and research." Pp. 5–27 in Hubert M. Blalock, Jr. and Ann B. Blalock (eds.), Methodology in Social Research. New York: McGraw-Hill Book Company.

Blau, Peter M., and Otis Dudley Duncan
1967   The American Occupational Structure. New York: John Wiley.

Bowles, Samuel S.
1968   "Towards equality?" Harvard Educational Review 38 (Winter): 89–99.

Bowles, Samuel S., and Henry M. Levin
1968a "Equality of educational opportunity: more on multicollinearity and the effectiveness of schools," The Journal of Human Resources (Summer).
1968b "The determinants of scholastic achievement—an appraisal of some recent evidence," The Journal of Human Resources 3 (Winter): 3–24.

Cain, Glen, and Harold Watts
1968   "Problems in making inferences from the Coleman report." Discussion paper 28–68, Institute for Research on Poverty, The University of Wisconsin, Madison, Wisconsin.

Center for Policy Studies
1968   The Quality of Inequality: Urban and Surburban Public Schools. Chicago: The University of Chicago Press.

Charters, W. W., Jr.
1963   "The social background of teaching." Pp. 715–813 in N. L. Gage (ed.), Handbook of Research on Teaching. Chicago: Rand McNally.

Clark, Kenneth B.
1968   "Alternative public school systems," Harvard Educational Review 38 (Winter): 100–113.

Cohen, Wilber J.
1967   "Education and learning," The Annals 373 (September): 79–101.

Coleman, James S.
1968a "Equality of educational opportunity: reply to Bowles and Levin," The Journal of Human Resources 3 (Spring): 237–246.
1968b "The concept of equality of educational opportunity," Harvard Educational Review 38 (Winter): 7–22.
1969   "Race relations and social change." Pp. 274–341 in Irwin Katz and Patricia Gurin (eds.), Race and the Social Sciences. New York: Basic Books, Inc.

Coleman, James S., Ernest Q. Campbell, Carol J. Hobson, James McPartland, Alexander M. Mood, Frederick D. Weinfeld, and Robert L. York
1966   Equality of Educational Opportunity. Washington, D. C.: U. S. Government Printing Office.

Conlisk, John
1969   "Determinants of school enrollment and school performance," Journal of Human Resources 4 (Spring): 140–157.

Cooley, Charles Horton
1909   Social Organization. New York: Charles Scribner's Sons.

Costner, Herbert L.
1969   "Theory, deduction and rules of correspondence." American Journal of Sociology 75 (September): 245–263.

Cowhig, James D.,and Charles B. Nam
1961   "Educational status, college plans, and occupational status of farm and nonfarm youths: October 1959." Farm Population, Series Census–ERS (P–27), No. 30 (August): 1–33.

Dahrendorf, Ralf
1959   Class and Class Conflict in Industrial Society. Stanford: Stanford University Press.

Duncan, Beverly
1965   Family Factors and School Dropout: 1920–1960. Cooperative Research Project No. 2258, Office of Education, U. S. Department of Health, Education, and Welfare. Ann Arbor, Michigan: The University of Michigan.
1967   "Education and social background," American Journal of Sociology 72 (January): 366–371.
1968   "Trends in output and distribution of schooling." Pp. 601–674 in Eleanor Bernert Sheldon and Wilbert E. Moore (eds.), Indicators of Social Change. New York: Russell Sage Foundation.

Duncan, Beverly,and Otis Dudley Duncan
1969   "Family stability and occupational success," Social Problems 16 (Winter): 273–285.

Duncan, Otis Dudley
1967   "Discrimination against Negroes," The Annals 371 (May): 85–103.
1968a "Ability and achievement," Eugenics Quarterly 15 (March):1–11.
1968b "Inheritance of poverty or inheritance of race?" Pp. 85–110 in Daniel P. Moynihan (ed.), On Understanding Poverty. New York: Basic Books, Inc.
1968c "Social stratification and mobility: problems in the measurement of trend." Pp. 675–719 in Eleanor Bernert Sheldon and Wilbert E. Moore (eds.), Indicators of Social Change. New York: Russell Sage Foundation.
1969   "Social forecasting: the state of the art," The Public Interest 17 (Fall): 88–118.

Duncan, Otis Dudley, Archibald O. Haller, and Alejandro Portes
1968   "Peer influences on aspirations: a reinterpretation," American Journal of Sociology 74 (September): 119–137.

Duncan, Otis Dudley,and Robert W. Hodge
1963   "Education and occupational mobility," American Journal of Sociology 67 (May): 629–644.

Eckland, Bruce K.
1964   "Social class and college graduation: some misconceptions corrected," American Journal of Sociology 70 (July): 36–50.

Educational Testing Service
1957   Background Factors Relating to College Plans and College Enrollment Among Public High School Students. Princeton: Educational Testing Service.

Featherman, David Lee
1969   The Socioeconomic Achievement of White Married Males in the United States: 1957–67. Unpublished Doctoral Dissertation for The University of Michigan.

Flanagan, J. C., W. W. Cooley, P. R. Lohnes, L. F. Schoenfeldt, R. W. Holdeman, Janet Combs, and Susan J. Becker
1966   Project Talent one-year follow-up studies. Final report to the U. S. Office of Education, Cooperative Research Project No. 2333. Pittsburgh: Project Talent Office, University of Pittsburgh.

Flanagan, J. C., J. T. Dailey, Marion F. Shaycoft, W. A. Gorham, D. B. Orr, and I. Goldberg.
1962a The Talents of American Youth. Vol. 1. Design for a Study of American Youth. Boston: Houghton Mifflin.

Flanagan, J. C., J. T. Dailey, Marion F. Shaycoft, D. B. Orr, and I. Goldberg
1962b Studies of the American High School. Final report to the U. S. Office of Education, Cooperative Research Project No. 226. Washington, D. C.: Project Talent Office, University of Pittsburgh.

Flanagan, J. C., F. B. Davis, J. T. Dailey, Marion F. Shaycoft, D. B. Orr, I. Goldberg, and C. A. Neyman, Jr.
1964 The American High-School Student. Final report to the U. S. Office of Education, Cooperative Research Project No. 635. Pittsburgh: Project Talent Office, University of Pittsburgh.

Folger, John K., Helen S. Astin, and Alan E. Bayer
1969 Human Resources and Higher Education. New York: Russell Sage Foundation.

Hauser, Robert M.
1968 Family, School, and Neighborhood Factors in Educational Performances in a Metropolitan School System. Unpublished Doctoral Dissertation for The University of Michigan.
1969 "Schools and the stratification process," American Journal of Sociology 74 (May): 587–611.
1970 "Context and consex: a cautionary tale," American Journal of Sociology 75 (January): 645–664.

Havighurst, Robert J.
1947 "The influence of recent social changes on the desire for social mobility in the United States." Pp. 97–105 in Bryson, Lyman, et al. (eds.), Conflicts of Power in Modern Culture, Seventh Symposium. New York: Harper and Bros.

Hertzler, J. O.
1952 "Some tendencies toward a closed class system in the United States," Social Forces 30 (March): 313–323.

Jaffe, A. J., and Walter Adams
1964 "College education for U. S. youth: the attitudes of parents and children," The American Journal of Economics and Sociology 23 (July): 269–283.

Janowitz, Morris
1969 Institution Building in Urban Education. Hartford: Russell Sage Foundation.

Jencks, Christopher and David Riesman
1968 The Academic Revolution. New York: Doubleday and Company, Inc.

Jensen, Arthur R.
1969 "How much can we boost IQ and scholastic achievement?" Harvard Educational Review 39 (Winter): 1–123.

Johnson, Charles E., Jr., and Aurora A. Zappolo
1969 "Factors related to high school graduation and college attendance: 1967," Current Population Reports, Series P–20, No. 185 (July): 1–10.

Katz, Irwin, and Patricia Gurin
1969 "Race relations and the social sciences: overview and further discussion." Pp. 342–378 in Irwin Katz and Patricia Gurin (eds.), Race and the Social Sciences. New York: Basic Books, Inc.

Killingsworth, Charles C.
1969 "Jobs and income for Negroes." Pp. 194–273 in Irwin Katz and Patricia Gurin (eds.), Race and the Social Sciences. New York: Basic Books, Inc.

Lenski, Gerhard
1966 Power and Privilege: A Theory of Social Stratification. New York: McGraw-Hill, Inc.

Lipset, Seymour Martin, and Reinhard Bendix
1959 Social Mobility in Industrial Society. Berkeley, California: University of California Press.

Lutterman, Kenneth G.
1968 "Effects of parental education, occupation and income on educational aspirations and attainment." Paper read at the Annual Meeting of the American Sociological Association in Boston.

Masters, Stanley
1969 "The effect of family income on children's education: some findings on inequality of opportunity," Journal of Human Resources 4 (Spring): 158–175.

Morgan, James N., Martin H. David, Wilbur J. Cohen, and Harvey E. Brazer
1962 Income and Welfare in the United States. New York: McGraw–Hill, Inc.

Pettigrew, Thomas F.
1968 "Race and equal educational opportunity," Harvard Educational Review 38 (Winter): 66–76.

Pettigrew, Thomas F.
1969 "The Negro and education: problems and proposals." Pp. 49–112 in Irwin Katz and Patricia Gurin (eds.), Race and the Social Sciences. New York: Basic Books, Inc.

Porter, John
1968 "The future of upward mobility," American Sociological Review 33 (February): 5–19.

Rhodes, Albert Lewis, Albert J. Reiss, Jr., and Otis Dudley Duncan
1965 "Occupational segregation in a metropolitan school system," American Journal of Sociology 70 (May): 682–694.

Rosen, Bernard C.
1959 "Race, ethnicity and the achievement syndrome," American Sociological Review 24 (February): 47–60.

Rosenthal, Robert, and Lenore Jacobson
1968 Pygmalion in the Classroom: Teacher Expectation and Pupils' Intellectual Development. New York: Holt, Rinehart and Winston, Inc.

Ryder, Norman B.
1965 "The cohort as a concept in the study of social change," American Sociological Review 30 (December): 843–861.

Sewell, William H.
1967 "Review symposium: equality of educational opportunity," American Sociological Review 32 (June): 475–479.

Sewell, William H., and J. Michael Armer
1966 "Neighborhood context and college plans," American Sociological Review 31 (April): 159–168.

Sewell, William H., Archibald O. Haller, and Alejandro Portes
1969 "The educational and early occupational attainment process," American Sociological Review 34 (February): 82–92.

Sewell, William H., and Vimal P. Shah
1967 "Socioeconomic status, intelligence, and the attainment of higher education," Sociology of Education 40 (Winter): 1–23.

Shaycoft, Marion F.
1967 The High School Years: Growth in Cognitive Skills. Interim Report 3 to the U. S. Office of Education, Cooperative Research Project No. 3051. Pittsburgh: Project Talent Office, American Institutes for Research and University of Pittsburgh.

Shaycoft, Marion F., J. T. Dailey, D. B. Orr, C. A. Neyman, Jr., and S. E. Sherman
1963 Studies of a Complete Age Group—Age 15. Final report to the U. S. Office of Education, Cooperative Research Project No. 635. Pittsburgh: Project Talent Office, University of Pittsburgh.

Sibley, Eldridge
1942 "Some demographic clues to stratification," American Sociological Review 7 (June): 322–330.

Siegel, Paul M., and Robert W. Hodge
1968 "A causal approach to the study of measurement error." Pp. 28–59 in Hubert M. Blalock, Jr. and Ann B. Blalock (eds.), Methodology in Social Research. New York: McGraw-Hill Book Company.

Sorokin, Pitrim A.
1927 Social and Cultural Mobility. New York: Harper and Bros.

Spady, William G.
1967 "Educational mobility and access: growth and paradoxes," American Journal of Sociology 73 (November): 273–286.

U. S. Commission on Civil Rights
1967 Racial Isolation in the Public Schools, Vols. I and II. Washington, D. C.: U. S. Government Printing Office.

U. S. Department of Labor
1965 The Negro Family: The Case for National Action. Washington, D. C.: U. S. Government Printing Office.

Wilson, Alan B.
1967 "Educational consequences of segregation in a California community," Appendix C3 in U. S. Commission on Civil Rights, Racial Isolation in the Public Schools. Washington, D. C.: U. S. Government Printing Office.

Wise, Arthur E.
1969 Rich Schools, Poor Schools: The Promise of Equal Educational Opportunity. Chicago: University of Chicago Press.

Socioeconomic Achievement and Religion: The American Case

BRUCE L. WARREN
Eastern Michigan University

Religious preference at several points in the life cycle is examined with regard to its affect on socioeconomic achievement and with regard to how religious preference is influenced by education, occupation, and income. The importance of considering the several major denominations separately instead of as a single category is demonstrated. When this is done Jews, Presbyterians, and Episcopalians have above average socioeconomic achievements; Methodists and Catholics are near the mean; and Baptists are below the average. Controlling for social origins and early achievements greatly attenuates the differences, but does not remove them with regard to education and income.

The relationship between religious preference and socioeconomic achievement has held the attention of the sociologist since the time of Karl Marx and Max Weber. Both the theorist and the research worker have attempted to explain and describe the way in which religious preference influences socioeconomic achievement, and vice versa. It is appropriate in the discussion of a topic that has commanded investigation over such a long period to examine what relationships have been found and verified, what current problems need solving, and in what direction future investigations should move. In this essay the discussion of these various relationships and problems is restricted to the consideration of their existence in current American society.

This essay has three objectives: (1) to discuss current problems in designing studies and obtaining data to investigate the connections between religious preference and socioeconomic achievement; (2) to review in a critical manner the recent empirical investigations of the relationship between religious preference and the various measures of socioeconomic achievement in terms of the appropriateness of the questions asked and the conclusions reached; and (3) to suggest a framework that will (a) specify the role of religious preference in terms of the total process of social stratification; (b) integrate and synthesize the empirical investigations pertaining to religious preference and socioeconomic achievement; (c) focus attention not only on the influence religious preference has in determining socioeconomic achievement, but also on the role socioeconomic achievement may have for influencing "religious mobility;" and (d) suggest some viable questions to be answered by future research.

130

SOURCES OF RELIGIOUS PREFERENCE DATA:
PROBLEMS AND PROSPECTS

Of all the major population characteristics, data about religious preferences of Americans are the most difficult to obtain. Both government and private sources obtain only limited data on religious preference.

Historically, the United States Bureau of the Census has taken several censuses of religious bodies which included church membership data reported by the churches themselves. Several weaknesses relating to the accuracy, completeness, and compiling of these data rendered them almost useless for most studies. Furthermore, no such census has been undertaken since 1936.

The Census Bureau has on two occasions collected data on religious preference from individuals. The first time was in the Current Population Survey (CPS) in March of 1957. Even though response to the survey was voluntary, less than one percent of the population failed to report a religious preference. Only part of the results were made public soon after the survey. The tables relating religious preference with socioeconomic achievement remained unavailable until very recently. The Census Bureau also collected data on religious preference of mothers who had teenage children. This was done by leaving a mail-in questionnaire with each mother in the October 1965 Current Population Survey sample. A return rate in excess of ninety percent was obtained. These two instances are the only times that the federal government has collected religious preference data from individuals.

The battle to place a question on religious preference on the decennial census has been a continuing one, and another defeat occurred with regard to the 1970 census. Some religious groups have opposed any attempt for the government to obtain religious preference data or lists of names by religious preference that could possibly be used to discriminate against them. Other religious groups have opposed a census question on religious preference because their beliefs prohibit the numbering or counting of their membership. Further discussion of the attempts to place a question on religious preference in the census is found in Foster (1961) and Goldstein (1969).

Non-governmental sources of religious preference data may be divided into two kinds: church record data based on membership roles and sample survey data obtained from individuals. Church membership data are not reported uniformly by the various churches. These data usually include people who are no longer members while excluding all who have a religious preference but are not formal members of any church. However, membership data have proved useful for indicating regional concentrations of the various religious groups (Zelinsky, 1961; Gaustad, 1962).

There are two major deficiencies in sample survey data on religious preference. First, most surveys include only a few thousand respondents. This
permits a detailed analysis of only a very few major religious groups because
low cell frequencies for minor religious groups are quickly encountered.
This is probably one of the main reasons why the investigation of Protestant-
Catholic differences has persisted for so long with little attention directed to
the various denominations. A second weakness exists since in most instances
religious preference has been of secondary interest in the design and analysis of studies. As a result, little attention has been given to determining
religious preference at more than one point in the life cycle. Usually only
current preference is obtained. However, for many investigations that posit
religious preference as an independent variable it would be more appropriate
to obtain childhood religious preference.

If the social scientist is going to do more than note the association between religious preference and socioeconomic achievement, he must seek
data about religious preference that will allow the analysis of several religious groups and permit the study of several variables simultaneously. It
appears that these data will have to be collected by non-federal agencies or
organizations. Attention should be devoted to establishing uniform questions and coding procedures for data relating to religious preference so that
the pooling of data from several national surveys could eventually provide
enough data for the detailed analysis that is necessary.

PREVIOUS RESEARCH AND THE PROTESTANT
ETHIC HYPOTHESIS

A review of the research on the association between religious preference
and socioeconomic achievement must begin by commenting on the role of
Max Weber's two essays that have been associated with this topic since
their publication. "The Protestant Ethic and the Spirit of Capitalism"
(1905) and "The Protestant Sects and the Spirit of Capitalism" (1920)
have shaped much of the research on the relationship between religious
preference and socioeconomic achievement. Much of this research has
merely attempted to prove or disprove the so called "Protestant Ethic
hypothesis." The nature of this hypothesis is succinctly summed up by
Organic:

Briefly stated, Weber took the position that (1) a belief-system stressing
mutually supportive "personal virtues" (economic asceticism, the intrinsic
value of work as a calling, thrift, industry and the delay of gratification, personal responsibility and rational planning, etc., which taken together are des-
ignated the Protestant Ethic) was instrumental in the emergence of modern
rational capitalism; (2) that possession and internalization of the peculiar

constellation of values making up the Protestant Ethic was facilitative to success in the economic and professional world; and (3) that Protestants, more than Catholics, have adopted these values (1963).

The "Protestant Ethic hypothesis" as stated above is inaccurately attributed to Weber. Organic correctly states that Weber was interested in demonstrating that the Protestant belief-system was instrumental in the emergence of modern rational capitalism. However, he goes too far by suggesting that Weber postulated that the degree to which a person has internalized this belief-system influences his socioeconomic achievement, and that Protestants have internalized this belief-system more than Catholics. Weber did not attempt to explain individual socioeconomic achievement by the presence or absence of the Protestant Ethic. In fact, he notes that many of the first Protestants already had socioeconomic advantages (which they passed on to their heirs) before they became Protestants (Weber, 1958:35). Actually, the "Protestant Ethic hypothesis" has been developed by those who have been attempting to understand differences in socioeconomic achievements that have been observed between Protestants and Catholics in some places and at certain points in time. Demerath and Hammond (1969) provide a persuasive analysis of the inherent problems in the "Protestant Ethic hypothesis" and the research based upon it. In addition, Greeley (1964) convincingly argues that further attempts to affirm or disprove the hypothesis should not be undertaken. We must acknowledge, however, that much of what we know about the relationship between religious preference and socioeconomic achievement has resulted from research that was concerned with the "Protestant Ethic hypothesis," ill-conceived though that research may have been.

PROTESTANT-CATHOLIC DIFFERENCES IN SOCIOECONOMIC ACHIEVEMENT BASED ON NON-NATIONAL DATA

Lenski's study, *The Religious Factor* (1961), provides one of the most thorough examinations of the relationship between religion and the other institutions of American society. Using data from a sample of Detroit residents in 1958 he concluded that Protestants are more likely than Catholics to rise in the economic system even when differences in father's occupational status are taken into account (Lenski, 1961:85). The differences are especially pronounced at the upper-middle class level. In addition, Lenski (1961:97, 357) found that Protestants view work differently than Catholics. Protestants are more inclined to adopt a rationalistic orientation while Catholics tend to accept a traditionalistic view of work.

Weller (1960) combined data from surveys of Detroit residents in 1952–1958 to specify further the Protestant-Catholic differences in achievement found by Lenski. Using data for white males raised in communities of

25,000 or more population in non-southern states, he found that Protestants advanced further in the job world than Catholics, holding constant ethnic and class origin. Furthermore, he concluded that these differences existed for younger as well as older men.

On the other hand, Burchinal (1962), using data for men who were married in Iowa between 1953 and 1957, concluded that there was little difference between the occupational distributions of Catholics and church-Protestants, except at the professional level. Furthermore, Catholic grooms have higher occupational statuses than Protestant grooms who are not identified with any specific denomination, and Catholic grooms also have higher occupational positions than grooms who specify no religious preference. Burchinal (1962:532) concluded that Lenski's finding of widening differences in achievement between Protestants and Catholics is probably not true for areas dominated by small and middle-sized cities and smaller metropolitan areas.

Lenski was criticized for not taking into account that Detroit Catholics differed in ethnic background from Catholics in the nation as a whole (Babbie, 1965:47). A greater weakness found in most non-national studies is the attempt to compare Protestants with Catholics in terms of achievement without taking into account the vast differences from one location to another in the denominational composition of the "Protestant" category.

Table 1 compares the denominational composition of the "Protestant" category found by Lenski in Detroit with the denominational composition of the "Protestant" category for the nation as indicated by a survey conducted in 1960. The over-representation of Episcopalians, Presbyterians, and Lutherans and the under-representation of Methodists, Baptists, and "other Protestants" in Detroit is obvious.

Even if Detroit and Iowa Catholics are the same in terms of socioeco-

Table 1

DENOMINATIONAL DISTRIBUTION OF WHITE PROTESTANTS IN DETROIT, 1958, AND THE UNITED STATES, 1960

Denomination	Detroit 1958	United States 1960	Difference Detroit—U.S.
Episcopalian	9.8	4.7	5.1
Presbyterian	16.1	9.6	6.5
Lutheran	25.4	10.7	14.7
Methodist	12.7	23.2	−10.5
Baptist	17.2	26.9	− 9.7
Other Protestants	19.5	25.0	− 5.5
Total	99.9	100.0	

SOURCE: *The Religious Factor* by Gerhard Lenski, 1961, p. 397, and "The Relationships Between Religious Preference and Socioeconomic Achievements for American Men" by Bruce L. Warren, 1970.

nomic achievement, we would expect Burchinal and Lenski to reach different conclusions. The term "Protestant" does not have the same meaning in Detroit as it does in Iowa or in most other parts of the country. Zelinsky (1961) and Gaustad (1962) have described the regional segregation by religious preference that exists in the nation and the differential preference of the followers of some denominations for urban residence (e.g., Baptists in the South, Lutherans in the rural North Central states). These denominational differences in regional and size-of-place locations cause the denominational composition of the "Protestant" category to vary from place to place. This compositional variation is very important when studying socioeconomic achievement because there exists a very wide range among the denominations in socioeconomic status. It is for this reason that nonnational studies that fail to take account of the denominational composition of the "Protestant" category will reach equivocal conclusions about differences in socioeconomic achievement among religious groups.

PROTESTANT-CATHOLIC DIFFERENCES IN SOCIOECONOMIC ACHIEVEMENT BASED ON NATIONAL DATA

Five prominent studies have used national survey data to investigate Protestant-Catholic differences in socioeconomic achievement. Even using national data, the researchers have not been able to agree on whether Protestants obtain greater achievement, the same achievement, or less achievement than Catholics.

Cantril (1943) using public opinion poll data for 1939–1940 concluded that the proportion of Protestants, relative to Catholics, increases at each higher level of education and economic status. This relationship was true at each level except the lowest. Cantril explained this exception by pointing to the large number of southern Protestants in this group.

Lipset and Bendix (1962) using data for 1952 and 1955 state that occupational differences exist between Protestants and Catholics only for first and second generation Americans. When parental foreign origin is controlled differences in social mobility between Protestants and Catholics disappear.

Goldstein (1969) reporting on 1957 data collected by the United States Census Bureau indicates that in terms of educational achievement and percentage of men with white collar occupations Jews are at the top, followed by white Protestants, then Catholics, and finally nonwhite Protestants. He also notes that standardizing for education and using only the urban population reduces the occupational differences, but does not eliminate them. Furthermore, he observed that Jews are ahead in income, but that little difference in income exists between Protestants and Catholics. Using just the urban population and standardizing for occupation sharply reduces the income differences among the groups.

Organic (1963) used data from the 1960 Growth of American Families Study (Whelpton, *et al.,* 1966), but restricted his analysis to white Christians with non-farm origins. He controlled for differences in ethnicity, as well as several other factors, and concluded that Protestants have higher occupational statuses than Catholics.

Glenn and Hyland (1967) made use of eighteen national surveys conducted between 1943 and 1965 to explore differences in achievement between Protestants and Catholics. They observed that at the end of World War II Protestants ranked well above Catholics in terms of income, occupation, and education. However, since that time Catholics have made such dramatic gains that they have surpassed the Protestants in most aspects of socioeconomic status. Only in the percentage who have been to college do the Protestants still excel (Glenn and Hyland, 1967:84–85). They suggest that this reversal between the two religious groups has occurred because the Catholics have overcome their immigrant handicaps and capitalized on their advantages in regional and urban location. In fact, Glenn and Hyland point out that in large non-southern metropolitan areas Protestants still hold the advantage.

If we accept the conclusions of Cantril and Glenn and Hyland that Protestants had higher socioeconomic statuses in the 1940s than Catholics, but that Catholics now have higher statuses than Protestants, then we can understand why the other investigators found differences and no differences during the interim period. However, in several of the studies the urban population or the non-farm population was examined separately and the conclusion reached was that Protestants still have higher statuses than Catholics in urban non-southern locations.

It seems appropriate, especially in the light of our earlier discussion of denominational composition of the "Protestant" category, to raise the issue of whether or not some of the denominations within the "Protestant" category lagged behind the Catholics and the remaining Protestant groups. The differences in social status, measured in terms of income, occupation, or education among the various major Protestant denominations, are larger than any documented variation between Catholics and Protestants, as a whole, as will be shown in the next two sections. Furthermore, Stark and Glock (1968) have found that major differences in religious beliefs, ritual, devotionalism, and religious knowledge exist among the several Protestant denominations. We can at least speculate that variation about beliefs that relate directly to the socioeconomic sphere of life also occurs among the denominations.

If understanding the relationship between religious preference and socioeconomic achievement is to be obtained, then combining several organizationally distinct religious groups (each having variation on both the independent and dependent variables under study) into a single religious category called Protestant is dysfunctional for research. The ambiguity that exists when evaluating Catholic socioeconomic achievements relative to Protestant achievements is eliminated when the question is restated in terms of Catholic achievements relative to the achievements of the various Protestant groups, as will be seen in the following section.

THE DENOMINATIONS CONSIDERED: RELIGIOUS PREFERENCE DIFFERENCES IN SOCIOECONOMIC ACHIEVEMENT IN NON-NATIONAL DATA

A very interesting study of eight churches in the San Joaquin Valley in California by Goldschmidt (1944) illustrates the differences in occupational status among the various denominations. He points out that those denominations in which the congregation places great importance upon "feeling the spirit" tend to have lower occupational statuses than those denominations with an educated clergy. Much heterogeneity in occupational status is observed for Catholics. Seldom does a small single community reflect the situation of the nation, but in this case definite variation among Protestant denominations in occupational status and the diversity within the Catholic group appears to be similar to the pattern found by researchers using national data.

Mayer and Sharp (1962) combine survey data about Detroit residents for the years 1954–1959. They rank religious groups on net achievement based upon the difference between an "achieved status" index and an "ascribed status" index. Their ranking places Baptists and Catholics at the bottom. They also present data on Negroes for four religious groups separately.

Laumann (1969) using data from a sample of white males 21–64 years old who were living in the Detroit metropolitan area in 1966 found that with regard to education, occupational status, and income, Jews and Congregationalists are at the top: Episcopalians, Presbyterians, Methodists, Lutherans, and no religious preference are all above the grand mean; Catholics are very near the mean; and Baptists and other fundamentalists are below the mean. As we shall observe in the next section, this ranking is also found by many of the most recent national studies.

THE DENOMINATIONS CONSIDERED: RELIGIOUS PREFERENCE DIFFERENCES IN SOCIOECONOMIC ACHIEVEMENT IN NATIONAL DATA

Six studies using national data merit discussion in this section. Each study investigated the differences in socioeconomic achievement among religious groups while distinguishing separate Protestant denominations.

Pope (1948) used 1939–1940 social poll data and 1945–1946 voter poll data. He concluded that in terms of educational achievement Baptists are the least educated and Congregationalists are the most educated. Catholics are above the Baptists and almost on a par with the Lutherans. Jews are near the top and almost at the same level as the Presbyterians. Since Pope was using a voter sample most southern Negroes were excluded.

Using data collected by the Survey Research Center of the University of Michigan in 1957, Lazerwitz (1961) stated that education, occupation, and income sort the religious groups into a social hierarchy with Episcopalians, Jews, and Presbyterians at the top; Methodists, Lutherans, and Roman Catholics in the middle; and white Baptists and Negro Baptists at the bottom. The "no-religion" group was found to be bi-modal with respect to socioeconomic status.

Bogue (1959) reached almost the same conclusions using 1953 and 1955 data collected by the National Opinion Research Center. He ranked the groups in terms of average educational attainment as follows: Episcopal, Jewish, Presbyterian, Methodist, Other Protestant, Lutheran, No Religion, Roman Catholic, and Baptist. Similar rankings were observed for occupational achievement and income. Also, Morgan and his associates (1962), while primarily interested in variables other than religious preference, provide data from a 1960 Survey Research Center survey that indicate a similar ranking of religious groups with regard to income.

Gockel's (1969) recent study of the relationship between religious preference and income should serve as a model for future studies, both in terms of methodology and types of relationships investigated. The ranking of religious groups by income, occupation, and education based on Gockel's data also is very similar to those found by Laumann, Pope, Lazerwitz, Bogue, and Morgan.

Using a regression analysis, with each of thirteen religious groups introduced into the regression equation as a dummy variable, Gockel examines the role of education, occupational SES, race, region, and size-of-place variations among the religious groups in accounting for differences in income. The results from this analysis indicate that the income differences are greatly attenuated when these variables are controlled, but that Congregationalists, Episcopalians, and Jews still have incomes that are more than $500 above the mean. Smaller differences remain for some of the other groups.

Finally, Warren (1970) reports that in terms of educational achievement Baptists and "Protestants, unspecified" have the least education, while Jews, Episcopalians, Congregationalists, and Presbyterians have the most education, with the remaining groups occupying intermediate positions. Similar rankings are obtained for occupational achievement and income. Data are from the 1960 Growth of American Families Study (Whelpton, *et al.,* 1966) and the 1960 Income and Welfare Study (Morgan, *et al.,* 1962).

Using a multiple-classification analysis (Hill, 1958; Melichar, 1965; Suits, 1957) Warren shows that much of the educational differences among the religious groups can be traced to variations in father's occupational status, respondent's race, and region of origin; but that interesting net educational achievements remain for some religious groups. Occupational achievement variations, on the other hand, can be almost completely understood in terms of social origin differences and educational attainments. Income advantages or handicaps among the religious groups become attenuated by controlling for variations among the groups in social origins, educational attainments, and occupational achievements; but as with education, advantages and handicaps for some groups remain.

Three generalizations can be drawn from the studies that have used national data to investigate the relationship between religious preference and socioeconomic achievement. First, there is much agreement as to the ranking of religious groups in terms of educational attainment, occupational achievement, and income. Second, large differences are observed among the Protestant denominations for all three measures of socioeconomic achievement, while the Catholic preference group is above the Baptists and on a par with, or below, most of the other major denominations. Finally, much of the difference in socioeconomic achievement among the religious groups can be attributed to differences in social origins and initial achievements, but for education and income some net variation among the groups remains.

RELIGIOUS PREFERENCE AND THE PROCESS
OF SOCIAL STRATIFICATION

It is imperative when examining the relationship between religious preference and socioeconomic achievement to make explicit the position of the religion variable in the process of socioeconomic achievement and to state the hypothesized direct and indirect influences. Blau and Duncan (1967) developed a basic model for the process of social stratification. Their model consists of social origin variables (namely father's education and father's occupational status) that influence educational attainment. These variables, in turn, influence indirectly (and in some instances directly) each suceeding measure of socioeconomic achievement in the life cycle. Building upon their basic model we consider the influence of an additional social origin variable: initial religious preference.

Figure 1 represents a first attempt to depict ways in which religious preference may influence education and occupational status. The same schematic notation used by Blau and Duncan in their basic model is used to show where religious preference enters the process of social stratification.

The advantage of specifying the various forms in which religious preference may influence socioeconomic achievement should not be underestimated. With our assumptions of causation made clear we can examine previous research to see which paths of influence tend to be supported, which ones do not, and which ones need to be investigated further.

The reader should be cautioned that the model is only as good as the rationale that it is based upon. Any amount of empirical investigation can only lend plausibility to the scheme, not verification, since it is possible that other variables not considered within the model may alter the proposed set of relationships. Furthermore, this model is only tentative. It specifies some of the more plausible means by which religious preference may influence socioeconomic achievement. If it spurs future research to explore any of the hypothesized relationships, it will have served its purpose well.

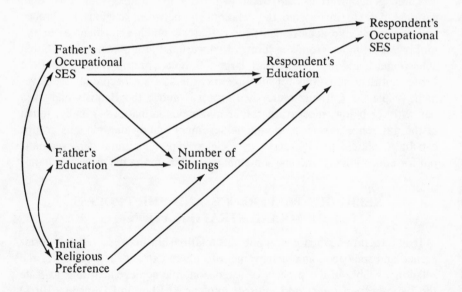

Figure 1. *A Model of the Process of Social Stratification as It Relates to Religious Preference*

The path diagram in Figure 1 indicates that initial religious preference is hypothesized to have a direct effect on number of siblings and education and indirect effects on each of these through father's education and father's occupational status. Initial religious preference also has indirect effects on the occupational status of the respondent.

In the following paragraphs we shall (1) discuss the rationale for hypothesizing the relationships that are shown in Figure 1, (2) summarize the available data that bear upon the specific relationships, and (3) indicate what kinds of data are needed to substantiate and clarify the possible relationships between religious preference and socioeconomic achievement.

EARLY RELIGIOUS PREFERENCE AND EDUCATIONAL ACHIEVEMENT

Father's education, father's occupational status, and respondent's early religious preference represent the socioeconomic and religious situation of men while in their family of orientation. In our model (Figure 1), we begin by assuming a correlation between each of these three social origin variables without specifying a causal interpretation. With regard to educational achievement, each of the three origin characteristics is hypothesized to have (1) a direct effect; (2) an indirect effect that is mediated through the number of siblings; and (3) a joint effect that is shared with the other two social origin characteristics.

The effects of father's education and father's occupation on respondent's education have been documented by Blau and Duncan (1967:chap. 5). It is possible that all or most of the correlation between religious preference and education can be explained by the correlations of religious preference with father's occupation, or father's education, or both. However, the data analyzed by Warren (1970) indicate that while a large part of the variation in educational achievement among the religious groups can be attributed to differences in father's occupational status, there still exist sizable differences (net of father's occupation) among some religious preference groups.

Furthermore, all or part of the net variation in education among the religious groups that remains may be due to the relationship between religious preference and number of siblings and the influence number of siblings has on educational attainment. The several national fertility studies demonstrate that there are differences between the Catholics and other religious groups in family size that are not due to differences in socioeconomic positions (Whelpton, et al., 1966:72). The effect of number of siblings on education is shown by Blau and Duncan (1967:chap. 9). How much of the relationship between early religious preference and education is a result of religion influencing family size, which in turn influences educational attainment, needs to be investigated further.

Since little variation in family size that cannot be accounted for by differences in socioeconomic characteristics has been found among the various Protestant groups, we hypothesize that a direct influence by religious preference on education will still have to be postulated in order to account for all of the observed relationship between early religious preference and education. This hypothesis is supported by the research by Featherman

(1969:214) which indicates that controlling for father's occupation, farm background, and number of siblings does not eliminate all of the differences in educational achievement among the religious groups.

In what ways might childhood religion directly influence educational achievement? One possibility is that some religious groups socialize their children to value education more than others. Indirect evidence offered in support of this position includes the differences in educational training required of the clergy of the various religious groups. Some select only laymen with no professional training while others require at least seven years of college training. This may indicate a difference in the value placed on education by the groups.

Morgan and his associates (1962) asked parents about the educational expectations for their children. They found that the non-Christian–no preference group (including Jews) had the highest expectations for their children, followed by the non-fundamentalist Protestants, the Catholics, and then the fundamentalist Protestants. Upon adjusting for several socioeconomic differences, as well as differences on several other characteristics, much of the observed variation disappeared. However, the non-Christian– no preference group still had somewhat higher expectations. The reader should be cautioned that the differences among the groups were not large, but still interesting enough to merit further investigation.

Veroff and his associates (1962) found some differences in need-achievement among religious groups. Unfortunately, they considered only Protestant-Catholic differences. Morgan and associates (1962:80) indicate that need-achievement for Catholics is intermediate between non-fundamentalist Protestants at the upper end and fundamentalist Protestants at the lower end. If further investigations indicate that differences in need-achievement are related to religious preference, then one might assume that parents with high need-achievement would instill values that would favor high educational achievement. Thus, if religious preference influences need-achievement and need-achievement influences educational attainment, then part of the observed relationship between religion and education can be understood in this manner.

Verifying and determining how religious preference influences educational achievement appears to be a very fertile area for research. First, an examination of the interrelationships between father's occupation, father's education, number of siblings, early religious preference, and educational achievement needs to be undertaken specifying the causal relationships as in Figure 1. Assuming that all of the correlation between early religious preference and education cannot be accounted for by the correlation between religious preference and father's education, father's occupation, and number of siblings, research needs to be undertaken to determine in what other ways religion may influence education.

One direction such future research might take is the analysis of differences in values and beliefs relating to education that are held by religious groups with the lowest and highest educational achievements, controlling for social origin characteristics. Warren (1970) reports that Baptists receive the least education and Jews the most, with Episcopalians and Presbyterians also obtaining higher educational achievements, after socioeconomic origin differences have been taken into account. Future research could examine in depth the values and beliefs relating to education that are held by these specific groups. If it could be shown that holding certain values and beliefs leads to higher educational achievement and that these beliefs are more widely held among followers of some religious groups than among others, then we would have greatly increased our understanding of the relationship between religious preference and educational achievement.

EARLY RELIGIOUS PREFERENCE AND OCCUPATIONAL ACHIEVEMENT

In the model shown in Figure 1, a direct effect of early religious preference on occupational achievement is not considered; but instead, any influence religious preference has on occupational achievement is assumed to be indirect through respondent's education and father's occupation. The two samples used by Warren (1970) indicate that most of the differences in occupational status among the religious groups disappear when differences in father's occupation and respondent's education are taken into account. Featherman (1969:chap. 8) also concludes that the influence of early religious preference does not directly, but only indirectly, affect occupational achievement. Furthermore, he shows that motivational and personality factors are of little importance as intervening variables between religious preference and occupational achievement (Featherman, 1969:247). Therefore, no direct path needs to be postulated to account for the relationship between religious preference and occupational achievement.

Future research should consider simultaneously the effects of early religious preference, socioeconomic origin characteristics, and educational attainment on occupational achievement. We shall postpone any discussion of the effect of religious preference on income pending a consideration of factors that determine religious preference at later stages of the life cycle.

FACTORS INFLUENCING RELIGIOUS PREFERENCE AT THE TIME OF MARRIAGE

The majority of American men have only one religious preference throughout their lifetime. However, there is a sizable minority of men (over seventeen percent) who change their religious preference. More than half of the men who do change their religious preference do so before or at the time of their marriage. Very few men (two percent) make more than one preference change in a lifetime (Warren, 1970).

We shall consider here only five variables out of the many that actually may help determine a man's religious preference at the time of his marriage. Initial religious preference, father's occupational status, respondent's education, as well as wife's religious preference and wife's education, are hypothesized as having such an influence. These variables are themselves interrelated in such a complex manner that a successful model depicting how they influence religious preference selection has not yet been developed. Furthermore, no such model can come forth until we are sure most all of the relevant variables have been identified.

Initial religious preference appears to have the greatest influence in determining a man's religious preference at the time of marriage. Over ninety percent of American men retain their original preference when they marry (Warren, 1970). Part of this influence by initial religious preference can be attributed to religiously based norms about selecting a mate. Specifically, it appears that the Jewish and Catholic religions have rigid norms discouraging the selection of a mate of a different religious preference; whereas the Episcopal, Congregational, and Presbyterian religions have less rigid norms that allow more freedom to select a mate of a different religious preference. (Of course, we have used the actual behavior to imply the norm, which is often a very risky thing to do.)

Norms also exist that indicate a married couple should be of the same religious preference. An indication of the importance of this norm is that in almost two out of every three couples the partners have the same religious preference at the time of marriage. Furthermore, out of the ten percent of the men who change their religious preference before they marry, seven out of every ten of these men change to the same preference as their bride. Still further evidence that such a norm exists is the fact that the percentages of couples with the partners having the same religious preference increases at each later point in the life cycle (Warren, 1970). Initial religious preference provides a set of norms about who is an eligible marriage partner with regard to religious preference and what is to be done with regard to changing one's religious preference if one chooses to marry a girl of a different religion. An indirect effect from initial religious preference through education is also probable, but most likely will have less influence than either the direct effect or the indirect effect that is mediated through wife's preference.

Wife's religious preference has an association with husband's preference at the time of marriage. Some of this association probably results from the wife's influence in persuading her future husband to change his preference.

How important religious homogamy is to her and how effective she is in persuasion will be determined in part by her own religious preference. The role of the wife's religious preference most likely is somewhat less important than the man's initial preference.

Previous writers have posed the question of whether socioeconomic achievement is related to religious mobility. We shall separate our discussion of this question into two parts: socioeconomic influences that may result in changes in religious preference at or before the time of marriage and socioeconomic influences that may lead to religious mobility at a later point in the life cycle.

The basis for assuming a relationship between socioeconomic achievement and religious mobility is the observation that there is a tendency for many religious groups (especially Protestant groups) to serve people primarily from one segment of the socioeconomic structure. This tendency for Protestant groups to develop as a result of differences in values among socioeconomic groups is the basic thesis developed by H. Richard Niebuhr in his classic book, *The Social Sources of Denominationalism* (1929). Goldschmidt also observed this tendency in his study of a California community (1944). Thus as one rises or falls on the socioeconomic ladder, we hypothesize that he has a tendency to become dissatisfied with his religious preference which fails to meet his new needs. Therefore, he seeks a religious preference that is more compatible with his new socioeconomic status.

Very few data are available to verify or disprove this line of reasoning. The work by Warren (1970) sheds light on the problem and leads to some speculations for future investigation. Table 2 shows the mean educational attainment for religious changers (early to current) among four religious categories and for the nonchangers using the combined Growth of American Families and Income and Welfare studies. The reader should be aware that these four groups were selected from an original set of eight groups (which included, besides the four listed in Table 2, Lutherans, Protestant unspecified, No religion, and Jews) in order to illustrate the possibility that socioeconomic achievement influences religious mobility. The men included in this table represent fifty-four percent of the changers and eighty-five percent of the nonchangers when all eight groups are considered.

The four religious categories in Table 2 are ranked according to the mean education of the nonchangers. With regard to religious destination, those who end up as Baptists or "Protestant others" have lower educational achievements than any of the other three destination groups, within each origin category (i.e., mean education in column 1 is less than that in columns 2, 3, or 4 for each row).

Similarly, those whose destination is Presbyterian or Episcopalian have higher educational achievements than those whose destination preference is one of the other three categories, within each origin group. The exception is the Presbyterian and Episcopal origin group, where there is little difference between those who remained Presbyterian or Episcopalian and those who changed to the Methodist, Congregationalist, or "Other religions" preferences. It follows, of course, that those with a Catholic, "Other religion," Methodist, or Congregational destination preference have educational achievements that are intermediate between those who are Baptists or "Protestant other" and those who are Presbyterian or Episcopalian, within each origin group.

Table 2

MEAN YEARS OF SCHOOLING FOR EARLY RELIGIOUS PREFERENCE
BY CURRENT RELIGIOUS PREFERENCE:
AMERICAN MEN, 1960

Early Religious Preference	Current Religious Preference			
	Baptist and Protestant Other	Catholic	Other Religions, Methodist, and Congregational	Presbyterian and Episcopal
Baptist and Protestant Other	10.0 (1412)	11.7 (32)	11.5 (129)	13.2 (53)
Catholic	10.1 (36)	10.8 (1178)	11.3 (43)	12.9 (18)
Other Religions, Methodist, and Congregational	9.6 (128)	12.0 (44)	11.5 (778)	12.6 (61)
Presbyterian and Episcopal	10.9 (28)	12.3 (21)	12.9 (34)	12.8 (268)

SOURCE: Data are from the combined samples of the Growth in American Families Study by Whelpton, et al., 1966, and the Income and Welfare Study by Morgan, et al., 1962. Lutherans, "Protestant, unspecified," No religious preference, and Jews are excluded from this table. The actual number of cases for each cell is shown within the parentheses.

In addition to the ranking by educational attainment just described, it appears in Table 2 for nine of the twelve cells signifying religious mobility that the average educational attainment of the movers more closely resembles the educational level of the nonmovers in the destination group than it does the level of the nonmovers in the origin group. It appears that those changing their religious preference seek a religious preference that is more compatible with their educational attainment than their previous one. Both on theoretical and empirical grounds we are led to assume a direct influence by educational achievement in determining religious preference at later points in the life cycle. However, we must not exclude the possibility that important indirect influences could account for part of the association between educational achievement and religious preference at the time of marriage.

As a result of educational attainment's role in the mate selection process, a man's education may indirectly influence his religious preference at the time of his marriage. If a man obtains more or less education than the mode of his religious group, he is less likely to marry a girl who shares his religious preference than a man who obtains the typical educational level of the group. Since at the time of mate selection educational attainment sorts people into different social and geographic spaces, it follows that the ratio of girls of the same religious preference to girls of all other preferences will be reduced in the locations of those men who obtain more or less education than is typical for their religious group. As a result of the importance of propinquity in the mate selection process, the lower ratio of girls of the same religious preference reduces the chances of a man with an atypical educational attainment for selecting a mate who shares his religious preference. In addition to educational attainment sorting people into different locations at the time of mate selection, there also appears to be a conscious selection of a mate with a similar amount of education (Warren, 1966). Thus for a man whose educational achievement is atypical for his religious preference group, the tendency of educational homogamy reduces the probability of him selecting a wife who shares his religious preference.

Extending our hypothesis one step further, we would expect not only a tendency for men with atypical educational achievements to marry women with religious preferences different from their own, but also a tendency for them to change to the wife's religious preference. Two reasons point to this result. First we hypothesize that a religious preference change would take place because of the emphasis placed on religiously homogamous marriages in our society. Second we would expect that in this situation the husband would be the most likely to change religious preference, rather than the wife. If we are correct in assuming that people attempt to bring all of their social statuses in line with each other, then the characteristics of the wife's religious preference are most consistent with the educational level of the man than are those of his own religious preference. Thus by changing to the wife's religious preference, he has not only created a religiously homogamous marriage, but has also changed to a religious preference that is consistent with his new style of life.

Educational achievement may not be the only socioeconomic variable that influences religious preference at the time of marriage. Father's occupational status may also have influence in determining religious preference at this point. Table 3 indicates the average father's occupational status (as measured by Duncan's [1961] Index of Socioeconomic Status) for the religiously mobile and nonmobile using the same origin and destination preferences as in Table 2. It is not just atypical education that influences religious mobility; in addition, father's occupational status appears to have a direct or indirect role in determining the religious preference at the time

Table 3

MEAN OF FATHER'S OCCUPATIONAL STATUS FOR EARLY RELIGIOUS
PREFERENCE BY CURRENT RELIGIOUS PREFERENCE:
AMERICAN MEN, 1960

Early Religious Preference	Current Religious Preference			
	Baptist and Protestant Other	Catholic	Other Religions, Methodist, and Congregational	Presbyterian and Episcopal
Baptist and Protestant Other	22.7 (1412)	32.8 (32)	28.1 (129)	37.6 (53)
Catholic	27.6 (36)	27.5 (1178)	29.9 (43)	31.6 (18)
Other Religions, Methodist, and Congregational	24.3 (128)	29.6 (44)	28.7 (778)	32.7 (61)
Presbyterian and Episcopal	25.0 (28)	43.7 (21)	39.8 (34)	37.9 (268)

SOURCE: Data are from the combined samples of the Growth in American Families Study by Whelpton et al., 1966, and the Income and Welfare Study by Morgan, et al., 1962. Lutherans, "Protestant, unspecified," No religious preference, and Jews are excluded from this table. The actual number of cases for each cell is shown within the parentheses.

of marriage. In fact, it appears that the same general pattern observed for educational achievement and religious mobility exists for father's occupational status and religious mobility.

One hypothesis that merits investigation is that much of any observed relationship between father's occupational status and respondent's later religious preference may be due to an indirect effect mediated through education. Fathers with higher or lower socioeconomic achievements than the norm for their religious group may not change religious preference themselves. However, as a result of the causal relationship between father's occupational status and son's educational achievement, the son may receive more or less education than the mode for those in his early preference group. This differential educational attainment, in turn, could lead to a change in religious preference at the time of marriage, as described above.

In addition, father's occupational status may influence the son's religious preference (observed at the time of marriage) in another way. Father's occupational achievement might also influence the father to change his own religious preference. (Hypotheses relating respondent's occupational achievement to religious mobility are discussed in the following section, but are equally applicable to the fathers.) In most cases, if a father changes his religious preference, it is likely that his children will also change their religious preference if they are in the early or middle years of childhood. Thus father's occupational status influences the son to change his religious preference from his initial one to another at a point in the life cycle prior to his marriage. If we only obtain information about initial religious preference and preference at the time of marriage, then it appears as if father's occupational status has a direct effect on the latter. However, we would predict that if intermediate observations of religious preference were obtained between initial preference and preference at marriage that any direct effect by father's occupational status would be on the intermediate religious preference rather than on preference at the time of marriage.

CHARACTERISTICS THAT INFLUENCE CURRENT RELIGIOUS PREFERENCE

We postulate three immediate antecedent variables contributing to the determination of a man's current religious preference: his earlier religious preference, his wife's religious preference, and his occupational achievement. No doubt, the greatest influence on a man's current religious preference is his religious preference at an immediately earlier point in time. Less than ten percent of the men in the Growth of American Families sample changed their preference after they had married (Warren, 1970).

Wife's religious preference also continues to exert an influence on the husband's religious preference at a later point in the life cycle, independent of any influence at the time of marriage. For the Growth of American Families sample, the percentage of couples with a religiously homogamous marriage increases from sixty-four percent at the time of marriage to seventy-five percent at the time of the survey (Warren, 1970). It is unlikely that this increase in religious homogamy after marriage results completely from wives changing to husband's religion and no husbands changing to the wife's preference.

Occupational achievement also appears to influence current religious preference. The net deviations from the average occupational SES score indicated in Table 4 for each of the origin by destination religion categories reveals that occupational achievement has some influence of its own on current preference, over and above that which is due to father's occupation and respondent's education. Although there are exceptions, the same basic patterns that were observed for father's occupation and respondent's education with religious mobility are also observed here. For example, those whose current preference is Baptist or "Protestant other" have less occupational achievement than all others, within a given origin group.

How might occupational achievement influence current religious preference? We would expect occupational status to indicate the current style of life of a man more so than his education because of the imperfect correlation between education and occupational status and the fact that education precedes occupation. As we reasoned earlier, if a person rises substantially above the norm for his religious group or falls substantially below it, he

Table 4

NET OCCUPATIONAL SES DEVIATIONS* FROM THE MEAN FOR
EARLY RELIGIOUS PREFERENCE BY CURRENT RELIGIOUS
PREFERENCE: AMERICAN MEN, 1960

Early Religious Preference	Current Religious Preference			
	Baptist and Protestant Other	Catholic	Other Religions, Methodist, and Congregational	Presbyterian and Episcopal
Income and Welfare Sample				
Baptist and Protestant Other	−2.8 (516)	0.0 (11)	− .2 (80)	.4 (36)
Catholic	−7.0 (19)	.1 (423)	3.1 (20)	3.9 (8)
Other Religions, Methodist, and Congregational	− .7 (80)	− .2 (22)	.5 (291)	5.1 (36)
Presbyterian and Episcopal	−2.4 (18)	−2.6 (8)	6.4 (15)	2.5 (93)
Growth of American Families Sample				
Baptist and Protestant Other	−2.3 (896)	1.9 (21)	2.9 (49)	4.6 (17)
Catholic	−6.7 (17)	.6 (755)	4.9 (23)	4.3 (10)
Other Religions, Methodist, and Congregational	− .8 (48)	−4.4 (22)	− .4 (487)	6.8 (25)
Presbyterian and Episcopal	−2.1 (10)	3.7 (13)	7.1 (19)	4.3 (175)

*Net deviations from the mean Duncan occupational SES score of 35.1 for the Income and Welfare sample and 37.6 for the Growth of American Families sample; deviations are net of the effects of father's occupational SES and respondent's educational attainment. Lutherans, "Protestant, unspecified," No religious preference, and Jews are excluded from this table. The actual number of cases for each cell is shown within the parentheses.

may find that his religious preference no longer reflects his values nor meets his needs; and as a result, he may seek a new preference that will reinforce his new socioeconomic position. This tendency to seek a religious group with followers of a similar socioeconomic position seems plausible since we observe a similar phenomena in several other choices in life (e.g., in residential housing patterns [Duncan and Duncan, 1955]; in mate selection [Warren, 1966; Laumann, 1966: chap. 5]; in friendship groups and voluntary organizations [Barber, 1957; Laumann, 1969]).

Other ways can be postulated in which occupational achievement net of father's occupation and respondent's education may influence religious preference. Movement up or down on the occupational ladder frequently leads to geographic mobility. Geographic mobility, in turn, often involves severing ties with one set of friends and organizations and forming new ties at the new location. In terms of religious organizations, it means leaving one congregation and selecting another. It is possible that at this juncture in membership, not only will a new congregation be selected, but also a new religious preference. As a result of the differential distribution of religious groups by region and size-of-place, some people who move will not easily locate a church of the same denomination as in their former community and will select a new religious preference. In this case, geographic mobility acts as an intervening variable between occupational achievement and religious preference.

We have considered several possible ways in which a limited number of interrelated socioeconomic variables may influence current religious preference. The strength of these influences, or even their specific form and direction, are empirical problems not yet solved. Any additional variables introduced to explain current religious preference must specify not only how they affect current religious preference, but also how they are interrelated with the variables discussed above.

RELIGIOUS PREFERENCE AND INCOME

Both Gockel (1969) and Warren (1970) have observed differences among religious groups in income. Both have also demonstrated that much of the variation in income can be traced to differences in socioeconomic achievement, such as education and occupation, among the groups. However, in both studies differences in income among some groups remain after differences in earlier socioeconomic achievements have been taken into account. For this reason a direct relationship from current religious preference to income is hypothesized. Differences in values and attitudes toward obtaining wealth may exist among the religious groups and lead to differential incomes.

Based on the observation by Warren (1970) that initial religious preference has an influence on income that is not accounted for by father's occupational status, the respondent's education, or occupational achievement, we could also hypothesize a direct relationship between initial preference and income. Instead we have assumed that this influence will be transmitted indirectly from initial preference to preference at marriage to current preference to income. For four out of every five men their first religious preference is the same as their present one. By hypothesizing a direct influence from current preference we can also take into account any changes in values or attitudes for those men who do change their religious preference. Of course, initial religious preference is related to income through several other indirect ways involving the socioeconomic achievement variables.

RECAPITULATION AND TOPICS FOR
FUTURE INVESTIGATION

The primary objectives of this essay were stated as (1) to review recent investigations of the relationship between religious preference and socioeconomic achievement; (2) to consider problems in methodology and data collection that relate to the study of this relationship; and (3) to propose a framework that would integrate the previous findings as well as suggest future areas of investigation about the role of religious preference in the process of social stratification.

Little agreement was found among studies that compared only Protestants and Catholics with regard to socioeconomic achievement. On the other hand, in those studies that considered specific Protestant denominations, as well as Catholics and other religious groups, a high degree of consensus was found in the rankings of religious groups on several measures of socioeconomic achievement. Most researchers found that with regard to educational attainment, occupational achievement, and income the Jews, Episcopalians, Congregationalists, and Presbyterians rank at the top; Baptists are at the bottom; and Catholics, Methodists, Lutherans, and "other religions" are in the middle. Furthermore, recent studies have shown that large differences in beliefs, devotionalism, ritual, and religious knowledge exist among the Protestant denominations. All of these findings point to the importance of examining the several Protestant denominations individually rather than as a single category.

Several studies indicated that variations in social origins or in early achievements accounted for many of the differences in later achievement among the religious groups. However, while the variations in educational attainment and income among the religious groups were attenuated when other variables were controlled, some difference in achievement remained.

Although the role of socioeconomic achievement for determining religious preference is less well documented than is the influence of religious preference on socioeconomic achievement, there is an indication that socioeconomic achievement does have an effect. This finding indicates the importance of specifying how religious preference is related to the total process of social stratification, describing both how religious preference influences educational attainment, occupational achievement, and income and how it is, in turn, influenced by these socioeconomic characteristics.

Of course, all of these findings emphasize the necessity of collecting religious preference data that will not only take into account the various denominations, but will also be specific with regard to a point in the life cycle. Data on childhood preference, preference at marriage, and preference at later points in a man's career are needed in order to consider the complex relationships between religious preference and socioeconomic achievement. Some kind of coordination for the collection of religious data through private means is needed, since it appears that the federal government is not going to provide these data for the country in the near future.

We no longer should attempt to determine whether it was Marx or Weber who was right, but instead we should attempt to determine for current American society what specific ways socioeconomic position influences religious values, beliefs, ritual, and devotionalism, and vice versa. Specifically, future research should examine how religious differences in norms relating to childbearing and family size may affect educational attainments. In addition, the whole set of questions relating to who changes religious preference and for what reasons needs to be explored further. The direct and indirect influences of socioeconomic achievement on later religious preference have a strong theoretical basis and some empirical support, but they have had little detailed study. Any investigation of this topic would need to explore the influence of socioeconomic achievement on religious preference until the time of marriage separately from influences on religious mobility after marriage.

The main thrust of this essay is to suggest the importance of considering religious preference as one variable in a system of variables that describe the process of social stratification and, also, as a variable that is influenced by this process.

REFERENCES

Babbie, Earl R.
1965 "The religious factor—looking forward." Review of Religious Research 7 (Fall): 42–53.

Barber, Bernard
1957 Social Stratification. New York: Harcourt, Brace & World, Inc.

Blau, Peter M., and Otis Dudley Duncan
1967 The American Occupational Structure. New York: John Wiley and Sons.

Bogue, Donald J.
1959 The Population of the United States. Glencoe: The Free Press.

Burchinal, Lee B., and William F. Kenkel
1962 "Religious identification and occupational status of Iowa grooms, 1953–1957." American Sociological Review 27 (August): 526–532.

Cantril, Hadley
1943 "Educational and economic composition of religious groups: an analysis of poll data." American Journal of Sociology 48 (March): 574–579.

Demerath, N. J. III, and Phillip E. Hammond
1969 Religion in Social Context. New York: Random House.

Duncan, Otis Dudley
1961 "A socioeconomic index for all occupations." Pp. 109–161 in Albert J. Reiss, Jr. (ed.), Occupations and Social Status. New York: Free Press.

Duncan, Otis Dudley, and Beverly Duncan
1955   "Residential distribution and occupational stratification." American Journal of
       Sociology 60 (March): 493–503.

Featherman, David L.
1969   "The socioeconomic achievement of white married males in the United States
       1957–1967." Unpublished doctoral dissertation, University of Michigan.

Foster, Charles R.
1961   "A question on religion." The Inter-university Case Program Series. Number
       66. University of Alabama Press.

Gaustad, Edwin Scott
1962   Historical Atlas of Religions in America. New York: Harper & Row.

Glenn, Norval D., and Ruth Hyland
1967   "Religious preference and worldly success: some evidence from national
       surveys." American Sociological Review 32 (February): 73–85.

Gockel, Galen
1969   "Income and religious affiliation: a regression analysis." American Journal
       of Sociology 74 (May): 632–647.

Goldschmidt, Walter R.
1944   "Class denominationalism in rural California churches." American Journal of
       Sociology 49 (January): 348–355.

Goldstein, Sidney
1969   "Socioeconomic differentials among religious groups in the United States."
       American Journal of Sociology 74 (May): 612–631.

Greeley, Andrew M.
1964   "The Protestant ethic: time for a moratorium." Sociological Analysis 25
       (Spring): 20–33.

Hill, T. P.
1959   "An analysis of the distribution of wages and salaries in Great Britain."
       Econometrica 27: 355–381.

Laumann, Edward O.
1966   Prestige and Association in an Urban Community. Indianapolis: Bobbs-Merrill
       Co.
1969   "The social structure of religious and ethnoreligious groups in a metropolitan
       community." American Sociological Review 34 (April): 182–197.

Lazerwitz, Bernard
1961   "A comparison of major United States religious groups." Journal of the
       American Statistical Association 56 (September): 568–579.

Lenski, Gerhard
1961   The Religious Factor. Garden City: Doubleday & Co.

Lipset, Seymour Martin, and Reinhard Bendix
1962   Social Mobility in Industrial Society. Berkeley: University of California Press.

Mayer, Albert, and Harry Sharp
1962   "Religious preference and worldly success." American Sociological Review 27
       (April): 218–227.

Melichar, Emanuel
1965   "Least-squares analysis of economic survey data." American Statistical Associa-
       tion: 1965 Proceedings of the Business and Economic Statistics Section. Wash-
       ington, D.C. 373–385.

Morgan, James N. et.al.
1962   Income and Welfare in the United States. New York: McGraw-Hill Book
       Company, Inc.

Niebuhr, Richard H.
1929   The Social Sources of Denominationalism. New York: Henry Holt & Co.

Organic, Harold
1963   "Religious affiliation and social mobility in contemporary American society: a national study." Unpublished doctoral dissertation, University of Michigan.

Pope, Liston
1948   "Religion and the class structure." The Annals of the American Academy of Political and Social Sciences 256 (March): 84–91.

Stark, Rodney, and Charles Y. Glock
1968   American Piety: The Nature of Religious Commitment. Berkeley and Los Angeles: University of California Press.

United States Bureau of the Census
1958   Current Population Reports. Series P-20, No. 79 (February 2).

Veroff, Joseph, et al.
1962   "Achievement motivation and religious background." American Sociological Review 27 (April): 205–218.

Warren, Bruce L.
1966   "A multiple variable approach to the assortative mating phenomenon." Eugenics Quarterly 13 (December): 285–290.
1970   "The relationships between religious preference and socio-economic achievement of American men." Unpublished doctoral dissertation, University of Michigan.

Weber, Max
1905   "Die protestantische Ethik und der Geist des Kapitalismus." Archiv für Sozialwissenschaft und Sozialpolitik 20 and 21.
1920   "Die protestantischen Sekten und der Geist des Kapitalismus." Gesammelte Aufsätze zur Religionssoziologie.
1958   The Protestant Ethic and the Spirit of Capitalism. Translated by Talcott Parsons. New York: Charles Scribner's Sons.

Weller, Neil J.
1960   "Religion and social mobility in industrial society." Unpublished doctoral dissertation, University of Michigan.

Whelpton, Pascal E., et al.
1966   Fertility and Family Planning in the United States. Princeton: Princeton University Press.

Zelinsky, Wilber
1961   "An approach to the religious geography of the United States: patterns of church membership in 1952." Annals of the American Geographers 51 (June): 139–193.

Occupational Prestige in the Negro Subculture*

PAUL M. SIEGEL
University of Michigan

Do Negro Americans see the prestige hierarchy of occupations differently from whites? The known facts suggest contrary inferences. On the one hand, the well-documented differences between the experiences and achievements of whites and Negroes in the occupational world and the social isolation and spatial segregation of the Negro community from the white population would seem to provide the basis and setting for a Negro subculture in which a different prestige hierarchy of occupations would emerge, reflecting the Negro experience in the world of work. On the other hand, in the study of occupational prestige it is well established that within a given country there are *no* sizeable subgroups of the population which hold radically differing views of the occupational prestige hierarchy. This overwhelming agreement seems to contradict the notion that job discrimination and ghetto life have produced a distinct black subculture which includes occupational evaluations radically different from those of the modal society. The present paper explores some models which would permit prestige ratings by Negroes, based in a Negro subculture derived from Negro experience in occupations, to be highly correlated with ratings by whites.

That Negroes make and use evaluations of the prestige of occupations rests upon evidence every bit as strong as the assertion that whites do: ethnographic studies of small communities and a very few thorough studies in large cities. In the sixteen studies of stratification among Negroes reviewed by Norval Glenn (1963), occupation was mentioned as a major criterion of social standing within the Negro community in all but two. If an individual's occupation is a major component of his social standing in the community, then clearly the community must evaluate occupations, and thus there must be a community-wide prestige hierarchy of occupations.

That members of the Negro community experience a different world of work than whites should need no fresh documentation here. It has repeatedly been shown that Negroes differ from whites in levels of income,

*This is a much revised version of a paper read at the Annual Meetings of the Midwest Sociological Society in Des Moines, in May 1966. Much of the analysis was completed with the support of a grant from the National Science Foundation to the National Opinion Research Center (NSF #G85, "Occupations and Social Stratification").

educational attainment, unemployment, etc., and in the distribution of occupations they hold (Duncan, 1967; U.S. Bureau of the Census, 1968, 1967). Current understanding places these differences in the context of a model of the stratification process which holds individual educational attainment to depend upon social background, occupational achievement to depend upon both of these, and income level to depend, in turn, upon all three (Blau and Duncan, 1967). Part of the observed Negro–white difference in socioeconomic achievements is to be attributed to the fact that for any particular status characteristic, Negroes have, on the average, less of each of the factors which cause it than do whites. Thus, for example, part of the average difference between Negro and white average incomes can be attributed to the generally poorer standing of Negroes in occupation, education, and social background, and the color-blind "process of stratification." But in addition to these differences due to stratification, for any particular status dimension, Negroes get less than do whites with the same levels of the causal characteristics, because of discrimination. Thus, for example, the income return on a given increment in education is less for Negroes than for whites (Duncan, 1969; Siegel, 1965; Anderson, 1955). Clearly, if a Negro subculture contains evaluations of occupations based upon the experience of Negroes in the world of work, these two kinds of differences between white and Negro experience should carry over into differences between white and Negro occupational evaluations.

That ratings of occupational prestige are highly intercorrelated from country to country (Hodge, et al., 1966) or from subgroup to subgroup within a single country (Reiss, et al., 1961, chap. 7; Svalastoga, 1959) is in large part the basis of the claim that occupational prestige ratings constitute a social fact. Of particular relevance, Morgan Brown (1955) found that ratings of the prestige of sixty-five occupations by a sample of Negroes in Cleveland correlated .94 with the ratings based on a national sample published by North and Hatt (NORC, 1947). In the present analysis of data from the 1947 North–Hatt study and its 1963 replication by the National Opinion Research Center, even higher correlations are found between mean ratings by whites and Negroes, computed over the sixty-one occupational titles that can be matched with census-detailed occupational categories. Our task, in view of this high correlation, is to explain how it could be so high if Negroes evaluate the prestige of occupations upon the basis of the experience of Negroes in them.

The kernel of our attempted explanation lies in the model of the way Negro–white differentials are produced, as sketched above. For that model, while producing the large white–Negro differences we observe, in no way precludes rather substantial correlations between the experiences of whites and Negroes in occupations. Figure 1 is a path diagram which relies upon this aspect of the process of stratification to produce high correlations between occupational prestige ratings in a white and a Negro subculture while allowing those subcultures to conform to the model implicit in the work of Glenn and others (e.g., Drake and Cayton, 1945).

In the lower portion of the diagram, the prestige ratings of occupations given by Negroes (N) are functions of (caused by) the income of Negro incumbents of the occupations (I_n), the educational attainment of Negro incumbents (E_n), and the racial composition of the occupations, i.e., the proportion of their incumbents who are non-white, (C). The mechanism which produces the function relating these socioeconomic characteristics of occupations to their prestige is merely the evaluation of the educational and income status experienced by Negroes in occupations, according to the evaluation scheme of the Negro subculture.

In the upper half of the diagram, an analogous process is portrayed representing the prestige ratings given by whites (W) as evaluations of the income received (I_w) and the educational attainment (E_w) of white occupational incumbents, plus the racial composition of occupations (C). The

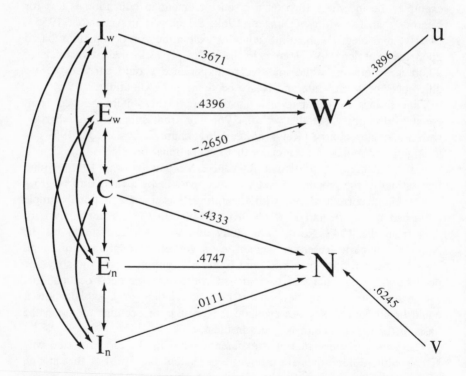

Figure 1. *Path Diagram for Simple Two Culture Model showing Occupational Prestige Ratings by Whites and Negroes based upon Racial Composition and Socioeconomic Characteristics of the White and Negro Occupational Incumbents, Respectively.*

unmeasured variables, u and v, represent the portions of W and N, respectively, which are not "caused" by the explicit antecedent variables in the diagram. As the diagram is drawn—i.e., with u and v uncorrelated (not connected by arrows)—u and v represent factors unique to their respective subcultures which exert further influence upon the prestige ratings in them. To the extent that u and v are found to be correlated, they can be taken as indicative of some factor common to the two subcultures, and independent of the socioeconomic characteristics of occupations, which has evaded measurement.

The curved arrows connecting the exogenous variables—income and education of white and Negro occupational incumbents—are the heart of our attempt to reconcile the high correlation between W and N with the existence of a separate Negro subculture. For they represent the correlations, taken as given, between the various factors which cause occupational prestige in the two cultures. These correlations are the outcome of the process of stratification alluded to above.

Before considering the numbers entered in the figure, let us examine these given correlations. To the extent that the educational attainment of occupational incumbents represents minimal skill requirements for holding the occupation, one would expect relatively high correlations between the educational attainment of Negro and white incumbents of the same occupations. Income, on the other hand, is much less determined by the technical requirements of the job itself. Rather it is free to vary with the conditions of demand and supply for labor, the seniority or replaceability of a particular worker in a particular position, or the tastes of the employer or the incumbent for various kinds of discrimination. The kinds of differentiation which can take place within an occupation and the factors which make the same job more desirable in some settings than in others (or in some industries than in others) are also likely to affect the wages paid. Considerations like these lead us to expect that the income of the Negro incumbents of occupations will not only be lower than those of their white co-workers, but also that the incomes of the two groups will be less highly related than their educational attainments.

Table 1 presents the correlations among several measures of occupational SES in 1950 over the sixty-one occupational titles which were reasonable approximations to census-detailed occupational categories from the ninty titles rated in the 1947 NORC Study of occupational prestige.[1]

---

[1] Similar calculations have been made based upon the 1960 Census and the 1963 replication of the NORC occupational prestige study. The correlation between entries in the 1950 correlation matrix, Table 1, and the corresponding figures from the later period is 0.98. The regression equation predicting the 1960 correlations (r^*_{60}) from the 1950 correlations (r_{50}) is given by $r^*_{60} = 0.96(r_{50}) + 0.03$. Because of this near identity of the basic data from the two periods, because the argument presented here

Our expectations are largely born out by the entries in the table. The educational attainment of white occupational incumbents (E_w) is highly correlated with that of Negro incumbents (E_n); and the correlation between the incomes of whites (I_w) and Negroes (I_n), is much lower. Further, we see that the jobs with large proportions of their incumbents nonwhite tend to require less education of both whites and Negroes and to pay less to both—correlations of I_n, I_w, E_w and E_n with C are all negative and large. Given this structure of relations among the characteristics of occupations that might be evaluated, and the high correlations between white and Negro prestige ratings, let us turn to our model of the two subcultures.

The numbers entered in Figure 1 are estimates of path coefficients obtained from the regression of W on I_w, E_w, and C; and the regression of N

Table 1.

INTERCORRELATIONS, MEANS, AND STANDARD DEVIATIONS OF PRESTIGE RATINGS BY WHITES AND NEGROES AND VARIOUS SOCIOECONOMIC CHARACTERISTICS OF 61 OCCUPATIONS, 1950

	W	N	I_w	I_N	E_w	E_N	C	D
W = White Prestige Ratings								
N = Negro Prestige Ratings	.9625							
I_w = Mean White Income (in $000's)	.8267	.8023						
I_N = Mean Nonwhite Income (in $000's)	.5962	.5970	.6793					
E_w = Mean White Education (in yrs.)	.8268	.7726	.7041	.7095				
E_N = Mean Nonwhite Education (in yrs.)	.7184	.6773	.6231	.8145	.9239			
C = Proportion Nonwhite	−.6864	−.6504	−.5661	−.4600	−.4859	−.4467		
D = I_N/I_w	−.4999	−.4474	−.5289	.1831	−.1674	.0663	.2875	
Mean	66.4	70.5	3.811	2.371	11.36	9.42	.085	.662
Standard Deviation	15.15	11.99	1.71	.95	3.06	3.57	.12	.17

SOURCE: U.S. Bureau of the Census, *U.S. Census of Population, 1950*, Vol. IV, *Special Reports*, Occupational Characteristics (Washington, D.C.: U.S. Government Printing Office, 1956), Tables 10, 11, and 19; and unpublished tabulations of the 1947 NORC-North-Hatt study of occupational prestige.

is cross-sectional and does not help us to make inferences about changes over time, because the cross-sectional models estimated yield essentially the same results in the two periods, and because the Negro prestige scores (N) for 1963 are based on ratings by roughly 60 Negro respondents, as opposed to approximately 250 Negro respondents in 1950, we shall discuss only the results for the earlier period.

on I_n, E_n, and C.[2] In the upper half of the diagram, white prestige ratings are seen to be composed of roughly equally weighted evaluations of the income and educational attainment of white occupational incumbents, and a moderately important negative evaluation of the presence of nonwhites in an occupation. In the lower half of the diagram we see that Negroes evaluate the characteristics of Negroes in occupations somewhat differently. First notice a strikingly important negative evaluation of the proportion of nonwhites in an occupation—in fact the absence of nonwhites is as important to Negroes as education or income are to whites, or education to Negroes. This relation is *independent* of the fact that the more nonwhites there are in an occupation the lower the income and the educational level, since the path coefficients are estimated by partial regression coefficients. That education is relatively highly evaluated by Negroes in assessing the prestige of occupations held by Negroes is consistent not only with Glenn's surmise based upon examination of distributions of income and education, but also with a vast literature on Negro occupational values and aspirations which tends to find Negro respondents stressing the value and importance of education far more than do whites (e.g., Rosen, 1956).

Negro income receives a surprisingly small weight in Negroes' evaluation of occupational prestige—in fact this coefficient is no larger than its standard error, and thus can be regarded as effectively zero. If these paths adequately represent the structure of Negro evaluations of occupational prestige, then Negroes would seem to have a quite different subculture— one in which education and working in occupations with few Negro incumbents are the desiderata. (A sort of assimilationist's dream of a subculture.) But while the path coefficients represent the relative causal importance of the variables entered *into* the model, the size of the residual paths, especially for Negroes, indicates that some major factors have been left out of this model.

The path diagram affords an heuristic for testing the adequacy of the model in another fashion than merely weighing the size of the R^2. The arrows drawn into the diagram represent the direct causal linkage between the variables they connect. Correlations observed between variables not linked directly by an arrow must therefore be explicable in terms of indirect linkage through variables which are directly linked in the diagram. Thus, for example, the observed correlation of .8023 between Negro prestige ratings and income to white incumbents (see Table 1) should be repro-

---

[2] We presume familiarity with the techniques of path analysis. The interested reader should consult Duncan (1966) or Land (1969) and references cited there. Path coefficients and correlations are reported to four place precision not because one could interpret differences in the third or fourth place, but in order to avoid rounding error in calculations based upon these reported figures.

ducible as the sum of the indirect paths from I_w to N. These indirect paths are, for example, the product of the correlation of I_w with I_n times the path coefficient linking I_n with N, etc. Thus the estimate of the correlation between I_w and N, shown in the first line of Table 2, is given by

$$r*_{I_wN} = r_{I_wC}p_{NC} + r_{I_wE_n}p_{NE_n} + r_{I_nI_w}p_{NI_n} =$$
$$-.5661(-.4333) + .6231(.4747) + .6793(.0111) = .5486,$$

a mere sixty-eight percent of the observed correlation $r_{I_wN} = .8023$).

This indicates that either there is some characteristic of Negroes in occupations that is highly correlated with white income in those occupations and which is left out of the diagram, or that Negroes are not evaluating the characteristics solely of Negro incumbents, but are taking the income of the majority of occupational incumbents (whites) into account.

Table 2 also shows that we have left out a variable which behaves somewhat like the educational attainment of white incumbents, though the discrepancy which prompts this surmise is smaller than that for income. On the other hand, the model seems to do too well in reproducing the correlations between white prestige ratings and the characteristics of Negro occupational incumbents. Finally, the model as drawn does very badly at predicting the correlation between white and Negro prestige ratings— only sixty-nine percent of the observed correlation is predicted by the model. This correlation is so low that in order to allow the present model to reproduce the observed correlation between N and W by allowing u and v to be intercorrelated, we would have to posit a correlation of 1.2326 between them. Thus, even the attempt to save the model by positing an unmeasured factor common to the evaluations of whites and Negroes, independent of the socioeconomic characteristics of whites and Negroes in occupations (the independent variables), fails.

In interpreting the failure of the model of Figure 1, there is some heuristic value in relaxing the assumptions made there about the residual variables, u and v. In that model u and v are assumed to be un-correlated not only with the measured "independent" variables in "their" equations, but also with the "independent" variables in the "other" equation. One way of interpreting the results in the top panel of Table 2 is to relax these assumptions and allow u to be correlated with I_n and E_n, and v to be correlated with I_w and E_w to the extent necessary to reproduce the observed correlations of W with I_n and E_n and N with I_w and E_w. The relaxation of these assumptions cannot change the value of any of the paths reported in Figure 1. The required correlations are

$$r_{vI_w} = .4062, \quad r_{vE_w} = .1851,$$
$$r_{uI_n} = -.2233, \quad \text{and} \quad r_{uE_n} = -.0896.$$

Table 2

ADEQUACY OF VARIOUS MODELS TO KNOWN CORRELATION

Correlation Between	Correlation Coefficients			
	Estimated from the Model	Observed	*Estimated* Observed	Required r_{uv}
	Figure 1			
N, I_W	.5486	.8023	.68	
N, E_W	.6570	.7726	.85	
W, I_N	.6832	.5962	1.15	
W, E_N	.7533	.7184	1.05	
W, N	.6626	.9625	.69	1.2326
	Figure 2			
N, I_W	.7880	.8023	.98	
N, E_W	.7355	.7726	.95	
W, I_N	.5728	.5962	.96	
W, E_N	.7044	.7184	.98	
W, N	.8089	.9625	.84	.9570
	Figure 3			
W, N	.8169	.9625	.85	.8368
	Figure 4			
W, E_N	.7533	.7184	1.05	
W, I_N	.6832	.5962	1.15	
N, E_N	.7021	.6773	1.04	
N, I_N	.6487	.5970	1.09	
W, N	.8065	.9625	.84	.8311

(The signs of these correlations must not be made much of, since they depend upon the signs of p_{Wu} and p_{NV} which are *arbitrarily* taken as positive.) These correlations are but another way of seeing what we have already concluded from Table 2, i.e., we sorely need a variable in the Negro subculture that behaves like white income.

Before taking up the search for the left-out variable, let me briefly discount two possible sources of discomfort. The measurements we have used to supply values of the income and education variables are means. Much previous research on the structure of occupational prestige ratings has employed different measurements to characterize the income and educational attainment of occupational incumbents, at least partly because of the well-known sensitivity of means to distortion by extreme values. All of the path diagrams estimated in this paper have also been estimated employing alternative measurements for income and education—percent high-school graduates and percent reporting income greater than the national median income for all males in the experienced civilian labor force. The alternate measures make absolutely no difference in the path coefficients obtained.

Hyman (1953) has shown, with data from the 1947 NORC study, that members of different "classes" claim to put different emphasis upon material and immediately useful rewards from occupations as opposed to more long-range and less tangible aspects of them in their evaluations of occupational prestige. In order to investigate the possibility that differences between Negro and white ratings arise not from racial subcultures but from social class subcultures, I have constructed a set of "standardized" Negro prestige scores by weighting the group of Negro raters differentially according to their occupations, so that they have the same occupational composition as the group of white raters, and recomputing prestige scores for the sixty-one occupational titles we are dealing with. Employing the "standardized" Negro prestige scores in a set of parallel path analyses produced virtually no difference from the analyses shown. Thus, if there is a subcultural effect in these data, it is based on race and not social class.

Returning to our search for evidence of a Negro subcultural evaluation scheme, we have reached the conclusion that there is a factor, centered in Negro experience of the world of work, which is highly related to the income of white occupational incumbents and which is omitted from the analysis in Figure 1. A possible candidate for this position was suggested by the Hodges when, in their recent article on occupational assimilation, they suggested that there may be positive income advantages to whites of discrimination against Negroes (Hodge and Hodge, 1965). Since what we are looking for is a variable highly correlated with white income and highly salient to Negroes, this hint should not go unpursued. Further, if we measure discrimination by the ratio of Negro average income to white average income within occupations, we obtain an index of discrimination which possesses not only these properties, but which also affords a quite elegant test of the notion that Negroes are evaluating the characteristics of the jobs held by Negroes. A theory of subcultures which held that Negroes should highly evaluate occupations in which they were discriminated against would leave much to be desired in the credibility department. It should be the case, rather, that if Negroes are telling us about the world in which Negroes work, they should think highly of those occupations in which it is possible for a Negro to engage in relative social comfort and to avoid social and economic stigma. Thus, since the smaller the value of D, the ratio of Negro to white average income, the greater the discrimination, we would expect this measure of discrimination to have a positive impact on Negro prestige evaluations, if they are telling us about the world which Negroes inhabit.

If, on the other hand, Negroes see the same world as everyone else sees, which the general consensus on occupational prestige would seem to require, then discrimination, since it is highly related to the average income of whites or to the average income of *all* occupational incumbents, should appear as a surrogate for white income, particularly since Negro income is not a good indicator of average income to all incumbents. In this view we would expect a negative relation between this measure of discrimination and Negro prestige ratings.[3]

Figure 2 is the path diagram for a model which allows us to test this hypothesis. By including D, the ratio of Negro to white average income, as a cause of Negro prestige ratings, we provide either a surrogate for

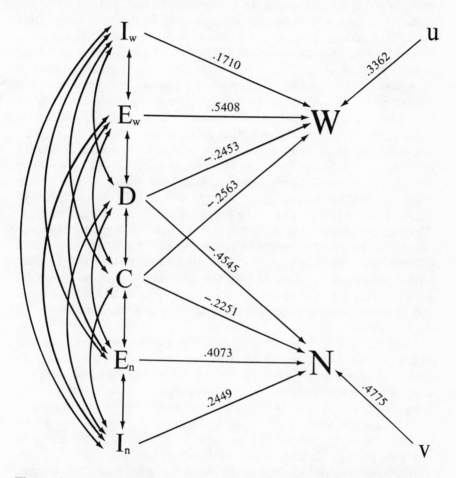

Figure 2. *Path Diagram for Two Culture Model Showing Occupational Prestige Ratings by Whites and Negroes based upon Racial Composition, Discrimination, and Socioeconomic Characteristics of White and Negro Occupational Incumbents, Respectively.*

---

[3] It should be pointed out that the measure of discrimination employed is at best a very poor interpretation of the model of discrimination and stratification discussed earlier. That model would require that we use the difference between the within-occupation slopes relating income to education for whites and Negroes to index discrimination. The data required for such an index are not available.

white income or an index of discrimination, according to whether or not there is a Negro subculture about occupational prestige. The large negative coefficient for D in the bottom half of the figure seems to offer dramatic proof that what Negroes are telling us about when they give prestige ratings of occupations is not the world in which Negroes work and live, but the world in which we all live and work, *even though* that forces them to upgrade occupations which discriminate against them. Further evidence that we have tapped an appropriate variable is offered by what has happened to the coefficient for white income in the part of the diagram pertaining to white prestige ratings. For whites, D can only be interpreted as income: on mechanical grounds, the high correlation between our measure of discrimination and white income (the highest correlation of those shown for D in Table 1) makes it difficult to separate their meaning. On substantive grounds, income discrimination against Negroes can at best make an addition to the reward derived from income by whites. Thus, putting D into the regression with I_w forces the effect of income on white prestige ratings to be divided among them, lowering the coefficient for white average income while only slightly increasing the multiple correlation (the coefficient of *u* goes from .39 in Fig. 1 to .34 in Fig. 2.) Finally, in Table 2 we see, in the panel corresponding to Figure 2, that we have managed to reproduce the observed correlations between I_w and N with this model—the model estimates ninety-eight percent of the observed correlation. While there are further conclusions to be drawn from this diagram, they involve treating D as white income. Rather than this, let us explicitly introduce white income and education into the equations predicting Negro prestige ratings, as we do in Figure 3.

The first thing to be noted in Figure 3 is that the equation predicting Negro prestige ratings has changed its form so that it quite closely resembles the equation for white ratings. All the emphasis is upon the characteristics of *white* incumbents of the occupations, and the coefficients for I_n and E_n are almost zero (in fact they do not exceed their standard errors). Thus we confirm what Figure 2 led us to expect—Negroes are not telling us about the occupational world inhabited by Negroes, they are telling us about the prestige hierarchy in the world we *all* inhabit.

While Negroes tend to emphasize education slightly more than income, the difference is, contrary to expectations based upon the work of Glenn, Rosen, and others, slight; and in any case, Negroes emphasize education less relative to income than do whites. The residual arrow in the Negro part of the diagram (v) is reduced quite strikingly from what we saw in Figure 1—from .62 to .48. This model accounts for a major portion (eighty-three percent) of the variance in Negro ratings of occupations.

The white half of the diagram does not look much different from what we have seen all along, save for the coefficient of Negro income which,

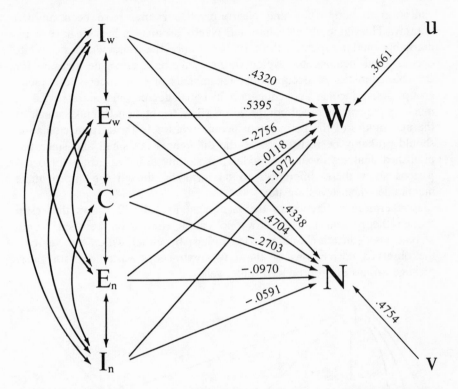

Figure 3. *Path Diagram for Two Culture Model Showing Occupational Prestige Ratings by Whites and Negroes based upon Racial Composition and Socioeconomic Characteristics of Both White and Negro Occupational Incumbents.*

though large, does not exceed twice its standard error. Reference to Table 2 will show that we still have not reproduced the correlation between white and Negro versions of the prestige hierarchy, but the fact that the residual arrows, u and v, are relatively small in absolute terms means that according to the theory of path coefficients we must posit an extremely large correlation between u and v (on the order of .84).

In turn this strong correlation can be interpreted as indicating that we have omitted a single major variable from the diagram. The similarity of the coefficients of u and v indicates that whatever this factor is, it is evaluated similarly by whites and Negroes. Duncan has observed (in conversation) that this left-out factor may well be the "prestige" as opposed to the socioeconomic standing of occupations.

The conclusions drawn from Figure 3 are perhaps best stated by reference to Figure 4, in which the negligible paths from nonwhite income and education to both white and Negro prestige ratings have been omitted entirely. The figure shows white and Negro prestige ratings to have a remarkably similar structure. Both are based upon the characteristics of white occupational incumbents—which we now take as a surrogate measure for the characteristics of occupational incumbents of both races. Both racial groups stress income and education in equal degree, and about twice as much as they stress racial composition. (The temptation to make much of the magnitudes of the paths from income relative to those from education should probably be resisted, since the differences are small and since unpublished analyses of similar models for slightly different groups of occupations show these differences to be unstable, though the approximate magnitudes themselves are not.)

Furthermore, reference to the last panel in Table 2 shows that even though the present model allows no causal connection between Negro income and education and prestige ratings by either whites or Negroes, the observed correlations of these two extraneous variables with those prestige ratings are reproduced quite well.

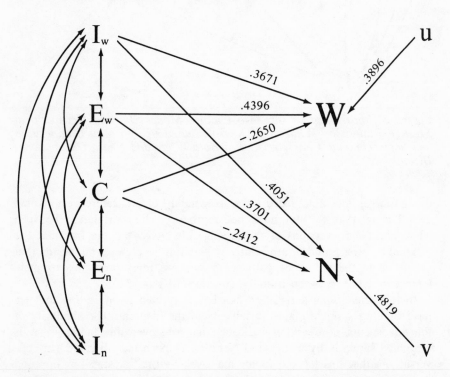

Figure 4. *Path Diagram for Single Culture Model showing Occupational Prestige Ratings by Whites and Negroes Both based upon Racial Composition and Socioeconomic Characteristics of Occupational Incumbents.*

Thus our attempt to preserve the dominion of a Negro subculture over Negro perceptions of occupational prestige, in the face of the similarity of those perceptions to those of whites, has failed. The assertion that there is a community-wide prestige hierarchy of occupations within the Negro community, based upon Negro experiences in occupations, just does not square with the facts. Instead, Negroes appear to be evaluating occupations in the same world as everyone else evaluates them and to be employing essentially the same information and the same combination of criteria as everyone else.

The argument presented here need not have employed the term "subculture." We could have asked simply whether Negro evaluations of the prestige of occupations reflect actual Negro experiences in working at such occupations. We would conclude that they do not, but that rather, occupational prestige seems based upon society-wide characteristics of occupations. We might then go on to speculate about the strains which these evaluations must place upon the management of socioeconomic achievement within the Negro subculture, and the impetus they might provide to demands for full equality and to dissatisfaction with American society as increasing numbers of Negroes achieve the levels of socioeconomic status where the discrepancies between these evaluations and their experiences become more marked.

But invocation of "subculture" as a basis for expecting what we did not find raises questions about the meaning and utility of that concept that must be answered first. How can it be that an area of life in which discrimination has been extreme—discrimination which has been a key element in shaping the Negro subculture (Ellison, 1964: 263–64)—is neither perceived nor evaluated differentially? In more general terms, what relations should one expect, *a priori,* between the forces which define the population of a subculture and the contents of that culture? What are the relations between society-wide cultural "universals" and the elements of its constituent subcultures? The present study shows that those aspects most important in "causing" a subculture are *not* necessarily treated by that subculture. How can one tell what aspects of life in the society are likely to be singled out for treatment by its subcultures? What, besides categoric membership, makes a group have a subculture? Is there any way to make more of "subculture" than an *a posteriori* excuse for deviance?

We must concur with Valentine (1968:104) that "clarification of these matters is very much overdue, if only because it has become so intellectually stylish to discover 'cultures' everywhere. . . ." The failure of the Negro subculture to reflect the very different experience of its members in this central aspect of living—earning a livelihood—can only be taken to indicate that we do not know enough about how subcultures work to employ them in explaining anything.

REFERENCES

Anderson, C. Arnold
1955   "Regional and racial differences in relations between income and education."
School Review 63 (January): 39.

Blau, Peter M., and Otis Dudley Duncan
1967   The American Occupational Structure. New York: John Wiley and Sons.

Brown, Morgan C.
1955   "The status of jobs and occupations as evaluated by an urban Negro sample."
American Sociological Review 20 (October): 561–566.

Drake, St. Clair, and Horace R. Cayton
1945   Black Metropolis: A Study of Negro Life in a Northern City. New York:
Harcourt Brace.

Duncan, Otis Dudley
1969   "Inheritance of poverty or inheritance of race?" Pp. 85–110 in Daniel P.
Moynihan (ed.), On Understanding Poverty: Perspectives from the Social
Sciences. New York: Basic Books.
1967   "Discrimination against Negroes." Annals of the American Academy of Political and Social Science. 381 (May): 85–103.
1966   "Path analysis: sociological examples." American Journal of Sociology 72
(July): 1–16.

Ellison, Ralph
1964   Shadow and Act. New York: Random House.

Glenn, Norval D.
1963   Negro prestige criteria: a case study in the bases of prestige." American
Journal of Sociology. 68 (May): 645–657.

Hodge, Robert W., et al.
1966   "A comparative study of occupational prestige." Pp. 309–321 in Reinhard
Bendix and Seymour Martin Lipset (eds.), Class Status and Power. (Second
edition). New York: The Free Press.

Hodge, Robert W., and Patricia Hodge
1965   "Occupational assimilation as a competitve process." American Journal of
Sociology. 71 (November): 249–264.

Hyman, Herbert H.
1953   "The value systems of different classes: a social psychological contribution
to the analysis of stratification." Pp. 426–442 in Reinhard Bendix and Seymour
Martin Lipset (eds.), Class, Status, and Power. Glencoe: Free Press.

Land, Kenneth C.
1969   "Principles of path analysis." Pp. 3–37 in Edgar F. Borgatta (ed.), Sociological Methodology: 1969. San Francisco: Jossey-Bass.

NORC
1947   "Jobs and occupations: a popular evaluation." Opinion News. 9 (September):
3–13.

Reiss, Albert J. Jr., et al.
1961   Occupations and Social Status. Glencoe: Free Press.

Rosen, Bernard C.
1956   "The achievement syndrome: a psychocultural dimension of social stratification." American Sociological Review. 21 (April): 203–211.

Siegel, Paul M.
1965   "On the cost of being a Negro." Sociological Inquiry. 35 (Winter): 41–57.

Svalastoga, Kaare
1959   Prestige, Class, and Mobility. Copenhagen: Gyldendal.

U. S. Bureau of the Census
1968   Recent Trends in Social and Economic Conditions of Negroes in the United States. (Current Population Reports, Series P-23, number 26.) Washington, D.C.: Government Printing Office.
1967   Social and Economic Conditions of Negroes in the United States. (Current Population Reports, Series P-23, number 24.) Washington, D.C.: Government Printing Office.

Valentine, Charles A.
1968   Culture and Poverty: Critique and Counterproposal. Chicago: University of Chicago Press.

Stratification and Ethnic Groups

STANLEY LIEBERSON
University of Washington

Ethnic stratification is compared with other forms of stratification, particularly those based on economic class. Using "ethnic" in its broadest sense, it is clear that such groups are most likely to move toward creation of their own separate nation-state. As a consequence, there are certain outcomes of ethnic stratification that cannot be accounted for in a general theory of stratification or one based solely on economic dimensions. An ethnic stratification system will also affect other forms of stratification in the society. For example, class alliances will be weaker if a given economic level is occupied by different ethnic strata. The added proliferation of statuses in a society with ethnic stratification compounds the political process. Other ways are also considered in which the presence of an ethnic hierarchy in the nation interacts with and affects age, sex, and economic stratification.

Does an ethnic stratification system differ significantly from those based on economic, age, or sex characteristics? Or is ethnic stratification but another form of general stratification? This paper compares ethnic hierarchies with other types of stratification in terms of two issues: first, the distinctive qualities of ethnic stratification; second, the ways in which ethnic stratification influences economic stratification in the same society. The term "ethnic" is used here in its broadest context, including groups that are differentiated on either cultural or physical criteria. This includes groups that are commonly called races, as well as populations that are distinguished on the basis of language, religion, foreign origin, history, or other cultural characteristics.

Most stratification theories are concerned primarily with economic dimensions such as the unequal distribution of rewards and privileges to labor and capital or to occupational groups. Indeed there are some who would hold that ethnic groups are not even a possible basis of stratification. But if, following Sorokin (1959: 11), stratification is defined as the differentiation of a population into a hierarchy of layers, and if this means an unequal distribution of rights and privileges, power and influence, then it is clear that ethnic differentiation may be the basis of a stratification system. To be sure, ethnic groups may differ in their aggregate positions on these dimensions without there necessarily being a system of ethnic stratification in the society. This would occur if the ethnic differences were *solely* a function of their positions on other characteristics such as education or occupation that were, in turn, not influenced by ethnic membership. However, it is clear that most often ethnic groups differ in their occupational opportunities as well as their positions of power and influence, rewards and privileges, at least in part because of their ethnic group membership *per se*. In such instances, the society can be viewed as stratified along ethnic lines as well as other dimensions. In other words, stratification exists *between* ethnic groups that goes beyond the stratification that occurs *within* each ethnic group.

Determination of an ethnic ranking system raises some serious methodological difficulties and the evidence on the United States is not altogether clear (see Jackson and Curtis, 1968: 125–126). It is difficult to decide whether ethnic groups should be classified in terms of prestige or political-economic position, or some other attribute. The dimensions used here are twofold: discrimination against a group in terms of economic opportunity or political power or both. This means that a society with two or more ethnic groups will be viewed as stratified along these lines if the ethnic groups have differential access to either economic position or political power in a way that cannot be explained through the operation of other forms of stratification in the society.

MAINTENANCE OF THE NATION

The most fundamental difference between ethnic and other forms of stratification lies in the fact that the former is nearly always the basis for the internal disintegration of the existing boundaries of a nation-state. On both theoretical and empirical grounds, only ethnic groups are likely to generate a movement toward creating a separate nation-state. Ethnic groups are the only strata that have the inherent potential to carve their own autonomous and permanent society from the existing nation without, in effect, re-creating its earlier form of stratification all over again. Political separatism offers a solution to disadvantaged groups in an ethnic stratification system that is not possible for groups disadvantaged on the basis of age, sex, or economic stratification.

In the case of sex stratification, it is clear that a crucial dependence exists between the sexes such that neither has the potential for maintaining a society without the other. Although there are striking analogies between the position of women and ethnic groups in societies generally (Hacker, 1951) and between Negroes and women in the United States (Myrdal, 1944: 1073–1078; Hodge and Hodge, 1965), they clearly differ with respect to the potential for maintaining separate nation-states. As a consequence, efforts to reduce or eliminate stratification along sex lines must occur within the context of the existing nation.

With respect to stratification based on age, no single age segment could maintain itself indefinitely in a society. If the age strata forming a new society was in the childbearing ages, then new age groups would be produced.

If past the childbearing ages, then it would not even be possible to produce a new generation. Under any circumstances, it is clear that separation would not eliminate age stratification since the new society, if it were to be viable, would soon re-create the age differences.

Likewise, it is not normally possible for an economic class to split off to form its own society since almost certainly this would re-create a set of economic classes. Except for the simplest systems, an economic group is normally not self-sufficient. Hence, it would be necessary for the abandoned functions to be re-created if a given class were to form its own nation-state. Unless a classless society were to be formed, a separatist movement among a subordinate economic class would be self-defeating except for those members of the new society who rise to the top.

By contrast, an ethnic group possesses the potential for creating an autonomous nation-state that would eliminate its subordination in an ethnic hierarchy. An ethnic group has all of the existing age and sex divisions. If subordinate in the existing economic system, then there are always members willing to assume the new opportunities for power and wealth that an autonomous state would offer. This theoretical potential for fission that marks ethnic strata also corresponds to the empirical reality. Generally, separatist movements or movements toward political decentralization are in fact based on ethnic group movements. In the former Belgian Congo, where Katanga province attempted to secede, there were distinctive ethnic factors as well as the influence of the outside mining interests. The creation of Biafra is a product of an ethnic group, the Ibos. The separatist threat in Canada is clearly an ethnic group movement. Likewise the political decentralization of India is deeply bound to linguistic issues that tear apart that nation. Ethnic forces were also the basis for the new nations that sprang into being after the First World War in Europe. To be sure, the ethnic divisions may mask or greatly overlap with socioeconomic divisions, but still the separation issue is normally cloaked in an ethnic form. Likewise, most regional forms of separation are usually based on ethnic differences between the groups residing in the various parts of the larger, established political union.[1]

In political terms, all nations are unions that incorporate heterogeneous populations with inherently conflicting goals and ambitions. In some nations these cleavages are based on forms of stratification that do not normally undermine the political boundaries of the nation. Although the means for seeking a resolution to these conflicting interests may vary from competition for power between political parties (or the wings of a one-party state) to demonstrations and revolution, the existing nation-state is generally main-

---

[1] The United States' Civil War is a notable exception to the role of conflicting ethnic groups in separatism.

tained. Political parties differ in their responsiveness to the conflicting demands within the nation, but they are geared to the continuity of the political union itself. Even the revolution in Russia had very little effect on the continuation of the Czarist position in Asia (Wheeler, 1960).

Although the probability of a separatist movement and its chances for success varies enormously between nations with ethnic stratification, the underlying potential for such movements exists in virtually all nations with diverse ethnic groups. Accordingly, the existing political union cannot be assumed to hold the inevitable and unvarying consent of those governed by it. The issue here, unlike economic stratification, is not replacement of one party by another or even a revolutionary change in the political system, but whether the ethnic segments will consent to participation within the confines of the existing nation-state. Nationalism is essentially an ethnic movement in which the distinctive characteristics of a "people" are emphasized and praised, and where the true and full expression of their unique qualities requires that a separate nation exist. To be sure, there may be economic interests compatible with such a movement, and international politics may play its role but the key to nation-making is ethnic groups. Ethnic groups can and do exist side by side in pluralistic nations, but nevertheless only such groups hold the potential for the creation of new, and separate, nations.

The position of each ethnic group is often an important source of conflict within the existing nation. One need only consider such nations as Belgium, the United States, Ceylon, and Malaysia to recognize that societies at all levels of development can be deeply torn by issues revolving about the positions of the various ethnic groups. To be sure these conflicts are often linked to economic stratification. Nevertheless, it is clear that a government's ethnic policy is often potentially a very sensitive issue for the stability of the nation. Language conflict, for example, can occur in such domains as: the official recognition of the language in the legislature, courts, and governmental documents; availability of government supported education in each group's mother tongue; government actions with respect to the discrimination against the speakers of a given language; maintenance of the language through mass media such as publications, radio and television; special budgetary privileges, and the like (see United Nations, 1950).

In short, the position of each ethnic group within the existing nation-state is often a major source of discontent which may, in turn, generate a movement towards political disassociation. In so far as the national government fails to meet the demands of its dominant ethnic group, a change in government provides a suitable mechanism for introducing reforms within the context of the present political union. For ethnic groups that are unable to achieve their goals through the existing nation-state, however, there is the possibility that they will seek to undo the political union which thwarts these goals. Barring the use of extremely repressive measures, no political party or coalition in power can afford to completely ignore a minority segment even if this segment is not the source of voting support.

IMPACT ON OTHER STRATIFICATION SYSTEMS

Obviously, the existence of an ethnic group hierarchy does not prevent a society from stratifying along other axes as well. Thus ethnic stratification is relevant to other forms of stratification even in nations where separatism is not a threat. There are a number of ways in which the presence of an ethnic stratification system modifies other forms of stratification and, in turn, is influenced by them. I shall describe several of these modifications, paying particular attention to the influence of ethnic stratification on economic stratification. This analysis is restricted to societies whose ethnic and economic strata are not mutually exclusive, but overlap to some degree. In the United States, for example, not all of the lower income positions are occupied by members of a single subordinate ethnic group, even if there is an obvious differential economic distribution between ethnic groups.

Class solidarity. There is reason to suspect that the presence of an ethnic stratification system will affect the development of class solidarity. It is clear that the existence of economic stratification does not automatically generate class unity with respect to either political or union activities. One may hypothesize that the presence of ethnic stratification that cross-cuts economic groups will tend to reduce the cohesiveness of the classes. If, for example, some members of the working class belong to one ethnic stratum and others belong to another ethnic stratum, then the unity within the economic class will be less developed than might otherwise occur in a nation with ethnic homogeneity.

The conflict between Negroes and whites in the United States, for example, undoubtedly undermines political unity between members of the groups who share common economic interests. This is particularly noteworthy in the South, where the conflict along ethnic lines definitely weakens both the union movement as well as a unified political approach. It is easy to understand how such divisions along ethnic lines might undermine or reduce economic classes. For the working class member of a subordinate ethnic group, there are two channels of social action that may be beneficial. Movements to raise the rewards available to either his economic or his ethnic group will offer rewards. Likewise, for working class members of the dominant ethnic group, any movement toward raising his economic group's position or reducing the position of subordinate ethnic groups offers rewards. By comparison, a homogeneous working class population does not face these conflicting and alternative paths for gains within the stratification system.

If one goes to a very simple extreme, it can be argued that the lowest economic stratum within the dominant ethnic group has a vested interest in ethnic stratification since it permits members of this group to look down on another segment of the population. But this perspective allows certain symbolic prestige advantages to override any economic advantages that the lower economic segment of the dominant group might gain through political or working alliances with other ethnic groups in the same economic position. Undoubtedly, symbolic advantages are of significance, but can be readily overdone. It would be of considerable value to work out models of the economic gains that might accrue to the economically subordinate sector of the dominant ethnic group in various settings. If these theoretical advantages are compared with the actual degree of cross-ethnic economic unity, it should be possible to determine the actual significance of such symbolic features for economic class behavior. Blalock (1967: 84–92) has offered a useful beginning to such an approach by adapting the coalition theories of Gamson and Caplow to the union situation in the United States.

The hypothesis is that class polarization tends to be reduced when such an alignment would conflict with ethnic stratification. In view of the rather wide variety of ethnic stratification systems existing in nations of roughly comparable economic and industrial development, it would be possible to test this proposition through a comparative study.

Mobility. There is an inherent linkage between economic mobility and the structural methods for maintaining ethnic stratification. In a society where there is no intergenerational mobility within each ethnic stratum, including the dominant one, then a caste-like situation exists in which discrimination is not necessary for the maintenance of ethnic stratification. The initial gaps between ethnic groups will remain unaltered over time and between generations without the need for discrimination against ethnic groups. If, however, the advantages enjoyed by one ethnic group over another are to be maintained in a system where intergenerational occupational mobility exists, then discrimination is necessary (see Lieberson and Fuguitt, 1967).

The importance of discrimination for maintaining ethnic stratification will vary with the magnitude of the intergenerational mobility patterns. If there is no relationship between father's occupation and those of his sons, to take the extreme case, then discrimination would be the only means whereby ethnic stratification in the occupational world could be maintained. If, however, the magnitude of intergenerational mobility is slight, then discrimination would be less necessary. Approaching mobility in terms of Markov chains, in the absence of discrimination the number of generations necessary to eliminate occupational differences between ethnic groups is a function of the rates of mobility. The level of difference at any given point in time would reflect the initial dissimilarity between the group in their occupational composition (Lieberson and Fuguitt, 1967: 199–200).

In effect, then, there is a relationship between the nature of the economic mobility system within the dominant ethnic group and the kinds of institutional activities necessary to keep some other ethnic stratum subordinate. If the actual rates of intergenerational mobility are high within the dominant ethnic group, then the maintenance of ethnic stratification will require severe forms of discrimination and repression in order to keep the subordinate ethnic groups from moving out of their subordinate economic positions. If, on the other hand, occupational mobility is less easily obtained, then such forms of discrimination are less necessary for maintaining ethnic stratification.

Creation of economic classes. New economic classes within a given ethnic population are sometimes created by the subordination of another ethnic group. The expansion of Europeans into the remainder of the world often meant the introduction of new economic enterprises that, in turn, created a new economic stratum of considerable wealth within the white group. The plantation economy, mining, and industries developed by Europeans overseas were often deeply dependent on large new labor forces that were supplied by other ethnic groups. Large-scale pineapple and sugar plantations in Hawaii, for example, required laborers from new ethnic groups (Lind, 1955:65–67). Africans and Asian Indians were used extensively in many parts of Africa as whites developed new industrial activities. The role of Indians in Natal provides a good illustration. They were first brought to South Africa to meet the new industrial needs created by whites. In no way were they encouraged to remain permanently, but only to meet these needs (Kuper, Watts, and Davies, 1958). Accordingly, the subordination of this ethnic group formed the basis of the creation of a wealthy economic class within the white population.

There are other instances where a new economic class within the dominant ethnic group is predicated on the availability of a cheap and subordinate labor force. The use of Negro slaves in the New World was undoubtedly crucial to the development of the cotton economy. Slave and quasi-slave systems of forced labor usually mean the subordination of one ethnic group by another. Hence, these systems are often an extreme illustration of the means by which an economic class within the dominant ethnic group creates and maintains its wealth through ethnic subordination. Since often not all members of the dominant ethnic group are able to use slaves to their advantage, it is noteworthy that the subordination of one ethnic group by another does not eliminate classes within the dominant ethnic group.

But even if the historical origins of a wealthy class are due to the initial ethnic stratification system, it does not necessarily follow that this wealthy

class later remains the main cause of ethnic stratification. A hierarchy may
continue long after the initial causes have disappeared. Initially, an ethnic
group may be used by a wealthy class exclusively and thus form no competition for other members of the dominant ethnic group. But the nature
of the situation can change radically. In the United States, due to technological and economic changes, the need for Negroes in the cotton fields
declined, but their threat to other economic segments of the dominant
white group increased.

In short, the historical origins of an ethnic stratification system are sometimes linked with basic characteristics of an economic system. But, on the
other hand, these earlier needs may later dissolve and may no longer
be the basic impetus for maintaining the ethnic hierarchy after it is established in a society.

Proliferation of statuses. Hughes (1962:162–175) has described the
wide array of status contradictions and dilemmas that may be formed when
the various stratification systems are combined. The occupational role of
a female Negro physician, for example, obviously clashes with her other
role expectations. If we consider a society in which there are various combinations of age, sex, economic, and ethnic stratification, it becomes clear
that the relative importance of each stratification system may vary considerably. This proliferation of status combinations can provide a powerful empirical clue to the nature of the stratification system since it is possible to attribute causal weights for each of these stratification factors as
determinants of, say, income. Moreover, it is not unlikely that "interaction"
effects will exist such that the importance of each status system will change
in different combinations. Siegel (1965) and Blau and Duncan (1967:
211–212) report such an interaction, for example, between education and
income for Negroes. Compared with whites, the more educated Negroes
suffer a greater income disadvantage than do those with lower levels of
education.

The presence of ethnic stratification also means that many of the conflicts involving economic, age, and sex strata are more complex. This, of
course, is not a unique quality of ethnic stratification since the same can
be said for each of the other stratification systems. However, in comparing
homogeneous with heterogeneous ethnic societies, issues are compounded
in the latter. Suppose, for example, there are three major economic classes
and three major age strata, then the homogeneous society will have eighteen age-economic-sex specific combinations. The addition of two major
ethnic strata means a doubling to thirty-six combinations. If there were
three major ethnic strata, then there would be fifty-four combinations and
so forth.

One significant question revolves about the development of unity within
an ethnic group that is potentially also divided by economic and other

forms of stratification. There are some basically conflicting interests if a subordinate ethnic group contains members of more than one economic stratum. The more prosperous members of the ethnic group face special issues that deal with the conversion of their income into the rewards normally enjoyed by equivalent class members within the dominant ethnic group. Such problems arise as housing, education, prestige, political power, recreation, and the like. For those members of the same ethnic group who also occupy poorly paying positions, employment and occupation may become the dominant issue. The conditions under which the different class segments of an ethnic group will unite on the ethnic stratification issue, as opposed to pursuing their somewhat independent class interests, requires further empirical study. This is a particularly crucial problem since it may atomize the potential power of the subordinate ethnic group. Such contradictions may also be confusing for the political leaders of the dominant ethnic groups.

The conditions under which class or ethnic stratification will become most salient for the dominant ethnic group also require further investigation. In the case of the South, for example, civil rights may override other issues and hence mold both the parties and the electorate accordingly. Other issues that are class-specific may become subordinated and neglected because of the confounding of ethnic stratification. In the case of public housing, welfare, and other forms of aid for the lower income segments in the United States, undoubtedly the issues are far more complex because any decision has ramifications for ethnic stratification independent of the class issues.

A CONCLUDING NOTE

There are two main points to this essay. First, ethnic relations is a distinctive form of stratification since only these strata hold the potential for forming their own separate nation-state. As a consequence, there are certain unique theoretical issues in the study of such groups that cannot be resolved through an application of other stratification theories. The conditions under which subordinate ethnic groups will accept or not accept the existing political entity is one that requires further elaboration. But it is also necessary to consider the ways in which the potential threat of separatism may modify and affect the existing nation-state in terms of its existing economic stratification and its power structure.

The second point revolves about the relations between ethnic stratification and other hierarchical systems in the society such as those based on age, sex, and wealth. Even when separatism is not a particularly salient issue, the presence of stratified ethnic groups will tend to alter and affect some of the remaining stratification systems. In this regard, for example, it is likely that economic class alliances will be weaker than in comparable countries that are homogeneous in their ethnic composition. Likewise, the presence of an ethnic stratification system is often a basic prerequisite to the creation of certain economic strata among the dominant ethnic group.

REFERENCES

Blalock, Hubert M., Jr.
1967 Toward a Theory of Minority-Group Relations. New York: John Wiley & Sons.

Blau, Peter M.,and Otis Dudley Duncan
1967 The American Occupational Structure. New York: John Wiley & Sons.

Hacker, Helen Mayer
1951 "Women as a minority group." Social Forces 30(October):60–69.

Hodge, Robert W.,and Patricia Hodge
1965 "Occupational assimilation as a competitive process." The American Journal of Sociology 71(November):249–264.

Hughes, Everett Cherrington,and Helen Macgill Hughes
1952 Where Peoples Meet. Glencoe, Illinois: The Free Press.

Jackson, Elton F.,and Richard F. Curtis
1968 "Conceptualization and measurement in the study of social stratification." Pp. 112–149 in Hubert M. Blalock, Jr. and Ann B. Blalock (eds.), Methodology in Social Research. New York: McGraw-Hill.

Kuper, Leo, Hilston Watts, and Ronald Davies
1958 Durban: a Study in Racial Ecology. London: Jonathan Cape.

Lieberson, Stanley,and Glen V. Fuguitt
1967 "Negro-white occupational differences in the absence of discrimination." The American Journal of Sociology 73(September):188–200.

Lind, Andrew W.
1955 "Occupation and race on certain frontiers." Pp. 49–70 in Andrew W. Lind (ed.), Race Relations in World Perspective. Honolulu, Hawaii: University of Hawaii Press.

Myrdal, Gunnar
1944 An American Dilemma. New York: Harper & Brothers.

Siegel, Paul M.
1965 "On the cost of being a Negro." Sociological Inquiry 35(Winter):41–57.

Sorokin, Pitirim A.
1959 Social and Cultural Mobility. Glencoe, Illinois: The Free Press.

United Nations-Commission on Human Rights
1950 Definition and Classification of Minorities. Lake Success, New York: United Nations Publications.

Wheeler, Geoffrey
1960 Racial Problems in Soviet Muslim Asia. London: Oxford University Press.

Social Integration, Psychological Well-Being, and Their Socioeconomic Correlates*

ROBERT W. HODGE
University of Chicago
and
University of Manchester

Unidimensional conceptions of socioeconomic status require that alternative indicators of one's position in the stratification system have similar effects upon the consequences of socioeconomic level. We show herein that different indicators of social participation and psychological well-being are in fact associated with different indicators of socioeconomic status. Thus, any attempt to combine these indicators—educational attainment, occupational pursuit, family income, or occupational origins—into a single index of socioeconomic status will prove unsatisfactory because its component parts have different consequences for the same variable. We also show in this paper precisely how certain formulations of the effects of inconsistency and mobility are wholly redundant and only represent a logically possible way of interpreting the linearly additive effects of the variables used to define inconsistency and mobility.

The recruitment of individuals to social positions and the motivation of individuals to perform satisfactorily the social roles they occupy are perennial problems of social organization. The existence of social inequality is often traced to these problems, being regarded as a solution to them. Davis and Moore (1945; 1961:470), for example, assert forthrightly in their now classic presentation of the functional theory of stratification, "the main functional necessity explaining the universal presence of stratification is precisely the requirement faced by any society of placing and motivating individuals in the social structure. As a functioning mechanism a society must somehow distribute its members in social positions and induce them to perform the duties of these positions. It must thus concern itself with motivation at two different levels: to instill in the proper individuals the desire to fill certain positions, and, once in these positions, the desire to perform the duties attached to them." They continue (1945;

---

*The research reported in this paper was supported by Contract PH3-66-960 from the National Institutes of Health, United States Public Health Service. The research was originally conducted at the National Opinion Research Center of the University of Chicago, which also collected the data upon which this report is based. The author wishes to thank Angela V. Lane and Karen Oppenheim for their assistance on this project.

1961:470), "it does make a great deal of difference who gets into which positions, not only because some positions are inherently more agreeable than others, but also because some require special talents or training and some are functionally more important than others. . . . Inevitably, then, a society must have, first, some kind of rewards that it can use as inducements, and, second, some way of distributing these rewards differentially according to positions." So stated, the functional theory of stratification provides some clue as to why individuals might incur the ordeal and expense of special training in order to secure certain positions: they obtain more from pursuing them. Having once achieved them, the theory also indicates why those in the functionally most important positions are motivated to continue pursuing them: they, too, receive more for their efforts. The theory gives us no clue, however, to the motivations of those in the least rewarded positions.

The place of individuals in modern society cannot be adequately characterized by reference to a single feature of its stratification system. This fact alone may secure the motivations of many who would otherwise be disenchanted. Empirically, there is no one to one correspondence between the prestige attributed to a position a man occupies and either the training or education required to enter it or the income received from pursuing it.[1] Thus, a man's occupational position is no certain clue to his education and income, achieved attributes which may provide access to rewards which are not directly derived from the nature of one's work and the prestige associated with it. The absence of a crystallized status system in which education, occupational prestige, and income are so closely interwoven that any one of them may be utilized as a surrogate for the others implies that the vast majority of individuals will have some legitimate claim upon the various rewards of a society. Those with a weak occupational or economic claim may make an appeal on the basis of learning; those lacking in objective educational and occupational achievements may still have the economic wherewithal to purchase a modicum of comfort. The rare individual is the one without economic means and neither the occupational training nor the educational attainment to improve his condition (cf. Nam and Powers, 1965).

The ties that bind an individual to his society and motivate him to fulfill his occupational role are not exhausted by differential rewards in the usual sense of the term. Our conception of personal and social integration covers a wide variety of attitudes and behaviors ranging from one's psychological

---

[1] Individual level correlations between years of school completed, family or personal income, and occupational status or prestige are usually around .4 to .6, indicating that no more than two-fifths of the variance in any one of these measures of socioeconomic position is common with any other of the measures. For a discussion of these matters, see Duncan (1961b).

sense of well-being to the extent and intensity of interpersonal connections. To be sure, the forms of personal and social integration open to an individual may be governed by his place in the stratification system. However, it is also possible that *different* aspects of an individual's location in the stratification system are permissive of different kinds of personal and social integration. Thus, while an uncrystallized status system contributes to social integration by reducing in some degree the numbers of those without any legitimate claims to status, differentiation in the forms of social integration may similarly contribute to its overall level by allowing different types of status claims to be associated with a corresponding type of personal or social integration. We explore these possibilities in this paper by examining the associations between several components of social status and various indicators of personal and social integration.

MEASURING SOCIAL INTEGRATION

We have already remarked that social integration, like socioeconomic status, is a multidimensional concept covering a variety of attitudes and behaviors. Data available from several sources enable us to investigate the effects of several components of socioeconomic status upon several dimensions of personal and social integration. Data collected in conjunction with a study of a widespread electric power failure along the Eastern seaboard on November 9, 1965, provide us with several attitudinal measures of psychological well-being. A description of the sample and other details of this study are available elsewhere (National Opinion Research Center, 1966). One's confidence in the performance of the social system is an important component of personal integration, since in complex societies the life pattern of every individual is dependent upon the effectiveness of a variety of institutions and their officials. Consequently, an individual's evaluation of the way in which critical public service organizations and private utilities usually perform their tasks can be regarded as one aspect of psychological integration or paranoia about social institutions.[2] Several other facets of per-

---

[2] For each of eleven public services, utilities, and related organizations (e.g., police, local newspapers, public schools) whose usual performance was evaluated, the respondent was given a score of one if he regarded the organization in question as, generally speaking, doing a "good" or "excellent" job and a score of zero if he thought it was doing an "average," "somewhat below average," or "poor" job. The respondent was also given a score of zero if he did not know what kind of job the organization was doing. The resulting index has a range between 11 and 0, taking on the former value if the respondent gave a positive evaluation to each of the eleven public services, utilities, and related organizations and taking on the latter value if the respondent accorded a positive evaluation to none of them. The index has a mean of 7.4 and a standard deviation of 2.5; each of the items comprising our index of positive evaluations of the usual performance of public service institutions and related organizations

sonal and social integration are covered by additional indices. One's sense of effectiveness in public affairs is measured by a scale of *powerlessness*,[3] while manifestations of stress and anxiety under ordinary conditions are tapped in part by reported psychosomatic symptoms.[4] In addition to these indicators, the blackout study provides us with a rough measure of one additional aspect of personal integration—work satisfaction. Employed respondents were asked, "Taking into consideration all the things about your job, would you say you are very satisfied, pretty satisfied, neither satisfied nor dissatisfied, pretty dissatisfied, or very dissatisfied with your job?" For purposes of computing the correlations reported below the five response alternatives to this question were assigned arbitrary scores ranging from 1 (very dissatisfied) to 5 (very satisfied).

---

has a substantial positive correlation with the total index. The index itself has a reliability coefficient of .7454, computed according to Case III of the methods proposed by Kuder and Richardson (1937).

[3] The questionnaire from the blackout study contains six items from a measure of alienation developed by Seeman. These items request the respondent to select one of two statements which is closest to his own view of things. For example, one question asks the respondent to decide which of the following two statements is more representative of his own view: "With enough effort we can wipe out political corruption" *or* "Some political corruption is a necessary evil of government." Selection of the latter alternative indicates that the respondent tends to feel little can be done to avoid political corruption. The remaining five items range over a variety of political affairs, domestic and international. As a measure of perceived powerlessness in political affairs, the face validity of the items seems apparent. On the one hand, individuals choosing the "alienated" or "negative" alternatives of the paired statements would appear to have felt a sense of powerlessness in political action, while, on the other hand, individuals with a felt sense of powerlessness in political action should find the "alienated" or "negative" statements attractive. In order to combine the six items into an index of powerlessness we assigned a respondent one point for selecting the "powerless" alternative to each pair of statements and no points for selecting the "powerful" alternative or being indecisive. The index, constructed in this way, has a range between 0 and 6, the latter value being achieved by respondents selecting the "powerless" alternative to each of the six items. The index of powerlessness has a mean of 2.3 and a standard deviation of 1.5; its reliability coefficient is .4983. For a discussion of the development of this index, see Seeman and Evans (1962).

[4] Respondents were asked whether they had been bothered frequently, sometimes, hardly ever, or not at all in the past few months by each of the following complaints: (1) general aches and pains, (2) dizziness, (3) headaches, (4) muscle twitches or trembling, (5) nervousness or tenseness, (6) rapid heart beat, and (7) cold sweats. For each of the seven items the response categories "frequently," "sometimes," "hardly ever," and "not at all" were assigned, respectively, the numerical scores 3, 2, 1, and 0. An index of psychosomatic symptoms was formed by assigning each respondent a score equivalent to the sum of his scores on each of the seven specific complaints. The resulting index has a range between 0 and 21 with a mean of 4.1 and a standard deviation of 4.1. The coefficient of reliability for the index of psychosomatic symptoms, estimated in a manner analogous to the procedure adopted above for indices constructed from dichotomous items, is .7700. For purposes of the present analysis we regard the prevalence of psychosomatic symptoms as an indicator, though not perfectly valid, of personal integration. Jackson (1962) uses an index of this kind in a similar way and offers a rationale for this interpretation.

The psychological and attitudinal features of personal integration derived from the blackout study are complemented by objective information on social participation derived from a probability sample of a suburb of Washington, D.C. Caplovitz and Bradburn (1964) provide additional information about these data. Four variables are available from this study—the number of times the respondent has gotten together with friends in the past few weeks (such as going out together or visiting in each other's homes), the number of different friends involved in the foregoing activities, the number of voluntary organizations (church and social groups, labor unions, social, civic, and fraternal clubs, etc.) the respondent belongs to, and the number of times the respondent has attended church services or church-sponsored events during the last month. These indicators of the extent and intensity of friendship and organizational ties provide objective readings upon the respondent's social involvements which may serve to engage him meaningfully in a segment of the society in which he lives.

REGRESSION AND CORRELATION ANALYSIS

The zero order correlations of the nine indicators of personal and social integration described in the preceding section with four common measures of socioeconomic status—education of the respondent, occupation of the respondent's family's main earner, family income, and occupation of the respondent's father—are shown in Table 1 for men and women separately. The income and education variables were continuously scored by assigning to each income and education category the midpoint of the intervals they covered. The reported occupations of the respondents' fathers and family main earners were coded according to the detailed occupational classification of the United States Bureau of the Census. In the blackout study, these occupational codes were subsequently assigned prestige scores derived from a recent national survey of occupational prestige which was designed to provide a prestige score for each detailed census occupation. Materials from the survey of a suburban county near Washington, D.C., were coded according to Duncan's (1961a) Socio-Economic Index, which, like the prestige study, provides a numerical score for every detailed census occupation. The utilization of different methods of scoring the occupational information derived from the two studies on which the present analysis is based is unlikely to affect the results reported herein in any substantial way, for there is a close correspondence between Duncan's Socio-Economic Index and the prestige scores (Duncan, 1961a). The correlations shown in Table 1 are computed over somewhat different case bases owing to slightly different response rates on the various measures of social and personal integration. The correlations involving job satisfaction are based

Table 1

ZERO ORDER CORRELATIONS BETWEEN MEASURES OF SOCIO-
ECONOMIC STATUS AND INDICATORS OF PERSONAL AND
SOCIAL INTEGRATION, FOR MEN AND WOMEN

Measures of Personal and Social Integration and Source	Measures of Socioeconomic Status				
	Respon-dent's Education	Family Income	Occupa-tion of Main Earner	Father's Occupa-tion	Number of Cases
	Men				
Blackout Study					
Evaluated usual perform-ance of public services	−.1514	−.0725	−.1071	.0228	699
Powerlessness	−.1833	−.2680	−.1070	.0468	699
Psychosomatic symptoms	−.1103	−.0531	−.0620	−.0253	699
Work satisfaction	.0699	.0356	.0944	.0401	543
Suburban Study					
Occasions for visiting with friends	.1480	.0503	.0768	.1406	564
Number of different friends	.2282	.1547	.1612	.1800	561
Number of voluntary organization member-ships	.3070	.3052	.2640	.1841	565
Frequency of church at-tendance, total men	.2024	.0660	.1778	.0769	564
Catholic men only	.3646	.1625	.2403	.1406	156
All other men	.1687	.0212	.1848	.0520	408
	Women				
Blackout Study					
Evaluated usual perform-ance of public services	−.1217	−.0732	−.1321	−.0870	443
Powerlessness	−.1806	−.2279	−.0867	−.0540	443
Psychosomatic symptoms	−.2856	−.1629	−.1231	−.0428	443
Work satisfaction	.1030	.0041	.1701	.1297	220
Suburban Study					
Occasions for visiting with friends	.2234	.1604	.1260	.1585	639
Number of different friends	.2110	.1821	.1341	.1285	637
Number of voluntary organization member-ships	.3136	.3008	.1873	.1889	640
Frequency of church at-tendance, total women	.1419	.0987	.1607	.1244	638
Catholic women only	.1805	.0846	.0892	.1458	166
All other women	.1483	.1176	.1753	.1424	472

on an appreciably smaller number of cases because the relevant question was
asked only of employed persons.

The correlations shown in Table 1 are at best modest in size and make
it quite clear that stratification variables alone are insufficient to account
for the observed variation in a variety of indicators of social and personal

integration. However, given the modest connections between stratification variables and measures of personal and social integration, there proves to be variation from one stratification variable to the next in the pattern of these relationships. Although detailed discussion of the zero order relationships is not warranted, we may still note some of the more striking patterns. In the upper panel of Table 1 for male respondents, we may observe that education has a pervasive influence on social integration, having modest correlations with all aspects of affiliation and attendance, as well as acting as a deterrent to the development of both one's sense of powerlessness and psychosomatic symptoms. Family income, by way of contrast, achieves modest correlations only with powerlessness, organizational memberships, and the extent of one's friendship circle. Both father's occupation and occupation of the family's main earner appear to exert influence only over the several aspects of social participation studied here. Even this cursory inspection of the zero order correlations for males in Table 1 suggests that different aspects of social status facilitate somewhat different aspects of social and personal integration.

The zero order correlations observed for women in Table 1 are patterned in much the same way as those observed for men. Thus, for women as for men, education achieves modest associations with most of the indicators of personal and social integration studied herein. For women, family income retains its significant associations with powerlessness, the extent of friendship networks, and voluntary association memberships. Unlike the pattern observed for men, however, among women family income proves to have a modest association with psychosomatic symptoms. Similarly, both father's occupation and main earner's occupation retain among women their modest associations with the several measures of social participation, but unlike the situation observed for men they also appear to be associated among women with several attitudinal and psychological measures of personal integration. Below, we will have occasion to comment upon the differences between the patterns observed for men and women, but we rest our discussion of the zero order correlations by noting again that a unidimensional conception of social status is not sufficient to account for the observed pattern of zero order associations. Instead, it appears that the various components of socioeconomic status and background have *dissimilar* effects on the various aspects of social and personal integration covered in the present study.

The net effects of each of the components of socioeconomic status studied here on the several indicators of personal and social integration cannot be inferred from the analysis of zero order correlations. Instead, recourse must be made to multiple regressions in which each of the social status indicators —education, family income, main earner's occupational prestige or SES, and father's occupational prestige or SES—is entered as an independent variable. For every measure of personal and social integration, multiple regressions of this form were computed separately for men and women. The partial regression coefficients in standard form achieved by each of the status variables in predicting each indicator of social integration are shown in Table 2, along with the associated multiple correlation coefficients. The regression coefficients in standard form are just the ordinary regression coefficients which would be associated with each independent variable if both the dependent and independent variables were normalized, i.e., expressed as variables with mean zero and unit variance, before computing the multiple regression. Unlike the partial regression coefficients in raw score form, i.e., the regression coefficients associated with the untransformed variables, the regression coefficients in standard form do not reflect the scale and relative dispersion of the independent variables. Like correlation coefficients, the regression coefficients in standard form may be compared directly. The multiple regressions are based on the same number of cases as the corresponding zero order correlations shown in Table 1.

The multiple correlations shown in the last column of Table 2 indicate that no more than fifteen percent, often as little as one percent and, typically, around five percent of the variance in the indicators of social and personal integration studied here can be explained by socioeconomic variables. However, several of the indices tapping psychological and attitudinal aspects of personal integration are not noteworthy for their reliability. Under the ordinary assumption of random errors, this implies that the multiple correlations shown in Table 2 understate the true variance in the relatively unreliable measures of social integration which may be explained by the doubtless more reliable measures of SES. Nevertheless, recomputing the multiple correlations from zero order correlations corrected for attenuation would not alter one's basic conclusion from the results shown in Table 2, to wit, that socioeconomic status by no means even appreciably, much less uniquely, determines one's level of personal and social integration. Our society, at least, partially resolves the problem of motivating and integrating workers in the stratified occupational world by placing the determinants of social integration and, hence, the rewards derived from felt psychological security and interpersonal involvement, outside the stratification system. But while variation in variables describing one's position in the stratification system does not appreciably affect one's level of social and personal integration, *participation* in that system, regardless of one's background, one's level of training, the prestige of one's occupation, and the income one derives from its pursuit, is still made essential. One must obtain the minimal necessities and amenities of living from some kind of work. These minimal requirements form the basis for continued participation and integration into society, but beyond the derivation of these minimum require-

Table 2

PARTIAL REGRESSION COEFFICIENTS IN STANDARD FORM AND
MULTIPLE CORRELATIONS OF SOCIOECONOMIC STATUS MEASURES
WITH INDICATORS OF PERSONAL AND SOCIAL INTEGRATION,
FOR MEN AND WOMEN

Dependent Variables: Measures of Social and Personal Integration	Independent Variables: Measures of Socioeconomic Status				
	Respondent's Education	Family Income	Occupation of Main Earner	Father's Occupation	Multiple Correlations
	Men				
Blackout Study					
Evaluated usual performance of public services	−.1507*	.0216	−.0492	.0682	.168†
Powerlessness	−.0943	−.2668*	.0540	.1101*	.297†
Psychosomatic symptoms	−.1164*	.0108	.0001	.0003	.111
Work satisfaction	−.0493	.0373	.1005	.0161	.105
Suburban Study					
Occasions for visiting with friends	.1191*	.0173	−.0237	.1019*	.176†
Number of different friends	.1527*	.0997*	.0122	.1137*	.270†
Number of voluntary organization memberships	.1715*	.2308*	.0698	.0854*	.397†
Frequency of church attendance, total men	.1514*	−.0063	.0952	−.0027	.217†
Catholic men only	.3092*	.0914	.0466	.0372	.380†
All other men	.1121	−.0681	.1545*	−.0276	.211†
	Women				
Blackout Study					
Evaluated usual performance of public services	−.0729	.0083	−.0929	−.0349	.154†
Powerlessness	−.1048	−.1921*	.0263	.0245	.243†
Psychosomatic symptoms	−.2922*	−.0333	−.0042	.0707	.294†
Work satisfaction	−.1781*	.1094	.1843*	.1111	.237†
Suburban Study					
Occasions for visiting with friends	.1574*	.0875*	.0283	.0759	.255†
Number of different friends	.1445*	.1160*	.0401	.0420	.250†
Number of voluntary organization memberships	.2109*	.2111*	.0375	.0596	.385†
Frequency of church attendance, total women	.0692	.0307	.1120*	.0652	.197†
Catholic women only	.1303	.0309	.0314	.1025	.209
All other women	.0646	.0425	.1174*	.0719	.213†

*Coefficients at least twice as large as their standard errors.
†Significantly greater than zero at .05 level by F-test.

ments variation in one's socioeconomic position does not substantially
affect one's level of social integration. Instead, individual variation in
personal and social integration is determined by variables exogenous to the

stratification system, so that no single class becomes the sanctuary of personal and social disintegration.[5]

Insofar as the present indicators of personal and social integration are affected by socioeconomic status, the partial regression coefficients in standard form exhibited in Table 2 make clear, as did the zero order correlations studied above, that different facets of integration are affected by different components of socioeconomic status. Looking first at the various social participation variables among males, we see that, excepting the church attendance of non-Catholic men, the coefficient associated with education is always significant. The same basic pattern is observed for women, save that education does not achieve a significant net association with church attendance either for all women combined or among the subsets of Catholic and non-Catholic women. Although it is widely known that social participation is related to social status, our understanding and interpretation of that connection is not wholly clear. This problem is compounded in some degree when one abandons a unidimensional conception of social status and assumes the responsibility of accounting for why only particular components of socioeconomic position have net associations with different types of social participation. In particular, we find it difficult to account convincingly for the relatively pervasive effect of education on associational phenomena, while plausible arguments may be advanced to account for the roles of other socioeconomic variables in the determination of participation. Persons of higher educational attainment maintain, as is well known, a higher level of interest in local and national affairs than individuals of lower educational attainment. These differences in interest levels between educational groups find expression in many facets of behavior ranging from reading habits to election turnout. The greater participation of more educated persons in church and voluntary organizations and their maintenance of more intensive and extensive friendship circles, net of income, main earner's occupation, and father's occupation, may represent yet another manifest expression of the known differences between educational groups in their levels of interest in community and national affairs. Such a suggestion, however, merely equates the explanation of the significant partial regression coefficients of education with the explanation of educational differences in public affairs and leaves the explanation of the latter phenomenon entirely unresolved. Attempting to move beyond this unsatisfactory state of affairs, Goode (1966) tries to explain the relationship be-

---

[5] Although a vast literature has purported to identify ecological bases of personal and social disintegration, a fair guess would be that the ecology of disorganization is no more rigid than the stratification of it. This, of course, does not deny that psychotics, delinquents, and other deviants are really concentrated; it does mean that they are probably no more concentrated by area than by socioeconomic variables, which is not very much.

tween church participation and social status by reference to involvement in voluntary activities. Hauser (1969) offers several suggestions about the causal relations between different types of social participation. At this writing, however, there is no wholly convincing explanation (specification) of the interconnections between one's social position and one's sociable activities.

Still focusing attention on the participation variables, we find among male respondents that family income achieves a significant partial regression coefficient only on the extent of one's friendship circle and organizational membership. Both the maintenance of extensive friendship circles and organizational ties require some monetary outlays in the form of entertainment expenses and dues. Consequently, there is ample reason to believe that these forms of social participation, unlike visiting with friends and church attendance which require expenditures of time without necessarily incurring corresponding expenditures of financial resources, should be curtailed in some degree by one's current income. Among women, family income exhibits a pattern of association with the several aspects of social participation which is nearly identical to that observed among men. The only exception is the significant relationship among women between family income and the extent of visiting with friends. Informal visiting among women may be largely a daytime activity, when their husbands are at work and their children at school. However, extensive visiting by mothers with pre-school age children would doubtless incur some babysitting expenses and, thus, make family income a constraint upon the frequency of visiting by mothers of young children. Such an effect of family income among a particular group of women could well be reflected, as in Table 2, in attenuated form among all women. There is no particular reason why the effect of income on visiting among women should spill over into church attendance patterns, because free babysitting services often are provided by churches.

Excepting church attendance among non-Catholic men and women,[6] occupational prestige of the family's main earner exhibits no significant net relationships with the participation variables. It is, of course, well known that churches, like occupations, are differentiated according to their prestige. This is particularly true of the several Protestant denominations, which not only enjoy a standing considerably above that attributed to Protestant sects, but also exhibit internal status differentiation with the Episcopalians, Congregationalists, and Unitarians enjoying superordinate

---

[6] The effect of main earner's occupational prestige on the church attendance of all women is apparently due to its effect on the church attendance of non-Catholic women, since there is no net relationship between church attendance and main earner's prestige among Catholic women.

status positions relative to Lutherans and Baptists.[7] It is also well known that the social standing of churches tends to correspond rather closely to the socioeconomic status of their members (cf. Lazerwitz, 1964). Thus, the positive association between church attendance and occupational prestige of the family's main earner may reflect a particular type of status consolidation, those deriving greater prestige from the occupational world tending to exhibit their occupational statuses at the community level by more frequent attendance at the more prestigeful churches. Such a process of status consolidation among non-Catholics is, of course, made possible by differentiation within the Protestant church and is not open to Catholics whose church attendance is more frequent and unaffected by occupational prestige.

The partial regression coefficients shown in Table 2 reveal that father's occupation affects the frequency of visiting with friends, the extent of one's friendship circle, and voluntary organizational memberships among male respondents. There is reason to believe that these net effects of father's occupation in fact conceal the operation of an intervening process, to wit, intergenerational inheritance of social participation patterns. Father's occupation probably exerts no *direct* influence over the social participation of sons. However, because father's occupation is correlated with father's social participation (an unmeasured variable) which in turn may be seen as affecting son's participation, a spurious, net effect for father's occupation is observed in Table 2. Although father's occupation does not appear to affect the social participation patterns of women in Table 2, women too may be subject to intergenerational inheritance of social participation patterns. The relevant alter for a woman, however, is her mother rather than her father. Thus, were mother's education entered into the regression equations, one might expect it to exhibit a significant regression weight among women, standing, like father's occupation among men, as a surrogate for the social participation of one's parent (cf. Hodge and Treiman, 1968; Hauser, 1969).

The relationships of the attitudinal and psychological indicators of social and personal integration to the several components of socioeconomic status are no less complex than the connections between social participation and measures of social status. For both men and women, only education proves significantly related to psychosomatic symptoms. Because only education exhibits an inverse association with psychosomatic symptoms, one must be especially wary of interpreting the observed associations as establishing a connection between socioeconomic status and anxiety. One may

---

[7] This statement is based on the results of a recent, unpublished study of the prestige standing of religious groups; ratings were solicited in this study from an area probability sample of approximately 500 adult Americans.

venture that education acts as a surrogate for the respondent's levels of general information and critical ability. Insofar as this is the case one might expect more educated persons to dismiss the minor somatic ailments tapped by the index of psychosomatic symptoms, while having recurrent symptoms professionally diagnosed and treated. Such a pattern would tend to generate an inverse correlation between education and *observed* psychosomatic symptoms at any particular point in time, even though the *occurrence* of these symptoms is uncorrelated with educational attainment.

Income is the only socioeconomic variable significantly related for both men and women to one's felt sense of powerlessness. Unlike education, occupational prestige, and social background, income is a resource which permits individuals some direct control over their immediate environment. Those with larger incomes have leeway in their choice of housing and life styles which is not possible for those with lower levels of income. It is not surprising that this direct control over one's life style which is facilitated by greater income should be transferred into a greater sense of control over affairs at large, as indicated by the inverse correlation between powerlessness and income.

Although income is inversely associated with powerlessness, we find among male respondents that powerlessness is positively associated with father's occupational prestige. An individual's own sense of powerlessness should be proportional to his sense of dependency upon others. If prestigeful fathers, who one may safely assume have more income to lavish upon their sons, continue to create opportunities for their adult sons or provide them with standards of living beyond what they could procure with their own achieved resources, they may do so at the risk of augmenting their sons' sense of powerlessness. As sons become increasingly engaged in a style of life dependent upon their fathers' support, they gradually lose their sense of control over their personal lives and affairs at large.[8] Although these ideas are consistent with the evidence reported in Table 2, they are clearly in need of refinement and replication with sets of data designed to explore them in depth.

Among male respondents, work satisfaction exhibits no significant relationships with any of the components of socioeconomic status studied here. This finding alone provides ample testimony that our society has, with reasonable success, instilled sufficient motivation among workers to perform the duties attached to their positions. Groups characterized by

---

[8] One does not expect the same phenomenon to be observed among married women. since their roles already largely assume financial dependency upon their husbands. One might, however, expect wife's father's occupation to have the same effect on the powerlessness of married men as that observed for father's occupation.

different socioeconomic positions are not clearly distinguished in their levels of work satisfaction, so that there is no one to one isomorphism between class configurations and the loci of work dissatisfaction. The work satisfaction of employed women, unlike that of men, is affected by several components of socioeconomic position. In Table 2, we first see that work satisfaction among employed women is positively and significantly associated with the occupational prestige of the family's main earner. Such an association has two apparent roots: for single women, the prestige of family's main earner is most likely the prestige of their own job, and one may surmise that women in prestigeful jobs find that work more rewarding; for married women, the prestige of the family's main earner is most likely the prestige of their husband's job, a factor which may contribute to the work satisfaction of wives by allowing them, since sufficient income and status is available from the husband's position, to be more selective in their employment and to accept only jobs with conditions and pay deemed satisfactory. Table 2 also reveals that, for women, education is significantly and inversely related to work satisfaction. Women, prone to leave the labor force through marriage or childbearing when young and return to the labor force in later life with often outdated skills or little experience, often find it difficult to secure employment commensurate with their educational attainment. Even if they are able to secure such employment they are seldom given the responsibilities and chances of advancement open to men of similar skill in similar positions. Insofar as women find that the rate of return upon their educational attainment and job skills are unequal to those obtained by men, one may expect them to experience job dissatisfaction. Since the more educated women have the largest investment in training and are, on the whole, more skilled, it is not surprising that they find their work least satisfying.

The results in Table 2 make it clear that none of the facets of social and personal integration studied here is even substantially explained by socioeconomic status and that different features of social and personal integration are associated with different components of socioeconomic status. For the most part, the results reviewed thus far also indicate that the effects of socioeconomic status on social and personal integration are largely salutary, persons in higher status positions generally evidencing higher rates of social participation and lower levels of stress, anxiety, or alienation. However, the correlations between the several features of social integration and social stratification are never so high as to exclude persons at lower socioeconomic levels from either developing a sense of personal well-being or participating fully in their communities. The system of social stratification *hinders* the full social integration of some individuals, but no one, *by reason of his class position alone,* is systematically excluded from full participation in his society.

STATUS CRYSTALLIZATION AND SOCIAL MOBILITY

In the preceding section we have reviewed the relationships between various indicators of social and personal integration and four commonly used measures of socioeconomic status: respondent's education, occupation of the family's main earner, family income, and father's occupation. However, much of the current sociological literature dealing with the connections between social status and social integration is preoccupied with the effects of occupational mobility and status crystallization, rather than with the effects of education, current occupation, income, and father's occupation per se (cf., Lenski, 1954, 1956; Goffman, 1957; Gibbs and Martin, 1958; Jackson, 1962; Jackson and Burke, 1965). As it turns out, however, many of the frequently employed measurements of both occupational mobility and status crystallization are only linear combinations of the status variables considered herein, a point which we now pause to develop in some detail.

Suppose we let the variables E_i, I_i, S_i, and F_i represent, respectively, the educational attainment, family income, main earner's occupational prestige, and father's occupational prestige of the ith individual. The means and standard deviations of these variables may be denoted, respectively, by $\overline{E}, \overline{I}, \overline{S}$, and $\overline{F}$, and by s_E, s_I, s_S and s_F. Subtracting the grand mean of each variable from each of the individual observations and dividing the result by the standard deviation of each variable yields the following transformed variables which have unit variance and mean zero: $e_i = (E_i - \overline{E})/s_E$; $p_i = (I_i - \overline{I})/s_I$; $s_i = (S_i - \overline{S})/s_S$; and $f_i = (F_i - \overline{F})/s_F$. The individual observations on any particular dependent variable, say Y_i, may be similarly transformed by the identity $y_i = (Y_i - \overline{Y})/s_Y$, where $\overline{Y}$ is the grand mean of the Y_i's and s_Y is their standard deviation. In the preceding section we considered regressions of the form,

$$y_i = k_i + a^*e_i + b^*p_i + c^*s_i + d^*f_i, \qquad \text{(Eq. 1)}$$

where k_i is a random variable with mean zero and the coefficients a^*, b^*, c^*, and d^* are the partial regression coefficients in standard form whose estimates were presented in Table 2.

An intuitively plausible measure of occupational mobility frequently employed in sociological research is obtained by simply subtracting the values of F_i from the corresponding values of S_i. This measure is obtained by simply arraying occupations of fathers and sons along a prestige or socioeconomic continuum and interpreting the difference between the raw scores attributed to father's occupation and to son's occupation as a measure of the son's intergenerational occupational mobility. Such an indicator of occupational mobility does not, however, take into account temporal changes in the occupational distribution. Over time, the occupational distribution has shifted in a generally upward fashion; employment in the professions and other white collar positions has expanded proportionally at the expense of employment in menial and farm occupations. Because the relatively higher prestige occupations have been expanding more rapidly, the prestige or socioeconomic status attributed to sons' occupations is on the average higher than the prestige or socioeconomic status of their fathers' occupations. Thus, on the average, all sons have experienced some net upward, intergenerational mobility. This mean shift is to be explained by the economic forces acting upon the occupational distribution and is no indication, for example, that sons are on the average more ambitious or more achievement-oriented than their fathers. A somewhat different measure of social mobility is considered herein, although it, like the simple arithmetical difference between the occupational prestige of fathers and sons, is also linearly dependent upon prestige attributed to father's and son's occupation. We consider for a measure of occupational mobility the difference between s_i and f_i, i.e.,

$$M_i = s_i - f_i, \qquad \text{(Eq. 2)}$$

rather than the difference between the raw prestige scores of fathers and sons. This measure of occupational mobility, unlike the arithmetic difference between father's and son's occupational prestige, has mean zero and considers the difference between the *relative* attainment of fathers and sons, rather than the difference between the *absolute* attainment of fathers and sons as an appropriate measure of occupational mobility. In sum, s_i provides a measure of the *i*th son's relative occupational attainment by expressing his absolute prestige in terms of the number of standard deviations it falls above or below the mean prestige of all sons, f_i provides a corresponding measure for fathers, and M_i gives a measure of occupational mobility by indicating whether the attainment of the *i*th son relative to all sons is greater or less than the attainment of his father relative to all fathers (cf. Blau and Duncan, 1967: 194 ff.).

Measures of status crystallization have been somewhat more diverse than measures of occupational mobility, including a variety of non-linear transformations of initial status variables such as income, education, occupational status, and ethnic background (cf. Lenski, 1954). However, most measures of status crystallization may be regarded as a summary index of the consistency of an individual's position in several hierarchies evolved from systematic comparisons of those positions. If we consider *only* the consistency between an individual's education and family income, then one plausible measure of the status consistency, C_i, of the *i*th individual is given by

$$C_i = p_i - e_i, \qquad \text{(Eq. 3)}$$

which expresses an individual's status consistency as the discrepancy between his relative income and relative education. The variable p_i gives a measure of the relative income of the ith individual by expressing his absolute income in terms of the number of standard deviations it falls above or below the average income, e_i provides a corresponding measure of relative education, and C_i provides a measure of status consistency by indicating whether the relative income of the ith individual is greater or less (and, if so, by how many standard deviations) than his relative education.

Both the measures of occupational mobility and status crystallization used here are *directed* measures. Thus, when $C_i = 0$, the ith individual has consistent levels of income and education, while *either* large positive *or* large negative values of C_i indicate the ith individual has vastly inconsistent positions in the educational and income hierarchies. The sign of C_i indicates, of course, whether the individual's inconsistency flows from having relatively higher income than education or from having relatively higher education than income. Similarly, M_i provides a directed measure of intergenerational occupational mobility, with positive values indicating relative upward mobility and negative values indicate relative downward mobility. Some students of occupational mobility and of status crystallization have preferred *undirected* measures of these phenomena, rather than the *directed* measures defined herein. Thus, if we took the absolute values of C_i and M_i, we would convert our directed measures of occupational mobility and status crystallization into undirected measures. If we used these undirected measures in a statistical analysis, we would be assuming that the effect upon an individual's behavior of a fixed amount of relative upward mobility is no different than the effect upon his behavior of an identical amount of downward mobility and that the effect upon an individual's behavior of, for example, being at the mean of the educational distribution and having an income two standard deviations *above* the mean level of income is no different than the effect upon his behavior of being at the mean of the educational distribution and having an income two standard deviations *below* the mean. Although there are some areas of behavior in which the assumptions underlying the use of *undirected* measures of mobility and status crystallization may be justified, the general area of social and personal integration does not appear to be one of them. On the whole, we would guess that the person whose relative income exceeds his relative education rejoices in the reasonable high rate of return upon his educational investment, while the person whose relative income is lower than his relative education experiences a corresponding degree of depression over the low rate of return upon his educational investment. Similarly, one might wager that the individual's response to upward occupational mobility is more likely to be euphoric than his response to an equal degree of downward occupational mobility. For these reasons, we regard directed measures of occupational mobility and status crystallization as more appropriate than undirected ones in the present context.

The particular definitions of occupational mobility and status crystallization adopted above are clearly linearly dependent upon the variables e_i, p_i, s_i, and f_i, whose effects upon various indicators of personal and social integration have already been examined in Table 2. Because of the linear dependencies between M_i, s_i, and f_i and between C_i, p_i, and e_i, it is not possible to attach unique effects to each of these six variables. Any model which attempts to accomplish that feat is not, in the statistical jargon, *identified* (cf. Blalock, 1966). Although it is impossible to attach simultaneously a unique effect to M_i, C_i, s_i, f_i, p_i, and e_i, it is possible to assign effects to certain combinations of these variables, *implicitly* setting the coefficients of the omitted variables at zero. For example, in the regressions already described the coefficients of C_i and M_i were implicitly set at zero (see Eq. 1). Other alternatives are, however, available which are as plausible as the solution already discussed. These alternatives will not, of course, alter the percentage of variation in the dependent variable which is explained by regression, but they will generate somewhat different coefficients for the variables explicitly entered in the regression equation and, in so doing, admit of somewhat different substantive interpretations than those advanced in connection with Table 2.

One of the most plausible rearrangements of the results based on regressions of the form considered above (see Eq. 1) follows from a conceptual decomposition of son's occupational prestige and income. One is at liberty to regard the occupational prestige or socioeconomic status of a son relative to all sons as the outcome of two prior factors: the relative occupational attainment of his father and his own occupational mobility, as indicated by the difference between his own relative occupational attainment and that of his father. Everyone enters upon life at a particular class level, represented by the relative attainment of one's father, and one's own relative attainment is completely determined, given this social heritage, by the extent of one's success or failure in improving upon it. This specification of the component processes which result in a man's relative occupational attainment may be symbolically represented by the addition of f_i to both sides of Eq. 2, yielding

$$s_i = M_i + f_i, \qquad \text{(Eq. 4)}$$

a form which makes clear the logical basis for regarding the relative attainment of sons as an additive function of the relative attainment of their fathers and their own success in improving on it.

Like relative occupational attainment, relative income is also subject to conceptual decomposition. By means of occupational pursuit and other gainful activities, individuals can convert their educational experiences into monetary gains. A man's relative educational attainment is, then, the initial determinant of his relative income position and, were the educational and income hierarchies perfectly consistent, would be the sole determinant of his relative income. However, individuals experience differential success in converting their educational experiences into the coin of the realm and one must regard the relative incomes of individuals as the sum of their relative educational attainments and the extents of their successes or failures in converting their relative educational attainment into superior, equivalent, or inferior relative positions in the income hierarchy. This conceptualization of the derivation of one's income, relative to others, may be symbolically represented by the addition of e_i to both sides of Eq. 3, yielding

$$p_i = C_i + e_i, \qquad (Eq. 5)$$

which makes clear the purely mathematical basis for regarding the relative income of individuals as an additive function of their relative educational attainments and the discrepancies between their relative positions in the income and educational hierarchies.

Substituting the identities given by Eqs. 3 and 5 into Eq. 1 yields the expression,

$$y_i = k_i + a^*e_i + b^*(C_i + e_i) + c^*(M_i + f_i) + d^*f_i, \qquad (Eq. 6)$$

which makes the values of y_i dependent upon education, father's occupation, status crystallization, and occupational mobility rather than upon education, father's occupation, income, and son's occupation. Multiplying out the expressions in parentheses on the right hand side of Eq. 6 by their respective coefficients and recombining terms yields an equation with explicit coefficients for e_i, C_i, f_i, and M_i:

$$y_i = k_i + (a^* + b^*)e_i + b^*C_i + c^*M_i + (c^* + d^*)f_i. \qquad (Eq. 7)$$

The coefficients of e_i, C_i, M_i, and f_i shown in Eq. 7 turn out to be the coefficients these variables would receive if we computed the regression of y_i on e_i, C_i, M_i, and f_i. In other words, if we considered regressions of the form,

$$y_i = k_i' + a'e_i + b'C_i + c'M_i + d'f_i, \qquad (Eq. 8)$$

then it may be shown that

$$k_i' = k_i, \qquad (Eq. 9a)$$
$$a' = a^* + b^*, \qquad (Eq. 9b)$$
$$b' = b^*, \qquad (Eq. 9c)$$
$$c' = c^*, \qquad (Eq. 9d)$$
and $\qquad d' = c^* + d^*. \qquad (Eq. 9e)$

These identities may be established by (1) writing out the normal equations associated with Eq. 1 and Eq. 8; (2) showing the equivalence of these normal equations; and (3) drawing the desired conclusion by invoking the theorem which states that n linearly independent equations in n unknowns have a *unique* solution.

The identities given in Eqs. 9b, 9c, 9d, and 9e enable one to derive the regression of y on e, C, M, and f from the regression of y on e, p, s, and f. Regressions of the latter form have already been computed and reported in Table 2; the coefficients in Table 2 may, therefore, be manipulated in the manner required by Eqs. 9b-9d in order to derive the coefficients which would be obtained from the regression of y on e, C, M, and f. The identities given by Eqs. 9b-9d make it perfectly clear, of course, that no new information is provided by studying the effects of f and M rather than f and s or studying the effects of e and C rather than e and p. Instead, replacing son's occupational attainment with a measure of occupational mobility and replacing income with a measure of status crystallization serves only to redistribute the known effects of father's occupational attainment, son's occupational attainment, education, and income in a somewhat different way.

The reader will recall that the coefficients a*, b*, c*, and d* associated with Eq. 1 are partial regression coefficients in standard form, since both the dependent variable—y—and the independent variables—e, p, s, and f—have been transformed to variables with mean zero and unit variance. However, not all of the independent variables entered in regressions of the form given by Eq. 8 have unit variance. The dependent variable—y—has mean zero and unit variance, as do e and f, the measures of education and father's occupational attainment. Consequently, the coefficient of e, i.e., $a' = a* + b*$, and the coefficient of f, i.e., $d' = c* + d*$, may be interpreted as partial regression coefficients in standard form. However, neither M nor C, the measures of occupational mobility and status crystallization, have unit variances and their coefficients—$c' = c*$ and $b' = b*$, respectively— must first be transformed before they can be interpreted as partial regression coefficients in standard form. The variance of C, the measure of status crystallization, is given by,

$$s_C^2 = s_{(p-e)}^2 = s_p^2 + s_e^2 - 2 \text{ Cov } [e, p],$$

where Cov [e, p] is the covariance between e and p, the measures of education and income expressed in standard form. Since e and p are in standard form, $s_p^2 = s_e^2 = 1$ and Cov [e, p] $= r_{ep}$, where r_{ep} is simply the zero order correlation between education and income. (Linear transformation of two variables does not affect the correlation between them, so $r_{ep} = r_{EI}$.) Consequently,

$$s_C^2 = 2 - 2r_{IE}.$$

A similar analysis reveals that the variance in M, the measure of occupational mobility, is given by

$$s_M^2 = 2 - 2r_{SF},$$

where r_{SF} is the zero order correlation between father's occupational prestige and son's occupational prestige. The partial regression coefficients in raw score form associated with C and M in Eq. 8 may be transformed to partial regression coefficients in standard form by multiplying them by the standard deviations of C and M, respectively. Thus, the value of

$$b'(2 - 2r_{IE})^{1/2} = b^*(2 - 2r_{IE})^{1/2}$$

is the partial regression coefficient in standard form associated with the measure of status crystallization and the value of

$$c'(2 - 2r_{SF})^{1/2} = c^*(2 - 2r_{SF})^{1/2}$$

is the partial regression coefficient in standard form associated with the measure of occupational mobility.[9]

Utilizing the information presented in Table 2, zero order correlations between income and education and between father's and son's occupational prestige (or socioeconomic status), and the logical relationships derived above, we have computed the partial regression coefficients in standard form associated with the measures of status crystallization, occupational mobility, respondent's education, and father's occupation when the various indicators of personal and social integration are regressed on them. These partial regression coefficients in standard form are given in Table 3, where the reader can see that the coefficients associated with education are always exactly equal to the sum of the coefficients associated with education and income in Table 2 and the coefficients associated with father's occupation are always exactly equal to the sum of the coefficients associated with father's occupation and son's occupation in Table 2. Because the effects of income and education in Table 2 are usually of the same sign, as are the effects of father's occupation and son's occupation, the coefficients associated with education and father's occupation in Table 3 are generally larger than the coefficients associated with them in Table 2. Since the zero order correlations between son's occupation and father's occupation and between income and education do not depart appreciably

---

[9] In general, when $b_{YX.Z}$ is the partial regression coefficient in raw score form associated with X in the regression of Y on X and Z (and any other variables), the partial regression coefficient in standard form, $b_{YX.Z}^*$, is given by $b_{YX.Z}$ (s_X/s_Y), where s_X and s_Y are the standard deviations of X and Y, respectively. In the present case, division by s_Y to obtain the partial regression coefficients in standard form is unnecessary, since the dependent variable has already been normalized to mean zero and unit variance.

Table 3

PARTIAL REGRESSION COEFFICIENTS IN STANDARD FORM FROM
REGRESSIONS OF INDICATORS OF PERSONAL AND SOCIAL
INTEGRATION ON FATHER'S OCCUPATION, OCCUPATIONAL
MOBILITY, EDUCATION, AND STATUS CRYSTALLIZATION,
FOR MEN AND WOMEN

Dependent Variables: Measures of Personal and Social Integration	Independent Variables			
	Respondent's Education	Status Crystalli- zation	Father's Occupation	Occupa- tional Mobility
Men				
Blackout Study				
Evaluated usual perform- ance of public services	−.1291	.0205	.0190	−.0591
Powerlessness	−.3611	−.2531	.1641	.0648
Psychosomatic symptoms	−.1056	.0102	.0004	.0001
Work satisfaction	−.0120	.0372	.1166	.1214
Suburban Study				
Occasions for visiting with friends	.1364	.0208	.0782	−.0286
Number of different friends	.2524	.1200	.1259	.0148
Number of voluntary organization member- ships	.4023	.2779	.1552	.0844
Frequency of church at- tendance, total men	.1451	−.0076	.0925	.1152
Catholic men only	.4006	.1153	.0838	.0578
All other men	.0440	−.0804	.1269	.1850
Women				
Blackout Study				
Evaluated usual perform- ance of public services	−.0646	.0083	−.1278	−.1095
Powerlessness	−.2969	−.1921	.0508	.0310
Psychosomatic symptoms	−.3255	−.0333	.0665	−.0050
Work satisfaction	−.0687	.1120	.2954	.2113
Suburban Study				
Occasions for visiting with friends	.2449	.1021	.1042	.0349
Number of different friends	.2605	.1354	.0821	.0494
Number of voluntary organization member- ships	.4220	.2540	.0971	.0461
Frequency of church at- tendance, total women	.0999	.0358	.1772	.1377
Catholic women only	.1612	.0364	.1339	.0425
All other women	.1071	.0495	.1893	.1390

from .5, the coefficients associated with occupational mobility and with status crystallization in Table 3 are, on the whole, about the same as the coefficients associated with son's occupation and income, respectively, in Table 2.

Rearranging the results exhibited in Table 2 by studying regressions of the form of Eq. 8 rather than those of the form of Eq. 1 leads one to assign substantial partial regression coefficients to our measures of status crystallization and occupational mobility only in a few instances. Among men, the coefficients of our measure of status crystallization exceed .2 only in two instances, while the coefficients of our measure of occupational mobility never exceed .2. As far as they go, the results for men suggest that, net of educational attainment, occupational mobility, and father's occupation, those whose relative income is higher than their relative education are more likely to join voluntary organizations and less likely to experience feelings of powerlessness than those whose relative income is less than their relative education. The coefficients of the measures of status crystallization and occupational mobility among women are quite similar to those observed for men, save that occupational mobility appears to make a substantial contribution to the work satisfaction of employed women. On the whole, these results are consistent with our previous discussion, though a detailed examination would require one to place a somewhat different emphasis on the roles of education and father's occupation and to replace descriptions of the effects of income and son's occupation with those of status crystallization and occupational mobility, respectively. However, whether one prefers to interpret the results in the form presented in Table 2 or in the form presented in Table 3, both arrangements make clear that the various components of a person's socioeconomic position neither contribute equally to any particular aspect of personal or social integration nor contribute in the same way to different aspects of personal and social integration.

SUMMARY AND CONCLUSIONS

In this paper we have reviewed the relationship between several components of socioeconomic status and various indicators of personal and social integration. The status systems of modern societies are not highly crystallized, the correlations between such components of socioeconomic status as income, occupational prestige, education, and social background factors being at best modest. Consequently, knowing a man's education is an important clue, but by no means a certain key to his occupational prestige and knowing both a man's education and his occupational prestige is only an ambiguous clue to his income. Because such status variables are only loosely intertwined, the vast majority of individuals in modern societies are able to advance some legitimate claims to recognition and the other rewards of society. Those with little education may still achieve ample income and those with modest incomes may land a prestigeful job. In this paper, we have shown that the various components of socioeconomic status contribute to different forms of social and personal integration. Thus, the vast majority of individuals not only have some claim to status, but that claim, whatever its basis, in turn facilitates some form of personal and social integration. Persons with different status configurations may, to be sure, have access to different types of social integration and experience somewhat different senses of well-being, but most status configurations are conducive to some form of social or personal integration. However, no form of social or personal integration is completely determined by status configurations. Thus, even those whose claims to social status are without objective support may still achieve a modest level of social and personal integration through other means. Since most status configurations facilitate one or another form of social or personal integration, most individuals have ample occasion to develop some sense of well-being and connect themselves with their society through social participation and interaction.

In addition to their bearing upon these global considerations, the results reviewed in this paper suggest a variety of specific directions for future research which go beyond the purview of this report. In particular, the observed relationships between powerlessness and father's occupation, between education and the work satisfaction of women, and between occupational status and church attendance among non-Catholics deserve replication and elaboration in future studies. The results of the present paper make clear, however, that those investigations will go awry if pains are not taken to distinguish both between the several components of socioeconomic status and the various features of social and personal integration.

REFERENCES

Blalock, Hubert M., Jr.
1966 "The identification problem and theory building: the case of status inconsistency." American Sociological Review 31(February):52–61.

Blau, Peter M., and Otis Dudley Duncan
1967 The American Occupational Structure. New York: John Wiley.

Caplovitz, David, and Norman M. Bradburn
1964 Social Class and Psychological Adjustment. Chicago, Ill.: University of Chicago, National Opinion Research Center.

Davis, Kingsley, and Wilbert E. Moore
1945 "Some principles of stratification." American Sociological Review 10(April): 242–249. Also, reprinted pp. 469–477 in Seymour Martin Lipset and Neil J. Smelser (eds.), Sociology: The Progress of a Decade. Englewood Clifts, New Jersey: Prentice–Hall, 1961.

Duncan, Otis Dudley
1961a "A socioeconomic index for all occupations." Pp. 109–138 in Albert J. Reiss, Jr., et al., Occupations and Social Status. New York: The Free Press of Glencoe.
1961b "Properties and characteristics of the socioeconomic index." Pp. 139–161 in Albert J. Reiss, Jr., et al., Occupations and Social Status. New York: The Free Press of Glencoe.

Gibbs, Jack P., and Walter T. Martin
1958   "A theory of status integration and its relationship to suicide." American Sociological Review 23(April):140–147.

Goffman, Irwin W.
1957   "Status consistency and preference for change in power distribution." American Sociological Review 22(June):275–281.

Goode, Erich
1966   "Social class and church participation." American Journal of Sociology 72 (July):102–111.

Hauser, Robert M.
1969   "On 'social participation and social status'." American Sociological Review 34(August):549–553.

Hodge, Robert W., and Donald J. Treiman
1968   "Social participation and social status." American Sociological Review 33 (October):722–740.

Jackson, Elton F.
1962   "Status consistency and symptoms of stress." American Sociological Review 27(August):469–480.

Jackson, Elton F., and Peter J. Burke
1965   "Status and symptoms of stress: additive and interaction effects." American Sociological Review 30(August):556–564.

Kuder, G. F., and M. W. Richardson
1937   "The theory of estimation of test reliability." Psychometrika 2(September): 151–160.

Lazerwitz, Bernard
1964   "Religion and social structure in the United States." In Louis Schneider (ed.), Religion, Culture, and Society, pp. 426–439. New York: John Wiley.

Lenski, Gerhard
1954   "Status-crystallization: a non-vertical dimension of social status." American Sociological Review 19(August):405–413.
1956   "Social participation and status crystallization." American Sociological Review 21(August):458–464.

Nam, Charles B., and Mary G. Powers
1965   "Variations in socioeconomic structure by race, residence, and the life cycle." American Sociological Review 30(February):97–103.

National Opinion Research Center
1966   Public Response to the Northeastern Power Blackout. Chicago: University of Chicago, National Opinion Research Center.

Seeman, Melvin, and John W. Evans
1962   "Alienation and learning in a hospital setting." American Sociological Review 27(December):772–782.

Industrialization and Social Stratification*

Donald J. Treiman
University of Wisconsin

This paper reviews the current state of knowledge about the effects of industrialization upon systems of social stratification. Taking societies as the unit of observation, we consider the relationships between level of industrialization and (1) the distribution of status characteristics in the population (the structure of stratification); (2) the pattern of interrelations among status characteristics (the process of stratification); and (3) the form of linkages between status characteristics and other aspects of social behavior (the consequences of stratification). A set of propositions is specified, a few of which are empirically well established but most of which yet require empirical testing.

Industrialization is perhaps the most pervasive and fundamental trend affecting national societies in the current era. Across the globe countries are industrializing as fast as they can muster the resources to do so. As this transformation takes place it necessarily entails changes in other aspects of social structure, and one of the social institutions most likely to be affected by industrialization is the system of social stratification. In this paper we will examine the interrelations between societal variations in extent of industrialization and societal variations in the nature of social stratification systems, reviewing what is known to date and offering suggestions for future empirical investigation. We will begin our review by considering variations in the *structure* and *process* of stratification and then will take up the *consequences* of these variations both for other social institutions and for the behavior of individuals.

By the *structure* of a stratification system we mean the composition of a population with respect to the possession of socially valued and scarce resources, or, to put it slightly differently, the *shape of the distribution* of these resources in a population. Three central components of stratification systems are education, occupation, and income, and we shall devote most

*Preparation of this paper was supported by a grant from the National Science Foundation to the University of Wisconsin (NSF #GS–2487, "Societal Development and Social Mobility"). Several of my friends read earlier drafts of the paper; their various expressions of dissatisfaction goaded me into making revisions which, I think, improved the thing considerably. I am indebted to Halliman H. Winsborough, Judah Matras, Robert Hauser, Kenneth Bryson, Peter Dickinson, Donald Holsinger, and my wife Michelle.

of our attention to these dimensions.[1] It is evident that societies vary with respect to the distribution of their populations over categories of educational attainment, occupational status, and income, and we will be concerned with the relation of industrialization to such variations.

By the *process* of stratification, or the *process of status attainment,* we refer to the principles or rules by which individuals are distributed over locations in the stratification structure. This leads directly to a concern with the interrelations among the various dimensions which comprise the structure. For example, the statement that occupational status is largely dependent upon educational attainment and only slightly dependent upon father's occupational status is a rule describing the process of stratification or the process of status attainment. And the assertion that the rate of occupational inheritance decreases as societies industrialize is a statement about a change in the process of stratification.

It is evident that both aspects of stratification systems are intimately interrelated: changes in *structure* necessarily imply changes in *process,* and vice versa. Nonetheless, for convenience of exposition we will attempt to separate this section of our review into the following topics: (A) the effect of industrialization upon the structure of stratification; (B) the effect of structure upon process; and (C) the effect of process upon structure. Then in the second section, we will consider how the relations between stratification and other aspects of social life are affected by variations in the level of industrialization of societies. Our procedure will be to review the principal issues associated with various substantive topics in order to formulate a series of propositions which either have substantial empirical support or which are suggested on theoretical grounds as warranting empirical investigation.

PROCEDURAL AND METHODOLOGICAL CONSIDERATIONS

Before beginning our substantive review we need to make explicit some of the assumptions underlying our approach and to deal with some methodological problems confronting comparative research.

First, we should make it clear that we conceive of the task of comparative analysis as *the discovery of covariation among properties of social systems.* Accordingly, the propositions we will offer have to do with the

---

[1] It is evident that these are not the only dimensions of stratification systems. A comprehensive exposition would necessarily consider the determinants of the prestige of individuals and groups and the role of ethnic and religious group membership in the process of status attainment, both of which topics we have ignored here. We have restricted our attention to education, occupational status, and income both because of limitations of space and because these dimensions are more amenable to comparative analysis than those we have not considered. Given the current state of the art, it would seem prudent to tackle the less recalcitrant topics first.

interrelations among various characteristics of social systems abstracted from the concrete nexus of traits characterizing any particular society. For example, we will be concerned with such things as the relation between the rate of social mobility and the likelihood of interclass conflict, considered independently of the peculiarities of political structure or local definitions of social class in the particular societies from which data happen to be drawn. While we recognize that most of the evidence we will be able to marshal in support of the propositions we present will in fact come from case studies of single countries or from comparisons of very limited numbers of countries, it is our contention that adequate understanding of intersocietal variations in stratification systems, or for that matter in any other social institutions, will ultimately depend upon the adoption of explicitly comparative approaches which take societies as the unit of observation and which study the covariation among their various characteristics.

The second point which demands comment is the issue of whether inferences about temporal changes in social structure within societies can be drawn from cross-sectional intersocietal comparisons. It is clear that it would be foolhardy to make the simple assumption that the process of societal development which the industrially advanced countries experienced during the nineteenth and early twentieth centuries will be repeated by the currently nonindustrialized countries (see Kuznets, 1954, for an excellent statement on this point). However, many of the concomitants of industrialization of relevance to the nature of a social stratification system may appear regardless of the exact process by which a country industrializes. For example, both cross-sectional and longitudinal data support the contention that as countries industrialize the availability of education increases (see Russett, 1964:283, for cross-sectional data and UNESCO, 1958, for longitudinal data). Thus, an assertion of the form "as educational opportunities increase the influence of social origins on educational attainment decreases" may be equally true as a description of a consequence of a *change* that takes place in a given society over time or of *variation* across societies at a given point in time. Because the phenomena we are concerned with here are the interrelations among various aspects of stratification systems as they appear at any given moment and because we wish simply to relate variations in these phenomena to variations in other aspects of social structure, notably degree of industrialization, it is not necessary to resolve the issue of whether variations in level of industrialization among contemporary societies simply reflect stages in a unilinear process of societal evolution; we contend that the patterns under discussion here would obtain regardless of the exact processes by which countries industrialize. Accordingly, we shall adduce both cross-sectional and longitudinal evidence in support of the propositions we put forth.

Our final task before turning to the substantive review is to define more precisely the variables we shall be considering. Despite variations in exact operational definitions, the meaning of the terms "education" and "income" is fairly straightforward. Education is ordinarily scaled in terms of categories of amount or type of formal schooling completed or attended; and income is usually scaled in terms of amount of money accruing to individuals (or sometimes to families) within a year or other fixed period. With suitable adjustments, both can be represented on interval scales. In contrast to income and education, the terms "industrialization" and "occupation" require some elaboration.

In this paper we accept Davis's definition of industrialization as "the use of mechanical contrivances and inanimate energy (fossil fuels and water power) to replace or augment human power in the extraction, processing, and distribution of natural resources or products derived therefrom" (1955: 255). While this definition refers simply to technological change, it is clear that such change is ordinarily accompanied by radical transformations of social structure, principally as a result of changes in the distribution of the labor force. This has led some authors to measure the level of industrialization by the proportion of the labor force not engaged in agriculture (see, for example, Golden, 1957; and Soares, 1966). However, for our purposes we prefer to stick to the definition of industrialization as the mechanization of production and to treat as problematic the association between industrialization and aspects of social structure, particularly the structure of stratification systems.

The remaining variable requiring definition is occupational status. Viable cross-national comparisons of occupational structures and of the process of status attainment require the utilization of standardized procedures for scaling occupational status. Unlike education and income, occupational categories have no intrinsic interval or even ordinal properties. However, it is possible to scale occupations according to their location in a hierarchy of resources and rewards. Most occupational scales seek to capture either the *prestige* or the *socioeconomic status* of occupations, that is, the average educational and income levels of the incumbents of each occupation. Fortunately, although they are conceptually distinct, the prestige and SES dimensions of occupations are highly correlated. Duncan (1961), for example, was able to account for over eighty percent of the variance in the prestige of forty-five occupations on the basis of the education and income levels of their incumbents ($R_{P(EI)} = .91$). Duncan's result subsequently has been replicated by Hodge and Siegel for all occupations in the United States Census 1960 detailed classification (reported in Treiman, 1968a:120) and extended to Canada by Blishen (1967) and to Great Britain by Treiman (1968a:120); $R_{P(EI)} = .89$ for both the U.S. and Great Britain and .92 for Canada. In work currently underway, Treiman is attempting to extend these results for a larger number of countries; so far education-by-detailed-occupation tabulations have been located for nearly twenty of the countries for which prestige data are also available, and income-by-detailed-occupation tabulations have been found for half this number. There is also some evidence that occupational status ratings formed on the basis of the impressions of expert judges are highly correlated with ratings derived from popular evaluations (see, for example, Hall and Jones, 1950:42). Hence, we are not likely to go too far wrong if we simply assume that the particular occupational status scales utilized by the various studies we will be reviewing all adequately represent the true occupational hierarchies in the populations referred to (for a discussion of this issue which reaches a similar conclusion see Duncan, 1966b:83–90).

This still leaves us with the question of how comparable occupational hierarchies are across countries. Recent work by Hodge, Siegel, and Rossi (1964) and by Treiman (1968a) indicates that occupational prestige hierarchies are substantially invariant across time and space. Hodge, Siegel, and Rossi found almost perfect agreement in occupational ratings derived from a series of surveys conducted in the United States from 1925 through 1963. Treiman, analysing data from thirty-eight countries varying widely in level of industrialization, found an average intercorrelation of .84 between pairs of countries. Thus, we can have reasonable confidence that intersocietal variations in aspects of the process of stratification which involve occupational structure are not simply artifacts of the way in which occupation is measured.

I. VARIATIONS IN STRATIFICATION SYSTEMS

We now turn to the body of this paper and consider the ways in which systems of stratification vary for countries at different levels of industrialization. We start with a selective review of the research literature on social mobility, since it is under this rubric that most of the work has been done that provides evidence about changes in the structure and process of stratification.

The comparative study of social mobility received its major impetus from the 1951 Conference on Social Mobility and Social Stratification sponsored by the International Sociological Association (ISA, 1951). As a result of that conference, some half dozen studies of social mobility were launched in as many European countries, and in subsequent years the number of national or regional studies of social mobility has grown to more than twenty-five (for reviews of most of these studies, see Miller, 1960:66–80; Lipset and Bendix, 1960:13–38; and Treiman, 1968b). The principal concern of the majority of these studies has been simply to establish rates of mobility in each separate country. Relatively little explicitly comparative work has been carried out; and until very recently, almost no attempt has been made to go beyond the internal analysis of individual zero-order mobility tables by investigating the complex process by which status is transmitted from one generation to the next.

Much of the comparative work to date has reflected preoccupation with the question of whether and in what way *rates* of social mobility vary across countries. On the basis of an analysis of rates of intergenerational crossing of the manual-nonmanual line in eight relatively industrialized countries, Lipset and Bendix (1960:13) concluded that *"the overall pattern of social mobility appears to be much the same in the industrial societies of various Western countries"* (italics theirs). And a somewhat more recent study by Svalastoga (1965) arrives at a similar conclusion. Comparing data for nine European countries by means of a correlational procedure, Svalastoga found striking similarity from country to country in the degree of correspondence between father's and son's occupational status; he reports correlations on the order of .4 for every country. On the other hand, Cutright (1968), using a procedure which purports to adjust for shifts in occupational distributions over time, found substantial variation in the mobility rates of thirteen nations. He concluded, moreover, that the rate of mobility is positively correlated with the level of industrialization of these countries. Studies by Fox and Miller (1965) and by Marsh (1963) reached substantially the same conclusion.

Unfortunately, each of these studies is technically flawed in some way. All but Svalastoga rely upon a simple manual-nonmanual dichotomy which does not adequately capture variability in patterns of mobility across societies (cf. Duncan, 1966b:86–90; and Lenski, 1966:411–412) and which cannot satisfactorily handle mobility from agricultural occupations. Also, Svalastoga's adjustment of his data to attempt to correct for intercountry variability in the distribution of the labor force was incorrectly carried out (Treiman, 1968b:38). Hence, we are left with no clear idea about the extent of intercountry variability in rates of mobility.

Moreover, even if we could resolve the simple question of *how much* mobility exists in various countries, this still would not take us very far toward an adequate understanding of the *process* of status transmission. For example, it is likely that the role of education as an intervening mechanism in the process of status transmission varies substantially across countries, depending upon the availability of educational opportunity. And, by the same token, the relationships among education, occupation, and income probably vary with the level of industrialization of countries.

Fortunately, however, recent work by Blau and Duncan (1967) has laid the foundation of a new and extremely fruitful approach to the study of social mobility that gives promise of stimulating substantial advances in our understanding of the process of status attainment. By recasting the tradi-

tional question of how much and what sorts of mobility characterize a
society as a problem of assessing the role of social origins in the process
of status attainment, Blau and Duncan have opened the way for investigation of the complex process by which status is transmitted from one generation to the next.

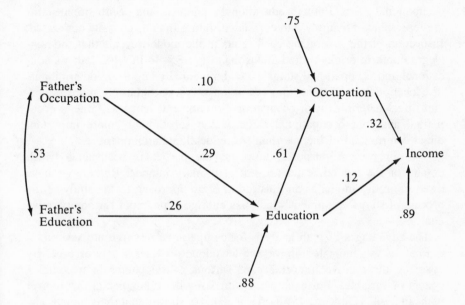

Figure 1. *The process of status attainment in the United States, 1962, for
non-Negro nonfarm origin males age 35–44 (adapted from Duncan, Featherman, and Duncan, 1968:53).*

Of even greater importance than the conceptual breakthrough, however,
is the *methodological* innovation represented by the use of path analysis to
decompose the correlation between father's and son's occupational status
into a set of causal linkages operating, in part, through intervening variables
(for an introduction to path analysis, see Duncan 1966a; and the papers in
Part I of Borgatta and Bohrnstedt, 1969). A basic model of the process
of status attainment in the United States, adapted from Duncan, Featherman, and Duncan's (1968) extension of Blau and Duncan's analysis, is
presented in Figure 1. While this model does not specify in full the details
of the process studied by Duncan and his associates, it is adequate to represent those parts of the process of special interest here and to provide a base
for speculation about the ways in which the process of status attainment
is affected by industrialization.

The model indicates that educational attainment depends directly upon both father's educational attainment and father's occupational status; that occupational status depends directly upon educational status and upon father's occupational status, but only indirectly upon father's educational attainment; and that income depends directly upon occupational status and educational attainment, but only indirectly upon father's educational and occupational status. Father's educational attainment and occupational status are represented as simply intercorrelated, rather than as causally connected. Inspection of the size of the coefficients in the model reveals that for non-Negro nonfarm origin United States males age 35–44 in 1962 father's educational and occupational status were about equally important determinants of educational attainment; that education was a substantially more important direct determinant of occupational attainment than was father's occupation; and that occupational status was a substantially more important direct determinant of income than was educational attainment.

For our present purposes, however, the particular coefficients which obtain for the United States are not of primary interest. Rather, we have dwelt upon this model as an illustration of an approach to the study of the process of status attainment which has enormous potential for comparative analysis.

The advantages of path analysis for comparative research are several.

First, as was indicated above, the technique provides a way of precisely assessing the relative importance of various causal chains in a complex system of variables. For example, by invoking the fundamental theorem of path analysis (Duncan, 1966a:5) it can be shown that only about one quarter of the observed association between father's and son's occupational status in the population depicted in Figure 1 can be attributed to the direct intergenerational transmission of father's occupational status, while fully three-fourths of the observed correlation can be attributed to the indirect linkage via education: the sons of higher status fathers go further in school, and those with more schooling obtain higher status occupations.

Second, direct intersocietal comparisons can be made of the sizes of any particular paths in the system, provided the variables are comparably measured. This feature provides a basis for testing propositions about the relations between variations in stratification systems and variations in other aspects of social structure. For example, it would be possible to estimate the parameters of some particular model of the process of status attainment (e.g., the one presented in Figure 1) for a number of societies. Then, assuming data for enough societies were available, the various parameters of the model could be treated as variables and correlated with other societal characteristics, such as the degree of industrialization or urbanization or the availability of education, thus providing precise estimates of the effect of such characteristics on the process of status attainment.

Third, since estimates of the parameters of a model (*path coefficients*) ordinarily are derived from the zero-order correlations among the variables in the model, it is often possible to use data from several sources in a single model. This last feature greatly increases the body of data potentially available for analysis, since for many foreign countries there are several sources of data on social stratification and social mobility, each source containing information on only a relatively small number of variables.

On the other hand, since legitimate comparisons of the parameters of a path model across populations require that the variables which enter the model be measured in comparable ways for each population, somewhat greater than usual demands are placed upon the researcher to insure that his data are indeed comparable. It would be extremely unfortunate if researchers were to rush blithely to the comparison of coefficients of path models, or for that matter any quantitative models, without expending the necessary prior effort to insure the comparability of the coefficients being compared. Fortunately, for the reasons given above, the problem of comparability is not insurmountable, provided appropriate care is taken. Procedures for improving the comparability of comparative data will be suggested in the summary section below. We now turn to the question of how industrialization affects the structure of stratification systems.

A. Industrialization and Structural Variation
Occupational structure

Perhaps the most obvious consequence of industrialization is a shift in the distribution of the labor force. Typically, as countries industrialize the efficiency of agricultural production increases and the proportion of the labor force engaged in agriculture decreases. Kuznets (1957:28–31) presents data for twenty-eight countries showing a decline in the proportion of the labor force in agriculture over approximately the past 100 years, which he attributes to the increasing industrialization of these countries. And among contemporary societies there is a very high negative correlation between the level of industrialization (as measured by per capita energy consumption) and the proportion of the labor force engaged in agriculture (rho = −.76 for 93 countries, computed from Ginsburg, 1961:Tables 10 and 34).

In addition to the shift out of agriculture, there is usually a shift in the occupational distribution of the nonagricultural labor force as well. This comes about in several ways. First, the increased productivity of labor resulting from mechanization allows a shift over time from the production of goods to the production of services (Jaffe and Stewart, 1951:254; Kuznets, 1957:28–31), which has the effect of increasing the ratio of nonmanual to manual workers. Second, technological changes tend to radically transform the nature of specific jobs and to give rise to entirely new occupations as well. The rationalization of production which accompanies mechanization ordinarily involves a shift from a craft system, in which all the tasks involved in the production of a given article are carried out by the same individual, to an assembly line system in which the manufacturing process is divided into a set of discrete operations, each of which can be carried out in a routine manner by a semiskilled workman or machine attendant. And, of course, mechanization implies the development of new occupations concerned with the design and maintenance of complex machinery (Jaffe and Stewart, 1951:256). What results is an enormous proliferation of occupational specialities such as has accompanied the process of industrialization in the United States (U.S. Department of Labor, 1965:xiii–xiv). Third, there is an increase in the scale of economic activity. Rising capital requirements and economies of scale result in an increase in the size of individual enterprises (Hoselitz, 1961), and improvements in transportation increase the size of the potential market for goods. The development of a complex production and marketing system requires an increase in clerical and administrative personnel, and this, together with increased productivity, results in an increase in the ratio of nonmanual to manual workers. Actually, the form this takes is the more rapid growth of the nonmanual than the manual sector, both of which grow at the expense of the agricultural sector (for cross-sectional evidence based on data from twelve Western Hemisphere nations see Soares, 1966:198; and for longitudinal data for four Anglo countries see Farrag, 1964).

Educational structure

A second concomitant of industrialization is an increase in the level of education in the population (Bowman and Anderson, 1963). Not only does the shifting labor market create increased demand for trained personnel, but educational opportunities tend to be more available in more industrialized countries. Such nations tend to have more extensive educational systems, and are more likely to make education available free of charge to the student. The popular desire for education tends to increase as well, as more and more jobs come to require explicit educational qualifications. And urbanization, which generally accompanies industrialization itself results in increased desire for education. Since an urban labor force has less need of child labor than does an agricultural labor force, urban parents are more likely to encourage their children to take advantage of educational opportunties—or, to put it in the opposite way, are less likely to prevent them from doing so. Also, with a shift from craft to factory modes of production, parents are no longer able to train their children directly for occupational roles and are less able to teach them the particular skills demanded by a fluid industrial labor market, notably literacy (Golden, 1957); hence, they are more likely to send them to school.

Income structure

Finally, industrialization results in increased per capita wealth. This is well known and in itself not very interesting. Of greater interest is the tendency for income inequality to be reduced as a consequence of industrialization. Kuznets (1963) presents both longitudinal and cross-sectional data showing a reduction in the inequality of family income as countries develop economically. This trend is probably due primarily to the shift of the labor force out of agriculture—traditional agriculture typically returns very low income, which reflects its extremely low productivity —and rising productivity of the remaining agricultural labor force. A second factor is the increase in education which accompanies industrialization. Rising educational levels tend to increase the supply of labor aspiring to nonmanual jobs and to reduce the supply of labor willing to accept manual jobs. To the extent that this shift is not matched by corresponding shifts in the demand for labor, differences in the wage scales of nonmanual and manual workers will be reduced (Reynolds, 1964:473–474). We shall have more to say about this point below.

We can summarize our conclusions about the relations between industrialization and the structure of stratification by stating them in propositional form. The following propositions are fairly well supported by both cross-sectional and longitudinal evidence, although more complete data will be required for them to be accepted unequivocably:

I.A.1. The more industrialized a society, the smaller the proportion of the labor force engaged in agriculture.

I.A.2. The more industrialized a society, the greater the number of different jobs in the occupational structure.

I.A.3. The more industrialized a society, the higher the ratio of nonmanual to manual workers in the nonagricultural labor force.

I.A.4. The more industrialized a society, the higher the proportion of children attending school.

I.A.5. The more industrialized a society, the higher the per capita income.

I.A.6. The more industrialized a society, the greater the equality of income.

B. Variations in the Process of Status Attainment

Having considered the ways in which the distribution of status variables vary with industrialization, we now turn to the question of the relation between industrialization and intercountry variations in the process of status attainment. It will be evident as we proceed through this section that most of the shifts in the process of status attainment we postulate are in fact consequences of shifts in the distributions of the three status attributes we have just considered. It is convenient to think of the model presented in Figure 1 (ignoring the coefficients) as a generic representation of the basic process of status attainment, even though we recognize that for particular societies the process might well vary somewhat. By restricting our attention to a single generic model, we can suggest some propositions about the ways in which various aspects of the process represented in the model can be expected to vary for societies at different levels of industrialization.

1. The direct (or net) influence of father's on son's occupational status should be weaker the more industrialized a society. The changes in labor force structure we have discussed above make direct occupational inheritance less likely in more industrialized countries. In particular, the greater bureaucratization of work (Moore, 1966) makes it more difficult for fathers to pass their own positions directly on to their sons or even to arrange for their sons to work at the same jobs they do. Also, in more industrialized economies the sheer number of jobs is greater, as we have indicated, and the labor market more complex, making it less likely on the basis of chance alone that a given individual will work at a job similar to that of his father.

2. The direct influence of education on occupational attainment should be stronger in more industrialized societies (cf. Anderson, 1958; and Hurd and Johnson, 1967:60). With the increased specialization of labor which characterizes industrialization, and the concomitant increase in the proportion of professional, technical, administrative, and clerical jobs, formal education probably becomes more important as a mechanism for the learning of occupationally relevant skills, and an increasingly important resource in job competition. This is particularly true of positions in public bureaucracies (Hurd and Johnson, 1967:60–61). Moreover, the demand of highly industrialized societies for a mobile and adaptable labor force likely results in a shift from ascriptive to universalistic achievement criteria as a basis for occupational role allocation.

3. In more industrialized societies parental status should play a less important role in educational attainment than in less industrialized places. Industrialized countries are more likely to have free mass educational systems; and where education is free the opportunity to continue with schooling tends to depend mainly upon academic success at the previous level of schooling, rather than upon financial capability. In addition, the greater degree of urbanization of industrialized countries should reduce the dependence of educational attainment upon social origins, since educational opportunities are more readily available to urban children and since there is less pressure upon the children of urban industrial workers to leave school at an early age to go to work.

Note that these three propositions taken together imply nothing about the effect of industrialization upon the gross association between father's and son's occupational status. The reason for this is that the three net effects are such as to potentially cancel each other out: while the direct intergenerational transmisison of occupational status should decrease with industrialization, the indirect linkage through education may either increase or decrease depending upon whether the increase in the importance of education for occupational attainment is stronger or weaker than the reduction of the influence of parental status on educational attainment.

4. However, while we cannot *deduce* the effect of industrialization upon gross occupational mobility rates from our previous propositions, there are theoretical grounds for expecting the rate of gross mobility to increase with industrialization. In the first place, the upward shift in the distribution of the labor force that occurs over time as countries industrialize, taken together with a negative association between occupational status and fertility (Wrong, 1958), necessarily requires that some sons have occupations different from those of their fathers. But even if the mobility implied by the shift in the occupational distribution across generations (sometimes called "structural" mobility; see, e.g., Hutchinson, 1958) is subtracted, we could still expect higher rates of net mobility (also known as "exchange" mobility) in more industrialized societies as a consequence of (a) more extensive education, (b) more pervasive mass communications, (c) greater urbanization, and (d) increased geographical mobility in such places as contrasted with less industrialized countries. Each of these factors operates to break down the rigidity of the class structure of traditional society, and thus to increase the ease of mobility; the following paragraphs elaborate this assertion.

(a) In addition to imparting skills with specific occupational payoffs, education serves to broaden individuals' acquaintance with alternative possibilities and to inculcate social skills which will enable them to take advantage of such opportunities. As Anderson (1958:4) points out:

> One must recognize that schools are acculturating as well as intellectual agencies. Individuals from the lower strata have an opportunity by association to learn the dialect, the social habits, the etiquette, etc., of the upper classes. . . . In some situations this result of schooling may be more important for mobility than the formal training. This is one reason why education could facilitate mobility even if every individual were to receive the same amount of schooling.

(b) The main consequence of the ubiquitous exposure of the population to mass media characteristic of industrial societies (Russett, 1964: 272, 274) is the development of a common culture and the diminution of regional, ethnic, and class differences in attitudes and behavior. Thus, in such societies occupational mobility is not likely to require acculturation to as radically different a style of life as would be the case in traditional societies.

(c, d) The increased urbanization and increased geographical mobility of industrial society should have the effect of reducing the ascriptive component in status attainment. Individuals migrating to new places or living in large urban centers must achieve success on the basis of their own talent, without either the help or the hindrance they would derive from the status of their parents in the smaller communities in which everyone knows everyone else.

We now turn to consideration of the effect of industrialization on the determinants of income and suggest three additional propositions.

5. The more industrialized a society, the stronger should be the direct effect of occupational status on income. The increased bureaucratization of work and the attendant increase in the specificity of job definitions and of occupational qualifications and perquisites probably results in a decrease in within-occupation variation and an increase in between-occupation variation in income (and, as noted above, education).

6. Following Smelser and Lipset (1966:35) and Anderson (1958:3), we would expect the direct effect of education on income to decrease with industrialization. Smelser and Lipset suggest that "the increase in the number of educated people in a developing economy necessarily means that as education becomes less scarce it should command less status and income." Actually, this assertion is only plausible on the assumption that the demand for educated personnel remains constant or at least does not increase as rapidly as the supply, for this is the circumstance that should reduce the increment in income expected from additional schooling.

7. The gross association between education and income should be smaller for more industrialized countries. As Anderson (1958:7) points out, while the effect of parental status on educational attainment should diminish with industrialization, the intergenerational inheritance of wealth should be largely unaffected by industrialization; hence, other things equal, the association between education and income would be expected to decrease with industrialization.

Evidence regarding the seven propositions we have specified here is extremely sparse. With the exception of the inconclusive studies of variation in gross mobility rates which we reviewed above, there have been no systematic cross-national investigations of any of these propositions. Hence, we are limited to the few specific results which can be pieced together from studies conducted in single countries. Duncan and Hodge (1963) present data for four cohorts of nonfarm origin Chicago men which show that both the gross association and the direct effect of father's on son's occupational status declined between 1940 and 1950, while the importance of education as an intervening mechanism in status transmission increased (on this point see also Blau and Duncan, 1967:180). This is the only investigation known to us which speaks *directly* to any of the first three propositions;

while relevant findings exist for a number of countries, incomparabilities in analytic procedures make direct intercountry comparisons impossible (see, for example, Duncan and Hodge, 1963; Carlsson, 1958:123–137; and Rocha, 1968, on the role of education in occupational attainment).

In support of the role of urbanization in facilitating mobility, we have two pieces of evidence. First, Ramsøy (1966:229) found the rate of "exchange" mobility of a cohort of young Norwegian males to increase sharply with the level of urbanization of community of residence. Second, Davis (1955:311) suggested that the association between caste and occupational status is breaking down in the urban areas of India, and specifically that urban factory work serves as a means of escape from the disability of low caste status which persists in the villages.

No evidence is available regarding any of the remaining propositions. Research currently underway by Treiman (1968b), which involves comparisons of the process of status attainment in approximately twenty countries by means of path analytic procedures, will hopefully supply some of the needed answers.

Again we summarize this section by stating our assertions in propositional form. None of the following can be taken as established; all require empirical verification.

I.B.1. The more industrialized a society, the smaller the direct influence of father's occupational status on son's occupational status.

I.B.2. The more industrialized a society, the greater the direct influence of educational attainment on occupational status.

I.B.3. The more industrialized a society, the smaller the influence of parental status on educational attainment.

I.B.4. The more industrialized a society, the higher the rate of "exchange" mobility. In particular,

a) The higher the level of education in a society, the higher the rate of exchange mobility.

b) The wider the distribution of mass communications in a society, the higher the rate of exchange mobility.

c) The higher the level of urbanization of a society, the higher the rate of exchange mobility.

d) The higher the rate of geographical mobility in a society, the higher the rate of exchange mobility.

I.B.5. The more industrialized a society, the stronger the direct influence of occupational status on income.

I.B.6. The more industrialized a society, the smaller the direct influence of education on income.

I.B.7. The more industrialized a society, the smaller the correlation between education and income.

C. Implications of the Process of Status Attainment for Occupational Structure[2]

Thus far we have considered changes in educational, occupational, and income structures resulting from industrialization, and the implications these *structural* changes have for the *process* of stratification. In doing this we attributed changes in occupational structure to shifts in the demand for various kinds of labor which result from the increasing mechanization of production. That is, we accepted the common assumption that changes in occupational structure over time are due to forces exogenous to the stratification process and that these changes condition the process of individual status attainment. However, it is possible to think of these relationships in an alternative way. Matras (1967; 1970) argues that shifts in occupational distributions can be viewed as *resulting from* the operation of a particular mobility process upon an initial occupational distribution. In such a formulation, what accounts for changes in occupational structure is not exogenous *demand* factors but pressures generated by changes in the *supply* of various kinds of labor. In this section we suggest some ways in which rising levels of education may generate pressures for change in the occupational structure by altering the supply of various types of labor.

There are two principal sources of pressure for expansion of educational opportunities in industrializing nations. First, as was mentioned above, the mechanization of production and concomitant shift in the organization of work require increased numbers of formally trained personnel. Second, because jobs in the modern sector, and particularly the highest status and best-paying jobs, tend to require formal education, education comes to be defined as the prime route to occupational success, and the demand on the part of the public for education increases. In response to political pressures brought to bear by those eager for education, many newly industrializing countries have expanded their educational systems more rapidly than is warranted by the ability of the economy to absorb trained labor. One well-known result is the underemployment of highly educated labor which is common in developing countries (Williams, 1965; Myint, 1965). We suggest that insofar as the supply of educated personnel entering the labor force exceeds the demand for individuals with such qualifications, the following kinds of pressures for change will be generated in the occupational structure:

Pressures for expansion of the nonmanual sector. As the supply of individuals trained for and eager to obtain professional, technical, managerial, and clerical positions increases relative to demand, the price of such labor

---

[2] This section owes its existence to Judah Matras's presence at Wisconsin during 1968–69.

presumably drops (Reynolds, 1964:473–74). This is particularly true because of the reluctance of educated persons in newly industrializing countries to accept jobs which are not commensurate with their level of training. The falling price of white collar labor should, all else equal, provide an incentive for employers to expand the number of such positions. Also, the prospect of large numbers of unemployed educated persons may induce governments to expand the number of positions in the public bureaucracy as a way of gaining the support of such individuals and of reducing the potential for social unrest which is inherent in the existence of a discontented, educated population (Tangri, 1962). It has been suggested that India has increased the size of its governmental bureaucracy for exactly this reason. As Davis (1955:282) points out, "the effort to avoid straight unemployment may lead in directions antithetical to efficient utilization. The 'make-work' attitude which emphasizes the 'necessity of a job' rather than the 'job to be done' is prominent in Indian thinking. . . ."

Pressures for contraction of the manual sector. As the educational level of the labor force increases, the supply of persons willing to do tedious and routine work tends to decrease. For example, in the West Indies the fact that so many young people have acquired a primary education has drastically reduced the supply of labor willing to cut sugar cane (Myint, 1965: 19). The reduction in the supply of manual labor should force wages up. Or, to find individuals willing to work for low wages, the employer must accept inferior personnel who may not be able to perform even routine tasks competently. Both alternatives provide incentives to reduce dependence upon labor by automating production as much as possible (Ross, 1967). Hence, it may well be the case that technological and organizational innovations which reduce the need for unskilled and semiskilled labor are as much a *consequence* as a cause of upward mobility.

It should be pointed out that just as increases in educational opportunity create pressures for an upward shift in the labor force by increasing the supply of educated labor relative to the demand, restrictions in educational opportunity may inhibit shifts in labor force distribution. Even if there is a demand for highly skilled workers, there can be no increase in the proportion of skilled workers in the labor force unless a supply of appropriately trained personnel can be found. This, of course, is why expansion of educational opportunity is often considered a fundamental prerequisite to economic development.

This section is not easily summarized in propositional form. Much of what we have presented refers to contingent responses to maladjustments of the labor market rather than to generic concomitants of industrialization. Moreover the empirical support for these ideas is at best scanty and impressionistic. Nonetheless we present the following as a guide to future investigation.

I.C.1. If the educational level of labor force entrants increases more rapidly than the demand for educated labor, the following kinds of pressures for an upward shift in the labor force distribution may be generated:

    a) The cost of nonmanual labor should drop, allowing low cost expansion of the white collar sector.

    b) Governments may enlarge the governmental bureaucracy to reduce the threat inherent in an unemployed, highly educated labor force.

    c) The cost of manual labor should increase, providing an incentive to replace labor with mechanical means of production.

    d) Alternatively, the quality of available manual labor should decrease, again providing an incentive to automation of production.

II. THE CONSEQUENCES OF STRATIFICATION

Having considered how industrialization affects the *structure* and *process* of stratification, we now turn to consideration of the impact of industrialization on the *consequences* of stratification. We will be concerned mainly with variations in the effect of social status on individual behavior, but also with consequences of the distribution of status characteristics in a society for other aspects of social organization, in particular the likelihood of political stability.

Probably more work has been done on the consequences of status for individual behavior than in any other area of research on stratification, but unfortunately, probably with less impact. What we have to date is an amorphous mass of findings that has not been integrated in any cogent way. These results tend to show that however status is measured, high status persons are more socially and politically involved, more tolerant of others and the views of others, enjoy better health, and show less evidence of social disorganization than lower status persons. In short, high status persons appear better able to cope with the exigencies of life and to have a broader perspective regarding their social world. (For a review of some of this literature see Bendix and Lipset, 1966:Part IV).

Wherever evidence exists, this general pattern seems to hold; and there is no reason to expect it to change as countries industrialize except that it is probable that status differences in behavior decrease with industrialization as a result of the increased interclass exposure which likely results from increased urbanization, extension of education to the general public, expansion of the coverage of mass media, and increased social mobility.

Of substantially greater interest than the analysis of individual status attributes is consideration of the behavioral entailments of simultaneous occupancy of particular combinations of statuses. A rather large literature has accumulated to date which posits a variety of consequences of social mobility on the one hand, and status discrepancy on the other, for the behavior of individuals. Essentially the same argument applies in both cases. Since particular behaviors are considered appropriate to any given position in a status hierarchy, individuals who are either socially mobile or who are "status discrepant" risk the possibility that their various statuses may require diverse behaviors. Two alternative theories of how people react to such situations have been posited:

(1) What we might call the "mean value theorem in sociology"[3] posits that, at the aggregate level at least, the behavior associated with any given *status configuration* will be a weighted average of the behaviors associated with each of the *component statuses* in the configuration.[4] For example, if in some sample the mean on a tolerance scale for those whose fathers are skilled workers is 5.0 and the mean on the scale for those who are themselves managers is 7.0, we would expect managers who are the sons of skilled workers to have a tolerance score somewhere between 5.0 and 7.0 (exactly where depends upon the weights for father's and son's status, which we will comment upon below). Or similarly, if sixty percent of Catholics and thirty percent of salesmen vote Democratic, the theorem posits that somewhere between thirty and sixty percent of Catholic salesmen will vote Democratic.

(2) In contrast to the notion that behavior is some additive function of component status variables is the popular theory that the effect of mobility *per se* or of status discrepancy *per se* has a disorganizing effect on individuals, engendering various pathological modifications in behavior. For example, it has been asserted that social mobility results in abnormally high rates of racial prejudice (for a review of this literature see Hodge and Treiman, 1966), suicide (Breed, 1963), mental disorder (Kleiner and Parker, 1963), political radicalism (Germani, 1966), etc. By the same token, status discrepancy is held to give rise to pathological behaviors, as a response to the abnormally great strain created by conflicts in the behavior appropriate to the various statuses occupied by discrepant individuals (see Treiman, 1966, for a review of status discrepancy theory). It is im-

---

[3] This phrase is due either to Robert W. Hodge or to Paul M. Siegel, and dates from the NORC occupational prestige project, around 1965.

[4] Individuals may strike a balance between the behaviors appropriate to each status; or may choose to act in terms of one status on some occasions and in terms of the other on other occasions, depending upon which status is more salient at the time; or may permanently resolve any conflict by always acting in a manner appropriate to whatever status is most salient in general. All of these alternatives imply an additive effect of status variables on behavior *at the aggregate level*. See Treiman (1966:653) for a more extended discussion of this point.

portant to note that the two alternatives are not contradictory, but that the social pathology theory requires that in addition to *additive* effects of the status variables on the behavior of interest there be *interaction* effects as well.

While virtually all the evidence to date which is based on methodologically adequate analysis is supportive of the mean value theorem but not of the social pathology hypothesis, this evidence is restricted to the United States. Moreover, there are theoretical reasons to expect the consequences of social mobility and of status discrepancy to vary for societies at different levels of industrialization. Starting with the consequences of social mobility, we can make several suggestions.

First, recognizing that the mean value theorem does not imply anything about the relative weight of parental status as against respondent's own status in determining behavior, we would expect the relative importance of parental status to vary inversely with the level of industrialization of societies. The increased neo-locality of young couples and increased likelihood of children living a considerable distance from their parents and seeing them infrequently which are characteristic of industrial society should reduce the strength of intergenerational ties and the influence that parents have on their adult offspring (but see Litwak and Szelenyi, 1969).

Second, it is probable that the disruptive effect of social mobility for individuals posited by the social pathology hypothesis varies inversely with the rate of social mobility in a society, and is thus more characteristic of less industrialized societies. Germani (1966:369–71) argues cogently that the strain induced by social mobility tends to be greatest in "traditional"— i.e., nonurbanized, nonindustrialized—societies, in which, he assumes (as we do—see proposition I.B.4), mobility rates tend to be low. In such societies, he suggests, mechanisms for mobility tend not to be institutionalized, thus providing no social support for the socially mobile individual. Moreover, one of the consequences of a high rate of social mobility in a society is a reduction of between-status differences in behavior and increasing heterogeneity within status categories. This follows directly from the mean value theorem: if behavior is a function of social origins as well as of current status, and if the social origins of members of a given status category vary widely, as would be expected in a highly mobile society, then the behavior of members of that status category should also vary widely. In consequence, definitions of appropriate behavior should be less rigid, reducing pressures for conformity on the part of each individual.

Third, as countries industrialize there should be a shift in emphasis from group to individual modes of mobility and hence a decline in support for leftist political organizations. Following Matras (1970:chap. 12) and Ramsøy (1969), we suggest that as educational opportunities become less dependent upon social origins and occupational attainment becomes more closely dependent upon educational attainment, both of which trends are presumably associated with industrialization (see propositions I.B.2 and I.B.3), success or failure comes to be defined as an individual matter rather than as a manifestation of a collective fate. Hence, leftist political groups which are oriented toward fundamentally changing the distribution of wealth and power should find it harder to gain support in industrialized countries (Lipset, 1960:45–47).

Turning to consideration of the consequences of status discrepancy, we can offer the following proposition, which is analogous to one of those suggested above: the greater the degree of status crystallization in societies, the greater the likelihood that status discrepant individuals will experience strain which manifests itself in pathological responses. In a highly crystallized society status categories are likely to be more homogeneous than in less crystallized societies and hence the range of appropriate behavior will be more narrowly circumscribed.

It should be noted that it is not possible to make an unambiguous prediction regarding the relationship between industrialization and the probability that status discrepancy will have disruptive consequences for individuals. The reason for this is that it is not clear whether the status structures of industrialized societies should be more or less crystallized than those of nonindustrialized societies; on the one hand, we expect the effect of education on occupation and of occupation on income to increase with industrialization (see propositions I.B.2 and I.B.5), but on the other hand, the association between education and income should decrease (see proposition I.B.7).

Turning from consideration of status discrepancy as a generic phenomenon to particular patterns of discrepancy, we can predict that in societies in which income and education are *perceived* to be highly correlated, those individuals with low income but high education will tend to feel frustrated by their lack of success, will blame the system for their failure, and will be drawn toward radical political organizations. Actually, this assertion makes a good deal more sense at the aggregate than at the individual level, since there is no particular reason to believe that an individual sense of failure will vent itself in radical political activity more than in other ways, such as withdrawal, self-blame, or passive acceptance. But at the aggregate level, it is not at all implausible to suspect that those groups which are composed of highly educated, poorly rewarded individuals will attempt to organize activity to change their situations. An example can be found in the role of intellectuals in radical political movements in Latin America (Germani, 1966:373) and in other underdeveloped areas; and Levy (1955) argues that "partially deprived" individuals are a major force for social change in developing nations. Finally, we can follow the discussion in Section I.C. about the pressures for social change inherent in rising education levels by noting that if governments are not responsive to the needs of unemployed intellectuals political stability is threatened (Smelser and Lipset, 1967:17).

There is one additional consequence of variation in the level of status crystallization which is worthy of note. It is likely that the strength of the association between "objective" status characteristics and subjective class identification depends upon the degree of crystallization of objective characteristics in a society—the more crystallized statuses are, the more likely subjective identification will depend upon objective characteristics, since the more consistently will objective characteristics be perceived by individuals. And, as a corollary of this, the degree of status crystallization of a society should determine the degree of class cleavage of the society, a point which has been recognized from de Tocqueville on but has never been empirically validated.

Once again we summarize our discussion by stating our assertions in propositional form. And once again the propositions we offer have virtually no empirical support to date aside from fragments of impressionistic evidence.

II.1.   The more industrialized a society, the less marked will be status differences in behavior.

II.2.   The more industrialized a society, the greater will be the effect of current status on behavior relative to the effect of parental status.

II.3.   The higher the rate of social mobility of a society, the smaller will be *inter-status* differences in behavior and the greater will be *intra-status* heterogeneity in behavior.

II.4.   Hence, the higher the rate of social mobility of a society, the smaller the likelihood that socially mobile individuals will experience disruptive strain resulting in pathological responses; that is, the smaller the likelihood of interaction effects consistent with a hypothesis of strain-induced behavior.

II.5.   The more industrialized a society, the greater the importance of individual as against group modes of mobility.

II.6.   Hence, the more industrialized a society, the less the support for leftist political organizations.

II.7.   The greater the degree of crystallization of statuses in a society, the greater the likelihood that status-discrepant individuals will experience disruptive strain resulting in pathological responses; that is, the greater the likelihood of interaction effects consistent with a hypothesis of strain-induced behavior.

II.8.   The greater the degree of crystallization of statuses in a society, the greater the likelihood that groups whose income is inferior to that commensurate with their level of education will be involved in radical political activity.

II.9. The greater the degree of crystallization of statuses in a society, the greater the dependence of subjective class identification on objective status characteristics.

II.10. The greater the degree of status crystallization in a society, the greater the degree of class cleavage.

SUMMARY AND CONCLUSIONS

This paper has constituted a review of what is known and what can be reasonably hypothesized about the relation between levels of industrialization and variations in systems of social stratification across societies. We have been concerned to specify the ways in which industrialization affects both the distribution of status attributes (which we termed the *structure* of stratification) and the *process* of status attainment, and the ways in which changes in the structure and process of stratification are interrelated. In addition, we have considered some ways in which industrialization alters the impact of status configurations on other aspects of social life.

If we can conclude anything at all from this review, it is that we actually know very little about the relation between industrialization and social stratification. Most of the propositions we have presented are simply hypotheses which as yet have almost no empirical support. The task before us is clear. If we are to move from a parochial concern with the structure and processes characteristic of a single society, the United States, to a concern with understanding the nature of social systems in general, we shall have to concentrate our energies on collecting comparable data from a large number of societies so that we can focus our attention upon covariations among characteristics of societies rather than upon characteristics of people or groups within societies.

Such a focus demands that we devote substantial effort to insuring that data collected in any given country are comparable to data already collected in other places. Since resources are currently not available, and are not likely to become available in the near future, to enable massive cross-national studies to be conducted by any given organization or individual, the best available substitute is for each researcher to make a concerted effort to design his study to enable the widest possible utilization of it. There are a number of specific things that can be done: (1) Whenever possible, data should be coded according to standard coding schemes. Occupations should be coded according to the International Standard Classification of Occupations (International Labor Office, 1969) and scaled according to the standard set of occupational prestige scores developed by Treiman (1968a)[5], thereby insuring inter-country comparability and facilitating comparison with census distributions in each country. (2) Data should be coded in as much detail as possible to provide the greatest flexibility to researchers wishing to recode the data for specific purposes. This is particularly true for education measures, which must reflect quite disparate educational systems. (3) Researchers planning studies should attempt to communicate with others sharing the same interests, and should attempt to include in their surveys data of interest to other researchers. While it is financially infeasible for any given individual to initiate data collection in a large number of countries, it is well within the realm of possibility to buy a few questions on a large number of surveys being conducted in various countries. In short, by making a concerted attempt to cooperate with one another, researchers with comparative interests can all gain substantially in their ability to carry out rigorous comparative analysis, to the great benefit of the field of stratification in general. For, as Duncan (1966b:83) points out, "until . . . *literal replication* can be applied to international studies, juxtaposition of data from various countries will require of the analyst as much skill in effecting comparability as in making comparisons." This circumstance probably accounts in large part for the relative paucity of systematic cross-national comparative stratification research, and must be modified if we are to have much hope of progress.

REFERENCES

Anderson, C. Arnold
1958   "Education and social stratification." English language version of article published in I Problemi della Pedagogia (Rome). Chicago: University of Chicago Press.

---

[5] Because intercountry correlations in occupational prestige evaluations are so high, it is feasible to construct a standard international occupational prestige scale by combining data from a number of countries. Such a scale will be available in the expanded version of Treiman (1968a) to be published in 1970. By combining data from a variety of sources it has been possible to assign a prestige score to nearly every occupation listed in the International Standard Classification of Occupations (1969) and to include prestige scores for a variety of specific occupations commonly found only in nonindustrialized countries. Thus, it will be possible for researchers conducting studies in any country to collect detailed occupational data and to scale it easily into status categories by reference to explicit and precise criteria. While some error undoubtedly will be introduced, simply because the prestige of occupations is not precisely identical throughout the world, such error in all likelihood would be smaller than that generated by coding occupations into gross categories which are arbitrarily assumed to form a status hierarchy or by utilizing existing prestige scales and guessing at the status of occupations which do not appear on the scales, both of which are common current practices. Moreover, for the researcher engaged in cross-national comparisons, utilization of a standard occupational status scale insures that results are not contaminated by differences in coding procedures.

Bendix, Reinhard, and Seymour Martin Lipset (eds.)
1966 Class, Status, and Power: Social Stratification in Comparative Perspective. Revised edition. New York: Free Press of Glencoe.

Blau, Peter M., and Otis Dudley Duncan
1967 The American Occupational Structure. New York: John Wiley and Sons.

Blishen, Bernard R.
1967 "A socioeconomic index for occupations in Canada." Canadian Review of Sociology and Anthropology 4 (February):41–53.

Borgatta, Edgar F., and George W. Bohrnstedt (eds.)
1969 Sociological Methodology 1969. San Francisco: Jossey-Bass, Inc.

Bowman, Mary Jean, and C. Arnold Anderson
1963 "Concerning the role of education in development." Pp. 247–279 in Clifford Geertz (ed.), Old Societies and New States. New York: Free Press.

Breed, Warren
1963 "Occupational mobility and suicide among white males." American Sociological Review 28(April):174–188.

Carlsson, Gosta
1958 Social Mobility and Class Structure. Lund, Sweden: C. W. K. Gleerup.

Cutright, Phillips
1968 "Occupational inheritance: a cross-national analysis." American Journal of Sociology 73(January):400–416.

Davis, Kingsley
1955 "Social and demographic aspects of economic development in India." Pp. 263–315 in Simon Kuznets, Wilbert E. Moore, and Joseph J. Spengler (eds.), Economic Growth: Brazil, India, Japan. Durham, N.C.: Duke University Press.

Duncan, Otis Dudley
1961 "A socioeconomic index for all occupations." Pp. 109–138 in Albert J. Reiss, Jr., et al., Occupations and Social Status. New York: Free Press of Glencoe.
1966a "Path analysis: sociological examples." American Journal of Sociology 72 (July):1–16.
1966b "Methodological issues in the analysis of social mobility." Pp. 51–97 in Neil J. Smelser and Seymour Martin Lipset (eds.), Social Structure and Mobility in Economic Development. Chicago: Aldine Publishing Co.

Duncan, Otis Dudley, David L. Featherman, and Beverly Duncan
1968 Socioeconomic Background and Occupational Achievement: Extensions of a Basic Model. Washington, D.C.: U.S. Department of Health, Education, and Welfare, Office of Education, Bureau of Research.

Duncan, Otis Dudley, and Robert W. Hodge
1963 "Education and occupational mobility: a regression analysis." American Journal of Sociology 68(May):629–644.

Farrag, Abdelmegid M.
1964 "The occupational structure of the labor force: patterns and trends in selected countries." Population Studies 18(July):17–34.

Fox, Thomas G., and S. M. Miller
1965 "Economic, political, and social determinants of mobility: an international cross-sectional analysis." Acta Sociologica 9 (No. 1–2):76–93.

Germani, Gino
1966 "Social and political consequences of mobility." Pp. 364–394 in Neil J. Smelser and Seymour Martin Lipset (eds.), Social Structure and Mobility in Economic Development. Chicago: Aldine Publishing Co.

Ginsburg, Norton
1961   Atlas of Economic Development. Chicago: University of Chicago Press.

Golden, Hilda Hertz
1957   "Literacy and social change in underdeveloped areas." Pp. 108–113 in Lyle
       W. Shannon (ed.), Underdeveloped Areas. New York: Harper and Brothers.

Hall, John, and Caradog D. Jones
1950   "Social grading of occupations." British Journal of Sociology 1(January):
       31–55.

Hodge, Robert W., Paul M. Siegel, and Peter H. Rossi
1964   "Occupational prestige in the United States: 1925–1963." American Journal
       of Sociology 70(November):286–302.

Hodge, Robert W.,and Donald J. Treiman
1966   "Occupational mobility and attitudes toward Negroes." American Sociological
       Review 31(February):93–102.

Hoselitz, Bert F.
1961   "Some problems in the quantitative study of industrialization." Economic
       Development and Cultural Change 9(April):537–549.

Hurd, G. E., and T. J. Johnson
1967   "Education and social mobility in Ghana." Sociology of Education 40(Winter):
       55–70.

Hutchinson, Bertram
1958   "Structural and exchange mobility in the assimilation of immigrants to Brazil."
       Population Studies 8(November):111–120.

International Labour Office
1969   International Standard Classification of Occupations. Revised edition, 1968.
       Geneva: International Labour Office.

International Sociological Association
1951   First International Working Conference on Social Stratification and Social
       Mobility. London: International Sociological Association.

Jaffe, A. J., and Charles D. Stewart
1951   Manpower Resources and Utilization: Principles of Working Force Analysis.
       New York: John Wiley and Sons.

Kleiner, Robert J.,and Seymour Parker
1963   "Social striving, social status, and mental disorder: a research review." Ameri-
       can Sociological Review 28(April):189–203.

Kuznets, Simon
1954   "Underdeveloped countries and the pre-industrial phase in the advanced
       countries: an attempt at comparison." Pp. 947–969 in Proceedings of the
       World Population Conference, Vol. 5. New York: United Nations.
1957   "Quantitative aspects of the economic growth of nations, II, industrial distri-
       bution of national product and labor force." Economic Development and
       Cultural Change 5(July, supplement): 1–111.
1963   "Quantitative aspects of the economic growth of nations, VIII, distribution
       of income by size." Economic Development and Cultural Change 11(January,
       part II):1–80.

Lenski, Gerhard
1966   Power and Privilege: A Theory of Social Stratification. New York: McGraw-
       Hill.

Levy, Marion
1955   "Contrasting factors in the modernization of China and Japan." Pp. 496–536
       in Simon Kuznets, Wilbert E. Moore, and Joseph J. Spengler (eds.), Economic
       Growth: Brazil, India, Japan. Durham, N.C.: Duke University Press.

Likwak, Eugene, and Ivan Szelenyi
1969 "Primary group structures and their functions: kin, neighbors, and friends." American Sociological Review 34(August):465–481.

Lipset, Seymour Martin
1960 Political Man: The Social Bases of Politics. Garden City, New York: Doubleday (Anchor Books).

Lipset, Seymour Martin, and Reinhard Bendix
1960 Social Mobility in Industrial Society. Berkeley: University of California Press.

Marsh, Robert M.
1963 "Values, demand and social mobility." American Sociological Review 28 (August):565–575.

Matras, Judah
1967 "Social mobility and social structure: some insights from the linear model." American Sociological Review 32(August):608–614.

1970 Populations and Societies. To be published by Aldine Publishing Co., Chicago.

Miller, S. M.
1960 "Comparative social mobility: a trend report and bibliography." Current Sociology 10(No. 1).

Moore, Wilbert E.
1966 "Changes in occupational structures." Pp. 194–212 in Neil J. Smelser and Seymour M. Lipset (eds.), Social Structure and Mobility in Economic Development. Chicago: Aldine Publishing Co.

Myint, H.
1965 "Education and economic development." Social and Economic Studies 14 (March):8–20.

Ramsøy, Natalie Rogoff
1966 "Changes in rates and forms of mobility." Pp. 213–234 in Neil J. Smelser and Seymour M. Lipset (eds.), Social Structure and Mobility in Economic Development. Chicago: Aldine Publishing Co.

1969 "Social mobility in Europe: a brief review of the 1960's." Paper read at the Cornell Mobility Conference, Ithaca, New York, April, 1969. To appear in R. McGinnis (ed.), Proceedings of the Cornell Mobility Conference. Forthcoming.

Reynolds, Lloyd G.
1964 Labor Economics and Labor Relations, fourth edition. Englewood Cliffs, New Jersey: Prentice-Hall.

Rocha, Fernando A. S.
1968 Determinants of Occupational Achievement, Income and Level of Living in Brasilia, Brazil. Madison, Wisconsin: University of Wisconsin, unpublished Ph.D. dissertation.

Ross, David F.
1967 "Employment and industrialization in developing countries: comment." Quarterly Journal of Economics 81(May):338–342.

Russett, Bruce M., Hayward R. Alker, Jr., Karl W. Deutsch, and Harold D. Lasswell
1964 World Handbook of Political and Social Indicators. New Haven: Yale University Press.

Sawyer, Jack
1967 "Dimensions of nations: size, health and politics." American Journal of Sociology 73(September):145–172.

Smelser, Neil J., and Seymour M. Lipset
1966   "Social structure, mobility and development." Pp. 1–50 in Neil J. Smelser and
        Seymour M. Lipset (eds.), Social Structure and Mobility in Economic Devel-
        opment. Chicago: Aldine Publishing Co.

Soares, Glaucio Ary Dillon
1966   "Economic development and class structure." Pp. 190–199 in Reinhard Bendix
        and Seymour Martin Lipset (eds.), Class, Status, and Power: Social Stratifica-
        tion in Comparative Perspective. Revised edition. New York: Free Press of
        Glencoe.

Svalastoga, Kaare
1965   "Social mobility: the Western European model." Acta Sociologica 9:175–182.

Tangri, Shanti
1962   "Urbanization, political stability, and economic growth." Pp. 192–212 in Roy
        Turner (ed.), India's Urban Future. Berkeley: University of California Press.

Treiman, Donald J.
1966   "Status discrepancy and prejudice." American Journal of Sociology 71(May):
        651–664.
1968a   Occupational Prestige and Social Structure: A Cross-National Comparison.
        Chicago: University of Chicago, unpublished Ph.D. dissertation. A revised
        version is to be published in 1970 by Markham Publishing Co., Chicago.
1968b   Societal Development and Social Mobility: A Cross-national Comparison of
        Systems of Social Stratification. Madison, Wisconsin: Department of Sociology,
        University of Wisconsin. Unpublished research proposal to the National Science
        Foundation.

UNESCO
1958   World Survey of Education, Volume II, Primary Education. New York:
        United Nations.

U.S. Department of Labor
1965   Dictionary of Occupational Titles, 1965. Volume 1, Definitions of Titles.
        Third edition. Washington, D.C.: U.S. Government Printing Office.

Williams, T. David
1965   "Some economic implications of the educational explosion in Ghana." Pp.
        479–494 in George Z. F. Bereday and Joseph A. Lauwerys (eds.), The Year
        Book of Education 1965: The Education Explosion. London: Evans Brothers
        Limited.

Wrong, Dennis H.
1958   "Trends in class fertility in Western nations." Canadian Journal of Economics
        and Political Science 24(May):216–229. Reprinted, pp. 353–361 in Reinhard
        Bendix and Seymour Martin Lipset (eds.), Class, Status, and Power: Social
        Stratification in Comparative Perspective. Revised edition, New York: Free
        Press of Glencoe, 1966.

Stratification in American Science*

HARRIET ZUCKERMAN
Columbia University

Although differential ranking in science is not readily visible to lay observers, American science is, in fact, sharply graded. Rewards and facilities for research are concentrated among relatively few investigators and organizations. This distinctive pattern of stratification, at odds with the egalitarian ethos of science, is not solely attributable to the distribution of talent in the scientific community. There is however a high correlation between assessed contributions to science and investigators' scientific standing. The present pattern of stratification is the outcome of processes of allocation of men and resources among various sectors of science which include selective recruitment and socialization of young investigators, differential access to publication and research facilities, and differential recognition of scientists' contributions through citations to their work and honorific awards. In a time when the legitimacy of reward systems in many social institutions is routinely challenged, scientists are apt to accept their own as just and correct.

There are now between 250,000 and 400,000 scientists in the United States (National Science Foundation, 1968; Greenberg, 1967a:6). It is indicative of the present state of knowledge that no better estimate can be made. Compared to other occupational groups in the United States, scientists[1] rank high, whatever criteria of evaluation one chooses. On the average, their annual income places them in the top fifth of Americans (National Science Foundation, 1968:2; U. S. Bureau of the Census, 1969:322). In growing measure, leading scientists have been involved in major national decisions which, in turn, have affected international relations. Trend studies of occupational prestige show dramatic increases in the social standing of scientific occupations as well as improvements in the proportion of Americans who know what these occupations are. The most highly rated scientific occupation, nuclear physicist, rose from eighteenth place in the 1947 ratings to third place in the most recent one, placing these scientists ahead of cabinet members, state governors and diplomats (Hodge et al., 1964). As a group, the scientific professions are located among the topmost layers of the social structure. But as we shall see, apparently small differences in income and in prestige accorded to the several kinds of scientists by the

---

*Research for this paper was supported by a grant from the National Science Foundation to the Columbia Program in the Sociology of Science. The paper may be identified as reprint no. A-563 of the Bureau of Applied Social Research, Columbia University.

[1] For my purposes, the terms science and scientist cover only the physical, biological, and earth sciences and the men who work in them.

235

general public only obscure the very significant differentiations that scientists themselves make among their colleagues. This seemingly uniform occupational group is, in fact, sharply stratified.

The first problem at hand, then, is to sketch out the main features of the stratification system in American science. Next, three issues need to be explored to move from describing the characteristically sharp stratification in science to accounting for it: (1) What criteria are used in ranking scientists and their work? (2) By what social processes are scientists allocated facilities and rewards? and (3) How do the various outcomes of these processes interact so as to enhance the opportunities of some to achieve high rank in science and to interfere with the chances of others? Finally, I want to comment on the extent of which stratification in science can be expected to remain the same or to move toward a more egalitarian allocation of recognition and rewards.

THE SHAPE OF THE STRATIFICATION SYSTEM IN SCIENCE

Each social institution has its own hierarchy of rewards for role-performance. Great contributions to science, like economic or political success, are apt to call forth both money and influence. These are not unimportant in science but prime significance is given to symbolic recognition by colleagues for work well done. Members of the scientific community are considered the only competent judges of the merits of an investigation and the significance of such knowledgeable judgments is continually reinforced in the socialization of young scientists and mature ones. They learn early to distinguish between a scientist's scientist and one who has merely earned public acclaim. (With occasional exceptions, public acclaim mirrors the judgments of the scientific community.) Differentials in recognition are not only fundamental to differential ranking in science but also provide the base from which scientists may acquire new facilities either in the form of resources for research or in increased influence. While these may, in turn, be used to gain even more recognition, they are not entirely transmutable. Influence in national politics, for example, is by no means underrated, but it does not give scientists the same esteem among their peers as discoveries of a higher order.

It is not easy to get at the degrees of recognition scientists accord one another. For one thing, they are ambivalent about recognition, at once coveting it and despising themselves for doing so. As a consequence, many deny any interest in it at all and assert that there are no inequalities among them except God-given ones. (For the basic discussion of recognition in science, see Merton, 1957c.) Others are less tortured but equally reluctant, for sociologists' sake, to rank their colleagues, feeling that it is at odds with the norms of science to do so. Still a third group is fascinated by social standing in science but their pleasure in public discussions of it evokes so much opposition from their peers that one suspects that their attitudes are deviant.

All one need do, however, is listen to the gossip in which scientists, like others, delight. One discovers that evaluations, sometimes of a most precise sort, are constantly made. Leo Szilard, the physicist and biologist, liked to measure himself by his opponents and claimed that he never argued with "third rate scientists, I quarreled [only] with the first rate scientists" (Gilman, 1965:143). In fact, the viability of modern science depends on there being a substantial consensus, arrived at through discussion, on the quality of scientific work and its producers. (See Ziman, 1968, for the significance of this consensus.)

Ranking is expressed in a variety of public estimates of scientific worth—the conferring of awards, major fellowships, citations to work, honorary degrees, distinguished lectureships, editorships and eponymy, the naming of scientific contributions after their discoverers.[2] These rewards for excellence, like excellence itself, are relatively rare. No more than a third of the physicists even in the most prestigeful university departments have, for example, ever received an honorific award (J. Cole, 1969:3–11). Similarly, most articles published in scientific journals are cited once but rarely more often (Zuckerman and Merton, 1969). And, of course, eponymy and the like are even harder to come by. To make the matter of scarcity even more extreme, it appears that receiving some honors more or less depends on having received others. Less prestigeful honors serve to lift investigators from obscurity into visibility, a prerequisite for receiving additional awards. Taking these two facts together, the rarity and the interdependence of scientific honors, the stratification of prestige and recognition is very sharply graded. Social honor in science is concentrated within a very small group of scientists.

Stratification and ranking are not, however, limited to individual investigators. Disciplines, publication in particular journals, types of research, organizations, and rewards are also ranked. Individual scientists can be located on each of these dimensions and their final rank is the sum or product of these and evaluations of their research. Taking these additional criteria into account does not change the picture appreciably, very few continue to have most of the scientifically meaningful rewards and the great majority have few or none at all.

---

[2] If it were possible to compare the gap between the maximum and minimum of scientists' earnings and their prestige, I suspect that the latter would by far be the larger. This would be so especially among university scientists whose top salaries are no more than two or at most three times as large as those of junior faculty but many of whom have world-wide fame.

At this point it may be useful to do a bit of sociological cartography on the understanding that the effort is more impressionistic than systematic. It is not entirely clear whether the stratification of science is comprised of one or several hierarchies but it seems now that various criteria for ranking—scientific achievement, influence in scientific politics, and contribution to the organization of science—are sufficiently interdigitated at the top at least to treat these several hierarchies as one.

Several types of men comprise the topmost stratum of science. First and most eminent are those whose scientific work has been significant enough to assure them high rank, present and future. Investigators like Pauling, Bethe, Wigner, Onsager, and Delbrück exemplify this type. These men happen to be Nobel laureates but this fact is incidental. Although very few question the quality of laureates' contributions, there is, of course, another cadre of very distinguished scientists who have not been tapped by the Nobel committees and never will be. These men are, very simply, great scientists and their achievements are mirrored in their prestige. With very few exceptions, they are members of the National Academy and have received one or several major scientific awards. (See Greenberg, 1967b for election procedures in the National Academy.) Other members of the Academy—particularly those who were elected for their scientific work—also may be included in this top layer, although they stand one or several notches below the very top. This second level group is apt to include major men at the highest quality universities or research laboratories who also have multiple honors. They are probably members of the American Philosophical Society and are well known in the world community of their particular fields. Just as one finds differences among Nobel laureates—and there are strong prizes and weaker ones—so, too, are there gradations in this larger elite and these are largely based on extent of contributions to science. For the most eminent, high standing, once achieved, remains with them through their lives—a pattern described as the 'ratchet effect' (Merton, 1968:57). They have contributed enough to avoid being subjected to accusations of being over the hill. Other scientists, however, whose standing is only somewhat slightly less lofty, feel pressed to demonstrate their worth time and again through continuous work (Zuckerman, 1967a: 401n).

These men do not exhaust the membership of the top group. Others belong who have occupied positions of influence in the major scientific organizations, have moved into academic administration or have served as liaison between government and science. (See Greenberg, 1967a for a knowledgeable view of these men.) They have very considerable influence in the politics of science which builds with each new position they acquire. These men who could not have risen as far as they have without having once made a respectable contribution, have not as a group had long careers of distinguished work. They are apt to be "scientist statesmen" rather than re-search scientists, though several, Glenn Seaborg or I. I. Rabi, for example, merit both titles.

These groups taken together can be construed as the national elite in science. They cover one or at the most two scientific generations for, on the average, they were elected to the Academy at 49 and are *en masse* now 62 or so (Greenberg, 1968:13). Within each discipline, most have come up through the ranks together and have shared a set of common experiences. Twenty or thirty years ago, when they were just beginning their careers, disciplines were very small, making it possible for each to have known the others since his twenties. The present group shared post-doctoral years at the great European and American laboratories. And they are also tied together by World War II experiences, which were most significant for the physicists and slightly less so for chemists and biologists. These long asso-ciations make for social solidarity among members of this group which integrates the various sciences even though disciplinary loyalties are strong. Not only do members of the elite share a set of commitments and interests, they also share the past.

The elite tends to comprise a gerontocracy (at least as compared to the age composition of the scientific community[3]) which plays a major role in allocating research funds, prizes, fellowships—in short, the facilities and rewards for doing science. This arrangement in useful activities is said to leave men still in their creative years free to work and to occupy those who have passed them. Whether this is true and if so, whether it will con-tinue, is still problematic. In any case, they are, to use an overworked term, the American scientific establishment.

Just below the top are two quite distinct groups which are not equiva-lently ranked. The first, and more esteemed, is composed of younger men destined to enter the elite as their work continues to win them recognition. These comers are fairly easy to identify by the time they are in their thirties; they have been made full professors early on and have become visible through numbers of important publications. The second group includes those who contribute to the ongoing operation of their fields by taking on the demanding administrative and editorial tasks. Their influence derives from their positions rather than from the personal authority of having done significant scientific work. They have probably accepted the fact that they will not do pathbreaking research but they have good enough sci-entific taste and sufficient energies to continue to do useful work as partic-ipants in disciplinary politics. These men are not younger versions of the scientific statesmen and are not apt to move up in the hierarchy.

---

[3] Half of those listed in the National Register of Scientific and Technical Personnel are under 40 and eighty percent under 50 (U.S. Bureau of the Census, 1969: 528).

The structural attributes of the foregoing groups are not precisely known but we do have some idea of what they are like. This is not the case for the strata below them. We do not know, for example, whether these strata are continuous or discrete. Opportunities for upward mobility are no doubt better for younger promising men in better universities and laboratories but less good for scientists past middle age who have not reached the middle level of their fields. There also seem to be separate and less sharply stratified clusters of industrial and government scientists as well as of men of all ages at middle level universities. They are not part of the competitive struggle for topmost scientific recognition but have, according to Glaser (1965), set their sights on respectable but undistinguished careers. (See Kornhauser, 1962: chap. 5 for an examination of the aspirations of scientists in different organizational contexts.) They can be differentiated in turn from scientists located at small colleges and minor universities who do some research now and then but who identify themselves as teachers of science rather than as research scientists.

We are only at the beginning now of understanding the ways in which age, prestige, and influence in science intersect in the process of stratification. We know something of the overall shape of each of these hierarchies but their details are still vague.[4]

BASES FOR RANKING IN SCIENCE

Scientists sometimes assert that differences in their standing derive primarily, if not exclusively, from differences in talent. And since great talent is very scarce, only a few scientists have the capacity to do great science and, in turn, be accorded great prestige. Others believe that the elitist character of science can be attributed to its culture, which favors markedly unequal rewards by emphasizing the contributions of one or several scientists to a particular discovery while underplaying antecedents and co-investigators. Neither of these satisfactorily explains the characteristic pattern of stratification in science.

Although we know little about the nature of scientific talent and its distribution, the data at hand suggest that significant scientific achievement is positively but not perfectly correlated with trained capacity (see Cattell, 1963, for one empirical study). The most striking examples of scientific genius—the Bohrs, Einsteins and Plancks—are apt to make us overlook

---

[4] These problems are even more acute if we shift our attention from the United States to foreign scientific communities and from the present to the past. Unsystematic observation suggests that science in more traditional societies is even more sharply stratified since there are fewer middle level posts available and it also seems that scientific rank and social rank are strongly linked in these contexts.

the much larger number of scientists whose work has brought them substantial recognition but who are no more than very able. At the same time, there have been appreciable numbers of gifted men who never quite fulfill their promise. Motivation and endurance seem to count for at least as much as intelligence in producing superior scientific work, and the most distinguished scientists have, by and large, worked enormously hard, leading some to propose a "stamina theory" of scientific success.

The distributions of abilities on the one hand and of rewards on the other may be related in other respects. Some scientists have complained that the increasingly large numbers who have entered science in the recent past have, on the average, been less able than earlier cohorts.[5] (Wigner, 1963:6). If so, then increasing recruitment into science will enlarge the differences between the most and least talented and produce considerable changes in their relative numbers. Until we learn something more than we know now about the distribution of abilities in different cohorts of scientists, these observations will remain more in the realm of speculation than of fact.

So much for the role of ability in producing stratification of scientists. The norms and values of science and, in particular, the emphasis placed on universalism and authority play a more significant role in the allocation of rewards. Universalism prescribes that performance will be appraised by the same standards wherever it is found. According to this rule, scientific work is to be judged on the degree to which it extends knowledge about nature and on no other grounds. Men should be free to enter science and to rise in it on their merits alone (see Merton, 1957a, and Storer, 1966: 75ff). Some have observed that scientists have never been thoroughly committed to this ideal norm (cf. Kaplan, 1964 for one) but the fact is that they nevertheless hold it as an ideal. In any case, if scientists judged one another on wholly universalistic grounds, there is no reason to suppose that their evaluations would lead to an equal distribution of rewards rather than an unequal one. Instead, rewards would be allocated so as to parallel the distribution of performance. Universalism, one principal institutional norm in science, does not then promote any single pattern of stratification.

In science, as in other social institutions, normative prescriptions do not always call for consistent actions (cf. Merton and Barber, 1963). Scientists are not only supposed to judge one another independently and on the merits of each case, they are also obliged to accept the standards set by scientific opinion or what is called "authority." Authority is the consensus among those most competent to judge on what is correct and significant; it has

---

[5] They believe that the new recruits are also less committed to science since they have, so to speak, been lured into science by "lavish" fellowships and promise of future income instead of experiencing science as a vocation. The truth of these claims has hardly been established to the satisfaction of anyone but the claimants.

coercive power and is, most of the time, what counts[6] (Polanyi, 1964:374–379). Luis Alvarez, a physicist given to plain talk, puts it this way, "There is no democracy in physics. We can't say that some second rate guy has as much right to [an] opinion as Fermi" (Greenberg, 1968:43). Authority holds sway since it is no easy matter for each scientist to judge the validity of new contributions to his own field much less to adjacent fields. This is particularly so when there are no grounds on which to assess the trustworthiness of the investigator involved. It is therefore assumed that work which runs counter to currently accepted, useful ideas, and which is presented by unknown scientists, is probably trivial and possibly misleading. The principle of authority guards science against cranks but it sometimes permits works of still unrecognised genius to be rejected out of hand. This dysfunction has been described as a small price to pay when one considers the relative number of unfounded claims and of works of overlooked genius (Polanyi, 1963). The application of authoritative judgments almost always favors the concentration of recognition among those who already have it; not only do the ideas they approve prevail, but these men also are the only ones ordinarily allowed to present apparently implausible versions of new knowledge.

Universalism and authority are institutionally prescribed criteria for evaluation. Beyond these, the culture of science gives high priority to originality and to humility, each of which affects processes of ranking. Merton (1957c) has so fully explored the significance of originality and priorities in science that only one comment is needed here. Being first in science is a major value and being second is a far cut below. This emphasis on priority derives from the high value placed on original contributions to science and, in its turn, gives rise to intense competition among scientists (cf. Hagstrom, 1965: 69ff; Watson, 1968). The fact that kudos go for discoveries, large and small, to the winner and little to the "also-rans" is another source of the pattern of sharp stratification in science.[7]

If one is fortunate enough to be first in making a significant discovery, according to scientific etiquette, one should at least be humble about it. While scientists recognize that great discoveries usually result from almost unendurable work, they also know that other scientists were often ready to make the same discoveries and that, to a degree, achieving recognition and priority is fortuitous. Whether, in particular cases, humility is warranted, the norms oblige scientists to be unassuming in confronting nature. They

---

[6] Polanyi is equally quick to point out that revolt against authority is also necessary for the making of great discoveries.

[7] This is not to say that scientists who contribute to their fields in a steady if unspectacular fashion are deprived of esteem. It is simply that the recognition received for discoveries is somewhat different in character from useful but not pathbreaking work.

believe that she has a way of confounding the arrogant. The emphasis on humility in science also appears in the belief that all investigators are joined in the collective enterprise of extending knowledge and are, in this sense, peers. Each man, no matter how small his contribution, adds to the common store of knowledge and is dignified in the process. (For only one version of this ideology, see the quotations from Sir Lawrence Bragg in Lonsdale, 1962). This view, which contrasts so sharply with the apparent facts of unequal contributions and rewards, serves to integrate the various strata of scientists and legitimates the efforts of rank and file scientists. It provides a degree of stability in a system which is highly competitive and grudging in its major rewards to all but a very few.

So far, we have crudely sketched out the structure of rewards in science and some bases for evaluation. We have not, as I have reiterated, succeeded in measuring differences in social rank. We know next to nothing about the actual distribution of scientists among the various strata, about rates of mobility between them and about the relations of these strata to one another. It may help to specify our ignorance a bit by turning now to examine the contribution of several social processes in science to the stratifying of its population.

ALLOCATIVE PROCESSES IN SCIENCE

The uneven distribution of rewards in science is the outcome of several processes which allocate facilities and rewards to individual investigators or alter their opportunities for attaining them. They include selective recruitment and socialization of young scientists, the allocation of scientists among different institutions and organizational sectors, access to resources for research and to publication, and finally, the allocation of honorific awards. Each of these processes both contributes to differential ranking and is a reflection of it.

Selective Recruitment and Socialization

We begin with the prosaic but important fact that large proportions of the scientific elite have been trained at a very small number of universities. About half of all the Nobel laureates who studied in the United States received their degrees from just four universities, Harvard, Columbia, Berkeley and Princeton, which during the same period produced just fourteen percent of all science doctorates (Zuckerman, 1967b:29). The same is the case for members of the National Academy of Sciences and for a sample of distinguished American psychologists (computed from Wispé, 1965:90). Just four universities managed to produce about half of each of these groups and these universities graduated only twelve and twenty-seven percent of comparable doctorates respectively. The top four are not the same institutions in each case but Harvard and Columbia are first or second in all. These data simply underscore the positive relation between scientific success and place of training.[8] One uncomplicated and apparently correct conclusion one might draw is that these institutions and others in the top rank attract more able students than the rest. (See Cartter, 1966 for university ratings field by field.) In an unusually pointed attempt to assess the contribution of intelligence to scientific achievement, Bayer and Folger (1966:388) report a low but positive correlation between measured ability of graduates and the quality of departments which trained them. Universalism in the form of allocating the more able students to better quality institutions seems to play some role in this process. This interpretation is not inconsistent with another that attributes the success of graduates of high quality institutions to their greater access to effective socialization.

Nobel laureates report that studying with distinguished scientists, as most of them did, was crucial to their intellectual development (Zuckerman, 1967a). The chance to see science at its best up close is apparently more important in shaping the careers of young investigators than is the larger university ambiance. This interpretation is supported by Diana Crane's (1965:711) findings that young men who have had sponsors with high prestige (and who are presumably superior scientists) are apt to gain recognition regardless of the quality of their graduate institutions, and by Wispé (1965:93) who reports that eminent psychologists were more often trained by distinguished teachers than were other graduates of the same institutions. Young scientists who had had the opportunity to learn "what matters" from eminent investigators start their careers with an early advantage. They continue to benefit from this experience not only because it has improved their research skills but also because it gives them visibility to those who make decisions on jobs, fellowships, research money, and awards. These young men have, so to speak, been properly launched and however universalistic in allocating resources and rewards the "gatekeepers" wish to be, they are bound to favor candidates they know and respect over others who might be equally able but who are unknown to them. This is defined by some as inadvertent particularism and by others as the efficient distribution of scarce resources. It is no easy matter to disentangle the effects of sponsorship from those of socialization. If nothing else, sponsorship is apt to speed the conferring of recognition. It turns out, for example, that Nobelists-to-be who as young men studied with older laureates, received their own prizes at an average age of 44, nine years earlier than men who had not had distinguished sponsors (Zuckerman, 1967a:393). Sponsorship apparently helps, but its absence is not an insurmountable obstacle. Ameri-

---

[8] The contribution of social origins to allocating young scholars among institutions is examined in Crane, 1969.

can science is then characterized by a mixture of Turner's ideal types (1960) of contest mobility, which emphasizes performance and is reinforced by the norm of universalism; and of sponsored mobility in which elites arrange for the selection of their successors. In both types, early leads acquired by some but not others begin the process of concentration of social honor among a small number of scientists.

The Allocation of Jobs

Over the course of their careers, the evaluation-system distributes scientists among various types and levels of institutions in accord with outward demonstration of talents. Positions in top universities and laboratories have a double significance, symbolic and instrumental. They are rewards for past achievements and they facilitate further research. Scientists are distributed among organizations at different levels of the stratification hierarchy roughly in accord with role performance. Their affiliation with these organizations is, in fact, a prime determinant of organizational standing. It is not easy to factor out how much talent contributes to role performance and to what extent access to sponsors and institutional prestige are also significant; it appears that some ability is indispensable to scientific achievement, but that these other attributes weigh heavily in producing differences in role performance.

There are no systematic studies of mobility of scientists over the course of their careers from academic origins to destinations. Data on affiliations of men at various stages of the scientific career suggest, as Berelson (1960: 114) puts it, that "where one ends up . . . depends a great deal on where one starts out." He is not exaggerating, since more than ninety percent of the arts and science faculties of the top twenty universities took their degrees at one of these same institutions (Berelson, 1960:115). By way of comparison, these institutions produced sixty-three percent of all doctorates during the period that these faculty members received their degrees. Their graduates are therefore overrepresented among their faculties.

The processes making for this distribution of scientists among various organizations are somewhat more complicated than it would first appear. For one thing, membership in the scientific elite is not settled at the beginning of scientists' careers, no matter where they were trained. It is the outcome of a series of evaluations in which talented men from lesser institutions are identified and come to change places with the less gifted who started out in the better universities. Hargens' (1969) reanalysis of Berelson's data on mobility of recent doctorates, from where they were trained to their first jobs, shows considerably more mobility from one prestige level to another than was suggested by previous studies dealing with scientists in all age groups (Hargens, 1969:31). Similar patterns of mobility have been found among Nobel-laureates-to-be. The small number of laureates who were trained at minor institutions moved out of them soon after they earned their degrees; each one had, by the time he was in his thirties, a position in a first-class university or research organization (Zuckerman, 1967b:29). Scientists are not then condemned to obscurity if their academic pedigrees are not quite correct, nor are they guaranteed maximum success if they are.

These findings are suggestive but they do not directly answer the crucial question. In what degree does the allocation of scientists among universities and industrial and independent laboratories correspond to the distribution of talent? Do graduates of the best universities get recruited almost automatically by these institutions or are they simply better scientists than those who find jobs elsewhere? Hargens and Hagstrom (1967:34) report that the prestige of degree-granting institutions is correlated with the prestige of current affiliations, regardless of the productivity (i.e. the number of papers published in the last five years) of individual scientists. This suggests that particularism is at work in some measure. Scientists who manage to rise from lesser institutions to distinguished ones, Crane finds (1965:710), are more apt to have been "recognized" than their colleagues who are graduates of high-ranking universities. Her data are, however, based on small numbers and lend themselves to competing interpretations. It may be that talented scientists will rise, but it also may be that scientists who are upwardly mobile must be even better than their colleagues in high-ranking departments who had no need to demonstrate the same degree of performance. These data may suggest a universalistic interpretation but they are also consistent with the view that institutional affiliations count for more than performance in achieving recognition in science. The Coles's work (1967:386), however, indicates that this is not correct, at least in physics. Although the sheer number of papers by physicists is correlated with other measures of scientific quality it is not, by itself, an adequate indicator. They find that the most prestigeful departments are more apt to hire "perfectionists" than "mass producers," physicists whose publications are relatively few but of very high quality as opposed to physicists who publish many papers which are seldom cited. In fact, the "perfectionists" were also more apt than the "mass producers" to have received honorific awards. It is difficult at this juncture to assess the significance of a universalistic interpretation suggested by the Coles's work and of a particularistic one suggested by Crane, Hargens, and Hagstrom. But whatever the determinants of the allocation of positions, being located in particular universities and laboratories facilitates work not only in the obvious sense of making better material resources available but also by providing stimulating colleagues who themselves have some control over the allocation of facilities and rewards. Both the allocation of students and of more mature scientists among institutions affects the stratification system directly and indirectly. Insofar as affiliations are bases for ranking, where one has been trained and where one is working contribute to social standing. At the same time, both provide opportunity structures which have second order effects on achievement and on upward mobility.

We know somewhat more about vertical mobility over the course of scientific careers than about choices scientists make among the academic, industrial, and government sectors. There is evidence that the several types of research laboratories are stratified much the same as universities; organizations such as the Bell Laboratories and the Institute for Advanced Study stand just as high as the top academic departments. Nonetheless, university science has had more prestige than has industrial and government research.[9] Academic scientists have pretty much cornered the market on honorific awards in science—having received three-fourths of the Nobel prizes going to Americans in the last twenty years[10] and four-fifths of the places in the National Academy of Sciences. By way of comparison, only thirty-five percent of the working scientists in the same fields are academics (National Science Foundation, 1969: computed from Table 4). These facts reflect the overall prestige of fundamental research relative to applied research and development and they also mirror career choices promising scientists have made. As we shall see, resources for research, in the aggregate, are more readily available for applied research and development than to more highly esteemed fundamental research—a factor which interferes with the strong tendency toward elitism in science. But within each type of research, the allocation of resources follows much the same patterns as we have already remarked on.

Allocation of Resources

Research expenditures and the quality of inquiry are no doubt related, but we do not know precisely how. Two things are certain: there are some kinds of research which simply require substantial sums of money; and expensive science is not necessarily good science.

Compared to the sums going to applied work and development—in all, about ninety percent of the more than $16 billions spent on science—relatively little is spent on fundamental or basic research (Greenberg, 1968: 8–9). Expenditures counter the existing stratification of types of research by making it difficult to finance research into fundamental problems—which is also the work most apt to pay off in prestige. At least this is the way things look at first glance. What is more to the point is that resources for fundamental research have become increasingly abundant since World War

---

[9] If life in American universities becomes increasingly chaotic, distinguished scientists may seek the tranquility of industry or research institutes in order to work in peace.

[10] If the then Rockefeller Institute and now Rockefeller University is counted as an academic organization, eighty-eight percent of the laureates were so affiliated.

II, and the more distinguished scientists have found such resources easy to get. On the principles of efficiency and of authority, it was inevitable that the government would seek to build on existing distinction so that "the rich did get richer" and, as Greenberg (1967:212n) continues, "it cannot reasonably be contended that they were undeserving of their happy fate." Data for the early sixties indicate that as few as ten universities[11] received more than a third of all federal expenditures in universities. This concentration is decisive since other sources of research funds contribute only a small share of the total. Hirsch, however, observes that the same ten produced about a third of all the doctorates and "shows a close correspondence between input and output . . ." (1968:105), suggesting that the allocation of funds may not be as disproportionate as it might seem. Moving from universities to individual scientists, Orlans (1962:94) observes that not all inequities are immediately apparent. It is not only a question of how much money is allocated to different grades of scientists but also a question of for what purpose? The best scientists, he notes, get support for what they want to do and the average ones for work the government wants done. Understandably, congressmen whose constituencies included the more than a thousand other colleges and universities pressed for changing the distribution of federal funds, so that by the early sixties, the distribution of funds was beginning to reflect a policy of upgrading many of the less effective universities rather than reinforcing excellence in a few.

As far as one can tell, the allocation of funds has not changed much since. Spending on the war in Vietnam has cut into funds for science. Data from official sources on the detailed allocation of monies are not yet available so that we shall have to see whether the anguished cries of academic scientists are, in fact, good indicators of their declining affluence and increasing competition for funds. Some research money is still around and it is apparently going to men who have already proved themselves, thereby enhancing the differences between the haves and the have-nots.

Differential Access to Publication

An easy way to assess scientists' contributions and, indirectly, their relative standing, is to count their publications. But as I remarked earlier, some have questioned the usefulness of this measure (cf. Cole and Cole, 1967; Bayer and Folger, 1966). Published productivity and scientific distinction are positively related since publications are the principal bases for evaluation of scientists. Productivity of individual scientists varies enormously. It runs the gamut from the usual single publication to the present world's record of 3,904 papers, held by the entomologist, Theodore Cock-

---

[11] These ten include, predictably, California, Caltech, Chicago, Columbia, Cornell, Harvard, Illinois, M.I.T., Michigan, and Minnesota. The same ten provided 37 per cent of the members of federal review panels (Hirsch, 1968: 106).

erell, who managed to do about two papers every week at his peak (Price, 1967:202).

More than forty years ago, Alfred Lotka (1926) proposed the simple inverse-square rule of scientific productivity—the chance that a scientist will produce as many as n papers is $1/n^2$. This means, as Price (1963: 45) indicates, that about sixteen percent of the scientists in an average population produce more than fifty percent of the publications by the entire group. (Cf. Price, 1963:47, for one modification of Lotka's law, and Price and Beaver, 1966, for another.) These figures hold, with minor deviations, for a variety of groups of scientists. Does this characteristic distribution result from real differences in rates of production of papers, as Price suggests, or is it the outcome of discrimination by journal editors who systematically favor papers submitted by a small elite over those submitted by other scientists?

Before confronting this question directly, it should be placed in context. Any scientist, with the double exception of those subjected to industrial and national security regulations, is free to submit his work to scientific journals. Given the prevailing low rates of rejection—they range between twenty and thirty percent in the physical and biological sciences—most will get their work published (Zuckerman and Merton, 1968:22). And, if papers are not accepted by the first journal to which they are submitted, authors are free to submit them elsewhere.[12] Interestingly enough, there seems to be an informal consensus on the order of journals to which submissions should be made so that the most demanding get them first and the least, last. (For a rank order of journals in sociology, see Lin and Nelson, 1969:49–50.)

These two observations touch upon the main question at hand but do not answer it. Merton and I have concluded after examining the files of one of the major journals in science that a mixture of universalism and particularism prevails in evaluation of submissions. Papers from distinguished scientists are sent, on the average, to fewer referees resulting in more rapid publication. Higher rates of acceptance combined with higher rates of submission from eminent scientists account for observed differences in published productivity. At the same time, problematic papers, that is, those whose correctness is questionable, are rejected at the same rate, regardless of the author's standing. And, finally, when rejection rates are examined according to the age and eminence of submitters, we found that the more eminent men within each age group had lower rates of rejection but the most distinguished *older* scientists, men past fifty, had no better chance of acceptance than rank-and-file scientists in their thirties (Zuckerman and Merton, 1968:55).

---

[12] Some claim that any paper will be published if its author simply submits it to a sufficient number of journals (cf. Price, 1967).

These findings indicate that if the system is not exclusively universalistic in the matter of assessing papers for publication, it is even farther from being particularistic. Opportunities for publication are only partly affected by procedures which enhance the standing of a selected few. On balance, the combination of low rejection rates and moderately universalistic assessments should make for a comparatively open—some think too open (cf. Price, 1967)—system of publication.

The Allocation of Honorific Awards

For my purposes here, two rather different matters can be considered under the rubric of honorific awards: the recognition of scientists' work by citation, and by honors such as prizes, eponymy, and election to academies. Both represent the assessments knowledgeable colleagues make about individual scientists and their work.

Citations. The measure of a scientist's contribution to his field is having other scientists acknowledge its worth by using it. "Being a successful scientist," Ziman (1968:25) writes—and he ought to know—"is having other scientists cite your work." Citations are, as those who have received them know, a reward; with all of their methodological faults (cf. Cole and Cole, 1967 for an assessment of these faults), they are the best measure of research quality we have at hand.

Since all authors are free to allocate citations as they please and since citations may be given to any scientist who has published (and, these days, to those who have not), they should be more evenly distributed than any other symbolic reward in science. As it turns out, citations are more widely dispersed than other types of recognition but, in the aggregate, they show the same pattern of clustering I have remarked on repeatedly. Nobel laureates, for example, are cited about thirty times as often, before they received the prize, as the average cited author with no more than two percent of all authors cited as much or more than they are (Sher and Garfield, 1965:6). Discrepancies in citations to the very eminent and the less so are enhanced by a continuity factor in which landmark papers by distinguished scientists are heavily cited over a long period of time, compared to the rapid aging of ordinary scientific publications (Garfield and Malin, 1969:5). Average cumulative citations to a sample of laureates, to recipients of the National Medal of Science and to members of the National Academy of Sciences array themselves neatly with the laureates having 199, medal winners 154, and academicians 127. By way of comparison, the average cited scientist in the same period received 5 citations (J. Cole, 1969:5–22).

We can begin to account for these patterns by noting that they are one manifestation of the Matthew Effect which "consists in the accruing of greater increments of recognition for particular scientific contributions to scientists of considerable repute and the withholding of such recognition from scientists who have not yet made their mark" (Merton, 1968:58). The Matthew Effect is one result of the greater visibility of publications by well-known scientists and the greater attention paid to them. Stephen Cole (1968:15ff.), in an effort to examine the Matthew Effect empirically, finds that the work of the topmost elite does in fact get cited sooner after publication and is thereby incorporated more quickly into the ongoing activity of science. He also finds that newly achieved eminence works retroactively; it brings attention to the earlier and more obscure work of the same men (S. Cole, 1969:27ff.). Similarly Garfield and Malin (1969:5) suggest that awards, the Nobel prize in particular, serve to focus attention on recipients' otherwise neglected work. The various components of the Matthew Effect bring about the concentration of recognition, in this case of citations, among a relatively small number of scientists. Since other honorific awards are also tied to the fruitfulness of an investigator's work, the enhanced visibility and speedier utilization of papers by eminent scientists—expressed in the Matthew Effect—have second order consequences for the allocation of recognition. We now turn to the distribution of honorific awards themselves.

Honorific Awards. The conferring of awards has a long tradition in science. Granting membership in academies—in, for example, the Royal Society, Académie Française, or Accademia dei Lincei, all founded in the seventeenth century—is as old as modern science itself. Election to an academy signals the scientific community as well as the candidate himself that distinguished investigators count him as a peer. These honorific awards have the dual character of being reward and facility at one and the same time. Symbolically, honorific awards help men to get on with their work by reassuring them that their efforts have not been misplaced. They are facilities in the sense that they can readily be converted into new resources for research.

The number of awards available varies from field to field and, apparently, among types of research. Every field, however, has at least one highly esteemed award, even though the absence of Nobel prizes in a number of fields has prompted complaints of neglect. Honorific awards themselves vary in prestige, with predoctoral fellowships falling at the lower end of the hierarchy, the great majority of honorific awards in the middle and, at the top, eponymy and the principal national and international prizes. Awards also vary with respect to their visibility. Cole (1969: chap. 5) reports that the majority of academic physicists know only the most celebrated honorific awards and that most have never heard of the vast array of lesser prizes, medals, and awards that are given. Only the winners of multiple honors who are, after all, deeply implicated in the reward system as judges as well as recipients, have extensive knowledge of the various awards available.

Honorific awards are distributed in much the same fashion as resources for research and citations. Eleven percent of academic physicists have seventy percent of all the awards held by this group (J. Cole, 1969: chap. 5), and although the figures no doubt would vary from field to field, all the evidence at hand suggests that the pattern in other disciplines is the same.

In part, the heaping of awards on a few scientists results from the self-definitions of awarding agencies. Very few make a point of identifying unknown scientists before they are widely recognized. Moreover, most of these groups are committed to honoring major contributions and, since there are few enough of these, awards tend to go to those who already have them. There have, understandably, been flurries of criticism about the selection of the same eminent scientist time and time again (cf. Gilman, 1965:144–145 for one such episode). Award winners sometimes play a role in selecting their successors, but more often award committees are comprised of scientists, each having multiple honors but not necessarily including the one they are charged with conferring. This accords with the principle of authority but it also makes selection committees vulnerable to charges of inbreeding and favoritism. In order to minimize these, the Nobel committees, for example, have extended the right to nominate candidates for Nobel prizes to several hundred reputable scientists, as well as to past prizewinners. The extent of consensus in the sciences involved is mirrored in the fact that these several hundred nominators propose only about thirty new names for Nobel prizes each year. (Nobelstiftelsen, 1962:160–165).

Up to now, the way the distribution of rewards and facilities in science contributes to its sharp stratification has been my main concern. I turn now to examine the stability and legitimacy of the present reward system in science.

SOME CONSEQUENCES OF DIFFERENTIAL REWARDS IN SCIENCE

Differential rewards in science serve much the same purpose as they do in other institutional spheres. They validate past role performance and provide a degree of motivation for the future. They bring attention to performance judged to be of high quality, thereby reinforcing the standards by which performance is to be assessed. (Cf. J. Cole, 1969: chap. 5 for a thorough discussion of the functions of the reward system in science.) But this does not give us any clue as to why, given the very unequal distribution of rewards in science, the majority of investigators has accepted its legitimacy and probably will continue to do so in the future, barring radical change in the social context of science.[13]

---

[13] These questions have been discussed at length with Jonathan Cole and other members of the Columbia Program of the Sociology of Science. Cole (1969: chap. 8) has examined some of them in detail.

Although most rewards that are highly valued by scientists are shared only by a small group, no scientist is deprived of all the good things of the scientific life. If scientists adequately discharge their role obligations in teaching, administration, and research, they are rewarded in a variety of ways. Beyond the respect accorded to them by the general public, they are recognized for their contributions by close colleagues and in varying measure by scientists in their disciplines. Since scientific recognition is not a zero-sum reward, the fact that top-level scientists have been substantially honored does not curtail the recognition available to scientists whose positions are less lofty. Middle and lower level scientists share in the compensations that go along with being in science. Their feelings of deprivation moreover are apparently not acute; Glaser (1963: 1964) suggests that the comparative reference groups of organizational scientists do not extend so far as to include the great discoverers but instead are limited to their colleagues and superiors in the same organizational setting. These scientists, more locals than cosmopolitans (Glaser, 1964), are probably not moved toward rebellion when they hear that Linus Pauling has been given still another distinguished professorship or that Arthur Kornberg may be on his way to a second Nobel prize. As Jonathan Cole (1969) has indicated, these rank-and-file scientists are not even motivated to acquire middle and lower level honorific awards; they do not even know they exist. The absence of deprivation and the selection of less lofty reference groups are not conditions which promote revolution.

Nor are these the only sources of stability in the system. From all that I can reconstruct, it appears that most scientists accept as legitimate authoritative evaluations of work and the criteria on which they are made. Although assessments of the interest and significance of particular inquiries are bound to vary, there is consensus on the importance of selected contributions such as the Crick-Watson model or the nonconservation of parity. Since the prevailing criteria for evaluation are taken as correct, scientists are apt to blame their failure to do significant research on themselves rather than on the system. Equivalent attitudes toward economic success, Merton (1957b) observed thirty years ago, lead individuals to experience a great deal of stress but leave the question of the legitimacy of the system unchallenged.

Not only do scientists subscribe to the evaluation system, but also they believe that significant contributions to science are rare events. They know from experience how difficult it is to have good ideas and they are apt to feel that their inadequacies are not uncommon. As a consequence, they are not reluctant to have multiple honors go to men who have done good research. But they are impatient with scientists who are past their prime but still try to exert their authority and with those who have been highly touted but have not lived up to their original promise.

Finally, science has its egalitarian ideology which, as I noted earlier, binds the various strata of scientists together in the common enterprise of understanding nature, and protects the scientific community from polarization.

This review of stratification in American science should indicate that we have come some distance in learning about the allocation of certain kinds of rewards, the bases for allocation, and some of their consequences for different parts of the scientific community. Mobility in science, especially over the whole life course, relations between the different strata of scientists, and, particularly the extension of detailed knowledge to include the middle and lower levels of scientists, are problems needing more attention. Beyond these, the malintegration of the reward system, on the one hand, geared as it is to recognize individual performance, and the organization of contemporary science, on the other, in which research is increasingly a collective rather than an individual effort, has disruptive potentials which may begin to undermine the stability of the present structure (cf. Zuckerman, 1968:277). And since science is no more exempt from criticism than other institutions, the reward system and the structure of opportunities, like their counterparts in the economy or the polity, will probably come under attack. These new conditions in the context of science may well alter a system of stratification which has stood for three hundred years.

REFERENCES

Bayer, Alan E., and John Folger
1966   "Some correlates of a citation measure of productivity in science," Sociology of Education 39(Fall):381–390.

Berelson, Bernard
1960   Graduate Education in the United States. New York: McGraw-Hill.

Cartter, Allan M.
1966   An Assessment of Quality in Graduate Education. Washington, D.C.: American Council on Education.

Cattell, Raymond B.
1963   "The personality and motivation of the researcher from measurements of contemporaries and from biography." Pp. 119–131, in C. W. Taylor and F. Barron, (eds.), Scientific Creativity: Its Recognition and Development. New York: John Wiley.

Cole, Jonathan R.
1969   The Social Structure of Science. Columbia University, Department of Sociology. Unpublished dissertation.

Cole, Stephen
1968   "The reception of scientific discoveries: the operation of the Matthew effect in science." Presented at the 1968 meetings of the American Sociological Association. To be published in the American Journal of Sociology.

Cole, Stephen, and Jonathan R. Cole
1967 "Scientific output and recognition: a study in the operation of the reward system in science." American Sociological Review 32(June):377–390.

Crane, Diana
1965 "Scientists at major and minor universities: a study of productivity and recognition." American Sociological Review 30(October):699–714.
1969 "Social class origin and academic success: the influence of two stratification systems on academic careers." Sociology of Education 42(Winter):1–17.

Garfield, Eugene, and Morton V. Malin
1969 "Can Nobel Prizes be Predicted?" Mimeo.

Gilman, William
1965 Science: U.S.A. New York: Viking Press.

Glaser, Barney
1964 Organizational Scientists: Men in Professional Careers. Indianapolis: Bobbs-Merrill.

Greenberg, Daniel S.
1967a The Politics of Pure Science. New York: New American Library.
1967b "The national academy of sciences: profile of an institution (I)." Science 156(14 April):222–229.

Hagstrom, Warren
1965 The Scientific Community. New York: Basic Books.
1966 "Competition in science." Presented at the 1966 meetings of the American Sociological Association.

Hargens, Lowell
1969 "Patterns of mobility of new Ph.d's among American academic institutions." Sociology of Education 42(Winter):18–37.

Hargens, Lowell, and Warren Hagstrom
1967 "Sponsored and contest mobility of American academic scientists." Sociology of Education 40(Winter):24–38.

Hirsch, Walter
1968 Scientists in American Society. New York: Random House.

Hodge, R. W., P. M. Siegel, and P. Rossi
1964 "Occupational prestige in the United States: 1925–1963." American Journal of Sociology 70(November):286–302.

Kaplan, Norman
1964 "Sociology of science." Pp. 852–881 in R. E. L. Faris (ed.), Handbook of Modern Sociology. Chicago: Rand McNally.

Kornhauser, William, with Warren Hagstrom
1962 Scientists in Industry: Conflict and Accommodation. Berkeley: University of California Press.

Lin, Nan, and Carnot E. Nelson
1969 "Bibliographic reference patterns in core sociological journals." American Sociologist 4(February):47–50.

Lonsdale, K.
1962 "Reminiscences." Pp. 595–602 in P. P. Ewald (ed.), Fifty Years of X-Ray Diffraction. Utrecht: N.V.A. Oosthoek's Uitgeversmaatschappij for the International Union of Crystallography.

Lotka, Alfred J.
1926 "The frequency distribution of scientific productivity." Journal of the Washington Academy of Sciences 16:317.

Margolis, J.
1967   "Citation indexing and the evaluation of scientific papers." Science 155 (March):1213–1219.

Merton, Robert K.
1957a   "Science and the democratic social order." Social Theory and Social Structure. New York: Free Press.
1957b   "Social structure and anomie." Social Theory and Social Structure. New York: Free Press.
1957c   "Priorities in scientific discovery: a chapter in the sociology of science." American Sociological Review 22(December):635–659.
1968   "The Matthew effect in science." Science 159 (January):56–63.

Merton, Robert K., and Elinor Barber
1963   "Sociological ambivalence." Pp. 91–120 in Edward A. Tiryakian (ed.), Sociological Theory, Values and Social Change: Essays in Honor of P. A. Sorokin. New York: Free Press.

National Science Foundation
1968   "Salaries and selected characteristics of U.S. scientists, 1968." Review of Data on Science Resources, No. 16 (December) NSF 69–5.

Nobelstiftelsen (ed.)
1962   Alfred Nobel: The Man and His Prizes. New York: Elsevier.

Orlans, Harold
1962   The Effects of Federal Programs on Higher Education. Washington: The Brookings Institute.

Polanyi, Michael
1963   "The potential theory of adsorption." Science 141(September):1010–1013.
1963   Personal Knowledge. New York: Harper Torchbooks.

Price, Derek J. deS.
1963   Little Science, Big Science. New York: Columbia University Press.
1967   "Communication in science: the ends—philosophy and forecast." Pp. 199–209 in A. de Reuck and J. Knight (eds.), Ciba Foundation Symposium on Communication in Science: Documentation and Automation. London: J. and A. Churchill, Ltd.

Price, Derek J. deS., and Donald Beaver
1966   "Collaboration in an invisible college." American Psychologist 21(November): 1011–1018.

Sher, Irving, and Eugene Garfield
1965   "New tools for improving and evaluating the effectiveness of research." Presented at the 1965 Conference on Research Program Effectiveness.

Storer, Norman
1966   The Social System of Science. New York: Holt, Rinehart and Winston.

Turner, Ralph
1960   "Sponsored and contest mobility and the school system," American Sociological Review 25(December):855–867.

U.S. Bureau of the Census
1969   Statistical Abstract of the United States. (90th edition) Washington, D.C.

Watson, James D.
1968   The Double Helix. New York: Atheneum.

Wigner, Eugene
1963   "Prospects in nuclear science." Oak Ridge National Laboratory Publication 16(November 8):6–8.

Wispé, Lauren
1965   "Of eminence in psychology." Journal of the History of the Behavioral Sciences 1(January):88–98.

Ziman, John
1968   Public Knowledge. Cambridge: Cambridge University Press.
Zuckerman, Harriet
1967a   "Nobel laureates in science: patterns of productivity, collaboration and authorships," American Sociological Review 32(June):391–403.
1967b   "The sociology of the Nobel prizes." Scientific American 217(November): 25–33.
1968   "Patterns of name ordering among authors of scientific papers: a study of social symbolism and its ambiguity," American Journal of Sociology 74(November):276–291.
Zuckerman, Harriet,and Robert K. Merton
1968   "Patterns of evaluation in science: institutionalization, structure and functions of the referee system." Presented at the 1968 meeting, American Sociological Association.
1969   Ongoing studies on the character of scientific journals.

What can Mathematical Models Tell us About Occupational Mobility?*

Thomas W. Pullum
The University of Chicago

A description is given of most models and methods which have recently been proposed for describing aggregate movement over a set of occupational categories, both during a single interval of time and over a sequence of intervals; contingency tables and Markov chains are emphasized. Substantial movement (in an aggregate sense) is "explained" by simple effects of supply, demand, age of respondent, etc., without knowledge of nondemographic variables such as respondent's education, aspirations, etc. Related but unpublished findings by the author and others are given and numerous possible directions for investigation are suggested.

INTRODUCTION

It is expected that most readers of this article will have a far better idea of what is meant by "social mobility" than of what is meant by "mathematical models." A brief description at the outset of the modelling concept and a broad classification of models which have been applied to social mobility will thus be useful.

A mathematical model is a theoretical framework which can be expressed and elaborated through mathematical techniques. At root it is a set of one or more assumptions. The utility of a model is dependent upon the availability of (1) methods for generating hypotheses from the assumptions, (2) methods for testing these hypotheses, and (3) appropriate data. A good model will also be derivative of a verbal analysis which is carefully conceptualized and concerned with mechanisms of human social behavior. A model is considerably more than an effort to "fit" data (cf. the objectives listed by Herbert Simon, 1957:142).

It is essential to recognize that the structure which a model brings to a sociological problem is more than a null hypothesis. Models also provide bases for comparison, the residual differences from which often form patterns in themselves. The criticism that a model's assumptions are too general is not always in itself a constructive criticism, as detailed assumptions can only evolve from a broader base. But we certainly do not mean to

---

*The author is grateful to several persons for their comments on an earlier draft, in particular Peter Blau, Leo Goodman, and David McFarland.

defend the use of general assumptions which seem to originate solely in the availability of mathematical methods for handling them, except insofar as the assumptions are subsequently refined.

We may initially classify the modelling of mobility according to two perspectives. Under the first perspective individuals are differentiated by an interval level variable, usually prestige. Multivariate techniques permit incorporation of additional qualitative attributes of the individual and a fairly sophisticated analysis. Svalastoga (1959) and others have used a continuous prestige scale, but the present state of the use of the general linear model, particularly, in this area is demonstrated by Blau and Duncan's *American Occupational Structure* (1968).

At the risk of seeming arbitrary, we shall exclude this perspective from the present paper, referring to it again only in the conclusion. The reason for this exclusion is simply that multivariate models for continuous variables are more accessible to sociologists than are the models to be discussed in this paper, but we believe the latter merit increased attention. The reader who wishes to pursue continuous models is referred to Blau and Duncan (1968) and their bibliography.

The second major perspective uses an ordinal or nominal level variable, usually occupational group membership. Again men are the unit of observation. Within this perspective two foci dominate. The first deals with a single pattern of movement (e.g., father's to ego's category). The second deals with a sequence of patterns of movement (e.g., grandfather's to father's to ego's category) and the interdependencies between patterns more than the interdependencies within specific patterns. This perspective will form the major concern of this paper.

Because of limitations of space we can only allude to a third and recent view, all work which can be attributed to Harrison White (1968). The "vacancy chains" model is applicable when a job is a "position" which exists whether or not it is occupied. An assignment of a man to a job in a given year indicates that a vacancy (perhaps of zero duration) existed in that job. The man who fills the job has left behind another vacancy, which must be filled, etc. Conversely, the man who previously held the job reported on will have moved to fill a vacancy elsewhere, etc. Thus each assignment of a man to a job is located on a chain of conceptual vacancies. The chain originates when a new job is created or when a person leaves the system permanently, creating an opening. The chain ends when a job is abolished (e.g., by merger with another job) or when a man enters the system. There is an analogy of this structure of movement within the system and exchange with the outside to Leontiev input-output theory in econometrics (see, for example, Kemeny and Snell, 1960, chap. 7).

White develops several sophisticated models along this theme, using a variety of techniques. Unfortunately, few of his results are conclusive, because of his small effective sample sizes, and it is likely that more straight-forward approaches to some of his questions are possible. Beyond this, applicability is limited to only a few man-job systems. However, the concept of the vacancy chain is, so to speak, orthogonal to the concepts of careers of men or of sequences of occupants of a job, and White is able to generate new questions and methods for answering these questions when the model does apply.

Our objective is to describe briefly and to interrelate most of the models under the second perspective above. Virtually none of the authors cited have provided the non-mathematical arguments for their models which we feel they require, and we cannot develop these arguments in this short space. But we shall try to be explicit about the assumptions that are made and some of the inferences that are of greatest interest to a less mathematical reader.

ORDINAL OR NOMINAL OCCUPATIONAL VARIABLE: SINGLE PATTERN

Once a number of states have been specified which can be accepted as sufficiently homogeneous internally, the presentation of movement by individuals between states is quite naturally given by a cross-classification table. This table is of a rather special type, however. On the one hand, its row and column categories refer to the same variable, with difference only in reference in time or generation. Consequently the table is square and if, for some reason, we wished to exchange positions of two rows, it would also be necessary to exchange the corresponding two columns. On the other hand, the mobility table does not describe a transaction flow, which also has the preceding properties, for immobility, as well as mobility, is recorded. When the number of categories is small, there may be some unambiguous ordering, e.g., according to prestige, so that ordinal level techniques will be available. With a dozen categories or more, however, there is usually reason to distrust a prestige ranking, and the researcher is limited to nominal level techniques; sometimes the occupational classification does not yield to a substantive ranking even with a small number of categories. It is thus useful to consider models at both the ordinal and nominal levels.

To make the discussion more specific, consider the data of Table 1, to which we shall refer repeatedly. These data were obtained by David Glass and associates (1954) for Great Britain; adult males were sampled and their own and their fathers' occupations were ascertained (our categories 1, 2, 3, 4, 5, correspond to Glass's categories 1–3, 4, 5, 6, 7, respectively). The first step in an attempt to find a pattern in this table is to standardize (i.e., divide each entry) by the total frequency, 3497, since the pattern is

Table 1.

INTERGENERATIONAL OCCUPATIONAL MOBILITY IN GREAT
BRITAIN, ADAPTED FROM GLASS (1954).

Category of father	Category of Respondent				
	1	2	3	4	5
1	297	92	172	37	26
2	89	110	223	64	32
3	164	185	714	258	189
4	25	40	179	143	71
5	17	32	141	91	106

presumably unaffected by the number of respondents in the sample. In this way we obtain Table 2. Denote the proportions in cell (i,j) of Table 2 by p_{ij}, the proportion in row i by $p_{i.}$ and the proportion in column j by $p_{.j}$.

The "density" in cell (i,j) can be obtained by a graphical representation in which the proportion of persons in that cell is shown by a three-dimensional block erected on a base which is $p_{.j}$ wide and $p_{i.}$ deep. Let R_{ij} be the height of the block; then $p_{ij} = p_{i.}p_{.j}R_{ij}$ or $R_{ij} = p_{ij}/p_{i.}p_{.j}$. Figure 1 shows these blocks from "above" and lables them with their heights, R_{ij}.

If Tables 1 and 2 were characterized by statistical independence then each of the R_{ij} would be unity and the collection of blocks in Figure 1 would comprise a unit cube. These heights are the ratios computed by Rogoff (1953), Glass (1954), and Carlsson (1958) in their cell-by-cell comparison of observed data with this model of "perfect mobility." Using this model as a standard, we observe from Figure 1 that (1) there is an excess of cases on the main diagonal, and if the classes are ordered along a prestige continuum, then (2) the excess is more pronounced at the upper and lower extremes (a "ceiling" and "floor" effect), and (3) there is a monotonic reduction in the values of R_{ij} as one moves from the diagonal toward the upper right and lower left corners of extreme movement; that is, there is a correspondence between the frequency of movement between

Table 2.

TABLE 1 STANDARDIZED BY TOTAL FREQUENCY, 3497.

Category of father	Category of Respondent					
	1	2	3	4	5	Total
1	.0849	.0263	.0492	.0106	.0074	.1784
2	.0255	.0315	.0638	.0183	.0092	.1483
3	.0469	.0529	.2042	.0738	.0540	.4318
4	.0071	.0114	.0512	.0409	.0203	.1309
5	.0049	.0092	.0403	.0260	.0303	.1107
Total	.1693	.1313	.4087	.1696	.1212	1.0001

Category of father	Category of Respondent 1	2	3	4	5	
1	2.81	1.12	.67	.35	.34	} .18
2	1.01	1.62	1.05	.73	.51	} .15
3	.64	.93	1.16	1.01	1.03	} .43
4	.32	.67	.96	1.84	1.28	} .13
5	.26	.63	.89	1.39	2.26	} .11
	.17	.13	.41	.17	.12	

Figure 1. *Ratios R_{ij} of observed frequencies to frequencies expected under statistical independence of origin and destination in Tables 1 and 2, expressed as heights of uniform-density blocks when viewed from "above."*

two categories (relative to the standard) and their prestige ranking. Property (3) is a manifestation of the underlying order of the occupational categories along a continuum—in this case, clearly, a prestige continuum. Except for minor variation, these observations hold for mobility tables from all countries and inclusion of any number of categories. A useful summary measure is the average deviation, in a given table, of R_{ij} from unity. For our data that quantity is .43, indicating that the average cell departs in frequency by 43% from the frequency implied by this first standard. Another indicator, the coefficient of dissimilarity (in which the terms in the preceding measure are now weighted by the base areas $p_{i.}p_{.j}$ and the resulting sum is multiplied by ½) is .30. That is, if 30% of the respondents in the table of perfect mobility were shifted then the observed table would be achieved;

the model correctly locates 70% of all individuals. Considering the simplicity of the assumption, however, we would not consider this a poor first step.

As Blau and Duncan (1967:93) have shown, this approach does not have the desirable effect of standardizing for the marginals, since by inverting the matrix of the R_{ij} it is easy to reconstruct Table 2. (Strictly speaking, it is possible that the matrix of R_{ij} will not be invertible, but properties (1)–(3) above make this possibility slight.) The model reorganizes Table 2, but does not reduce it in any sense, nor does it remove any effects of nonuniform distributions over categories.

Following this initial grip on the pattern, one could proceed in various directions. Strictly in terms of mathematical logic, there are two ways to modify the model of independence without discarding the possibility that the number of persons in a given mobility route (i.e., cell of a table) is proportional to both the origin and destination frequencies. Supply and demand, as measured by the latter frequencies, should and do have major impact, and it is worth trying first only minor modifications of the model of perfect mobility. The first modification is limitation of the model to a subset of mobility routes. This modification, due to White (1963) and Goodman (1965), is referred to as quasi-perfect mobility. The second possibility would be incorporation of additional factors of proportionality.

First consider quasi-perfect mobility. As mentioned earlier, a table such as Table 1 contains cases of immobility as well as mobility. Blumen, Kogan, and McCarthy (1955) were the first to suggest that these two phenomena be separated (in a different context). Table 1 can be expressed as the sum of two tables, one of which has the frequencies corresponding to immobility replaced by zeroes (the "mover" table), and the other of which has the frequencies corresponding to mobility replaced by zeroes (the "stayer" table). Immobility would first be conceived of as limited to the main diagonal, but could be generalized to include movement between categories which are "near" one another according to an overall ordinal ranking by which the R_{ij} decrease monotonically with movement away from the diagonal (as described above). Under such a pattern of the R_{ij} and with this expanded view of immobility, it is in fact necessary to count as immobile nearly all persons in the upper left and lower right quadrants of the table; at most one occupational group can have non-zero entries in both the upward and downward mobility portions of the "mover" table. (This is indeed a well-motivated implication and not a *post hoc* attempt to improve the fit; for a related discussion, see Goodman, 1965, and McFarland, 1968.) Thus as the number of categories increases, the proportion of cells on and near the diagonal which must be allocated to the "stayer" table approaches .50.

An alternative decomposition of a mobility table would consider only persons on the main diagonal as stayers, but would subdivide the movers

Table 3a.

THE RATIO R^*_{ij} OF EXPECTED TO OBSERVED FREQUENCY FOR THE QUASI-PERFECT MODEL*

Category of father	Category of Respondent				
	1	2	3	4	5
1	—	—	1.04	.90	.92
2	—	—	.99	1.14	.83
3	1.04	.94	—	.99	1.05
4	.92	1.17	.98	—	—
5	.80	1.21	.99	—	—

* Persons in cells marked "—" were considered to be stayers.

into "upward movers" and "downward movers." Methods for such a tripartite decomposition have been described by Goodman (1968a) and are currently being applied in this context by the present author. By separating these two types of mobility one can use all cells except those on the main diagonal, and can formulate and answer new questions about differences between upward and downward patterns of movement.

If we follow the model of quasi-independence, which assumes that in the mover table frequencies in cells not constrained to zero are the simple product of an origin effect and a destination effect, then we obtain the ratios R^*_{ij} of the observed values to predicted values given in Table 3a. It is clear that for these data, at least, the model fits the behavior of the movers quite well. Among the movers, the average departure of R^*_{ij} from unity is only .09, and 95% of the movers are correctly classified by this model. When the χ^2 test is applied to the observed and expected frequencies of the movers, we obtain a value of 7.9, with 7 degrees of freedom, indicating that on statistical grounds we certainly cannot reject this model for the movers.

Although the original model of quasi-perfect mobility was applied to movers only, we can also check for quasi-independence in the "stayer" table. Methods described by Goodman (1968a) yield the ratios R^*_{ij} for stayers given in Table 3b (one cell has an asterisk because no degrees of

Table 3b.

THE RATIO R^*_{ij} OF EXPECTED TO OBSERVED FREQUENCY WHEN THE CONCEPT OF QUASI-PERFECT MOBILITY IS APPLIED TO STAYERS RATHER THAN MOVERS*

Category of father	Category of Respondent				
	1	2	3	4	5
1	1.16	.69	—	—	—
2	.68	1.61	—	—	—
3	—	—	*	—	—
4	—	—	—	1.17	.77
5	—	—	—	.81	1.25

* Persons in cells marked "—" were considered to be movers. The center cell (marked "*") has no degrees of freedom for a prediction.

freedom were available for its estimation). For the stayers, the pattern of the R^*_{ij} is similar to the pattern of the R_{ij} in Figure 1, and it is clear that the model of quasi-independence does not adequately describe the movement of this sub-population.

If the quasi-perfect model holds for movers, then there is an openness to the occupational class structure to the extent that all persons who have changed class enough to lie inside the "mover" boundary have overcome any effect of "distance" from their class of origin (at least any effect which can be detected in a crude classification with only five categories). The "movers" are all in the same pool of individuals, their movement governed only by supply and demand, with no remaining impact by differential prestige, etc. Conditions of equal access to skills and positions over all origins would result in perfect mobility. If the bias in such access, which we know always exists, is limited only to class of origin or an adjacent class or two, then quasi-perfect mobility will result. The author has applied the model to a variety of tables and has found that it works best for industrialized societies, particularly when urban-farm movement is excluded. These findings are presumed to be due to the greater relevance of skills and lesser relevance of ascribed characteristics when the technology is advanced and education is widely available. The model does less well for a given country, however, when an increased number of occupational categories are employed. There appear to be special supply-demand relations between various pairs of categories under finer definitions of categories. At worst, however, the model draws our attention to these special relationships (Pullum, 1964).

Finally, note that the only sense in which the expected pattern for the movers is conditional upon, or is controlled for, the observed pattern of stayers, is in the adjustment for the marginal frequencies of the stayer subpopulation.

A second modification of the model of independence would incorporate some indicators of distance between categories; for example, the frequency of cases in mobility route (i,j) could be hypothesized to be inversely proportional to the "distance" from class i to class j. There seem to be at least three reasons why this direction has not received a place in the literature. The first is the conceptual difficulty associated with transference of distance from the physical world to the class structure. The second problem is that distance from class i to itself cannot be established, so treatment of diagonal entries is ambiguous. Thirdly, if estimates of cell frequencies under any model are required to add to observed frequencies for all origins and destinations, as they usually are, we would require different constants of proportionality for each cell. Evaluation of the model would then require evaluation of two arrays: the array of expected frequencies (to be compared with the observed) and the array of constants of proportionality ("gravitational" constants), which should be nearly equal if such a model were acceptable. Efforts by the writer, at least, to find a distance function in this categorical case which is plausible and corresponds well to observed data have not been fruitful. (Social distance is, of course, a concept which has received considerable theoretical and methodological attention. See, for example, Beshers and Laumann, 1967, and McFarland, 1969b.)

If one considered the bivariate density of continuous occupational prestige over the unit square with uniform marginals (in effect, "smoothing" Figure 1 to obtain a continuous surface), the result would be approximately a hyperbolic paraboloid (a "saddle"). An adequate conceptualization of the metric and its functional elaboration would be crucial to the value of any mathematical analysis of this density, but the reduction of the pattern to a few parameters could permit useful comparisons of patterns from different countries, etc., and might also yield a continuous distance function.

Another mode of analysis which, like the above, makes no *a priori* assumption about the ordering of categories, depends on statistical interactions (Goodman, 1969a). Suppose we have a $K \times K$ array of numbers $\{ a_{ij} \}$ which add to zero in each row and each column; if the mobility table is given by the array $\{ n_{ij} \}$ then a quantity of the form $\sum_{i,j} a_{ij} \log n_{ij}$ is defined to be an interaction. Subject to the constraints on the arrays $\{ a_{ij} \}$ there will be exactly $(K - 1)^2$ such arrays which are linearly independent; on the other hand, there is an infinite number of such collections of arrays, corresponding to different decompositions of the $(K - 1)^2$ degrees of freedom of the original $K \times K$ table. Two useful properties, among others, are that (a) the sum of two interactions (or a linear combination of interactions) is an interaction and (b) if the model of independence holds, all interactions will be zero. The estimated variance of an interaction is $\sum_{i,j} a_{ij}^2 / n_{ij}$, and if an interaction is divided by its estimated standard deviation it is referred to as a standardized interaction. Interactions are useful in the analysis of any contingency table, since hypotheses about subtables or combinations of subtables can be evaluated. They are particularly applicable to mobility.

The converse of property (a) in the last paragraph is that any interaction, no matter how complex its associated array $\{ a_{ij} \}$, can be expressed as a linear combination of interactions in 2×2 subtables of the main table. Thus if i and i′ are two distinct rows, and j and j′ are two distinct columns of the main table, then interactions of the form

$$(+1)\log n_{ij} + (-1)\log n_{ij'} + (-1)\log n_{i'j} + (+1)\log n_{i'j'} = \log(n_{ij}n_{i'j'}/n_{ij'}n_{i'j})$$

are the "fundamental" interactions by which it is possible to obtain *any* interaction through linear combinations.

The fundamental interactions with $i = j$ and $i' = j'$ can be used to relate pairs of categories. These have the form $d_{ij} = \log(n_{ii}n_{jj}/n_{ij}n_{ji})$, and the special properties (a) $d_{ij} = d_{ji}$ and (b) $d_{ij} = \infty$ if there is not some movement both from i to j and from j to i. As with all interactions, $d_{ij} = 0$ under independence; we know enough of the mobility pattern, however, to be sure that d_{ij} will always be positive. This index can be said to measure the immobility between categories i and j. The $\{ d_{ij} \}$ for Table 1 are given in Table 4, and show a monotonic decrease with movement from the (undefined) cases $i = j$, so that the measure is a partial validation of the ranking of the categories and may at first appear to be a distance metric. However, for several cases it happens that d_{ij} is greater than the sum $d_{ik} + d_{kj}$ for a class k ranked between i and j. We thus wish to forestall any use of d_{ij} as a distance metric.

Table 4.

INDICES OF IMMOBILITY d_{ij} FOR TABLE 1.

Category i	Category j			
	1	2	3	4
2	.602			
3	.876	.280		
4	1.662	.789	.345	
5	1.852	1.056	.453	.370

One can design arrays $\{ a_{ij} \}$ to yield interactions which, rather than relating a pair of categories, instead measure an attribute of a single class, although in a context of several categories. One possible array with this use is built up as follows. Consider any fundamental interaction which has $i = j$, and thus has the form $\log(n_{ii}n_{i'j'}/n_{ij'}n_{i'i})$. Such an interaction gives positive weight to persons who inherit category i and negative weight to persons who are mobile out of category i (to category j') or are mobile into category i (from category i'). It gives positive weight to the number of persons who move directly from i' to j' in order to balance the role that origin i' has had in the magnitude of $n_{i'i}$ and the role that destination j' has had in the magnitude of $n_{ij'}$. Thus this interaction is a partial, positive indicator of the inheritance of category i. It will be zero if simple supply and demand operate within the 2×2 subtable.

A plausible index of the inheritance of i would be the arithmetic average of all distinct interactions of this form with specified i, an index which is itself an interaction. A preferable index, however, would limit the averaging of subtables which did not include any cells (other than [i, i]) inside an admissible "stayer" blocking, discussed earlier. The index for category 1 of Table 1, under the blocking of Figure 1, would be defined by:

$$a_{11} = 1; a_{13} = a_{31} = -\frac{1}{2}; a_{14} = a_{15} =$$

$$a_{41} = a_{51} = -\frac{1}{4}; a_{34} = a_{35} = a_{43} = a_{45} = \frac{1}{4};$$

otherwise, $a_{ij} = 0$. In order both to obtain a measure which is invariant under multiples of the array $\{a_{ij}\}$ and which has unit normal sampling distribution when the standard of independence is used, we divide the preceding interaction by its standard deviation. The result is the intrinsic status inheritance of category i, as defined more generally by Goodman (1969a).

In column A of Table 5 we present these measures for all 5 categories of the British data. The results correspond in their horseshoe pattern with those given by Goodman for a collapsed version of Table 1 and are largely a second manifestation of the horseshoe pattern of the $\{R_{ii}\}$ of Table 2, with a pronounced "ceiling" and "floor" effect for the ranking used. The negative value for category 3 indicates a relative *dis*inheritance from this category. Any interpretation of this disinheritance must be tied to an understanding of the basis of the coefficient. For category 3, the total number of persons who have moved to (or from) categories 1 and 2 from (or to) categories 4 or 5 count just as heavily for inheritance as does the number of persons who actually inherit category 3. The fact that there are relatively few persons who make these fairly distant moves gives the measure its low—in fact, negative—value.

Goodman (1969a) has also proposed a new index of immobility for category i which is analogous to R_{ii} in that it is the ratio of an observed frequency to a predicted frequency. Specifically, it is the ratio of the observed diagonal frequency to the frequency predicted by the supply and demand effects in the mover portion of Table 3 when extended to the stayer position. This measure is listed in Column B of Table 5 and agrees substantially with the pattern of standardized interactions in Column A. An index of "persistence" of categories has also been suggested by Goodman (1969b).

Table 5.

COLUMN A: INTRINSIC STATUS INHERITANCE. COLUMN B:
INDEX OF IMMOBILITY FOR MOVER-STAYER BOUNDARIES OF
TABLE 3 (FROM GOODMAN, 1969A). COLUMN C: CONDITIONAL
UNCERTAINTY ABOUT DESTINATION, GIVEN ORIGIN.

Category	A	B	C
1	17.32	12.00	.57
2	4.85	2.62	.62
3	−1.85	.68	.61
4	12.43	3.15	.60
5	9.91	4.35	.61

Recently Mosteller (1968; see also Levine, 1967) has applied to mobility tables a longstanding technique associated with W. Edwards Deming and Frederick Stephan (Deming, 1943, chap. 7) for the adjustment of table entries to specified marginals in a manner which preserves all interactions (although not *standardized* interactions). Mosteller's motivation was indeed "adjustment" to render tables from different countries, etc., more comparable by giving them the same marginals—typically, uniform marginals. Obviously, comparability of occupational categories is a major requirement if such comparisons are to be worthwhile. Mosteller has found remarkable similarities of patterns for Great Britain and Denmark.

The author has considered an alternative motivation for this technique. Kahl (1957) argued that mobility has four components: class differential birth and death rates (actually, the role of death rates was overlooked by Kahl), immigration, and change in the occupational distribution—three structural components which "force" an amount of movement—and circulatory mobility. If we conceptualize circulatory mobility not as a residual, as Kahl did, but as the pattern of relations between categories, the present object of investigation, which is modified by structural components, then the various models should be compared with a table of circulatory movement, rather than total movement. As a first approximation for recent decades in the United States and other industrial societies we can ignore structural factors other than change of occupational distribution since, as we shall see, this is the dominant factor. We shall also overlook for this presentation the difficulty of overlapping generations (see Duncan, 1966). The problem then is to relate the observed table to a "stable" mobility table, representing the circulatory pattern, with the same origin marginals as are found in the observed table but with the same marginals for destinations as well.

To be specific, suppose that class j has increased in the observed table. We interpret this as an increase in the recruitment by that class from other classes, relative to the recruitment rates which would have maintained class j at the original level. The amount of increase is not immediately calculable, however, for simultaneously with this increase in recruitment, the out-flow rates from class j may have undergone adjustment. It is reasonable to assume that in order to effect the increase in class j, all frequencies of movement into j in the "stable" table were multiplied by a constant c_j; that is, the relative sizes of the contributions from other classes into class j have been unchanged but all contributions have been altered by a single multiplier. An analogous argument can be made for the changes in out-flow, with the effect that the circulatory frequencies differ from observed frequencies only by one multiplier effect for origin and another for destination. Given the restriction on the marginals of the circulatory table, and the observed entries, the circulatory table is uniquely determined by compu-

Table 6.

THE "STABLE" OR CIRCULATORY TABLE CORRESPONDING TO
TABLE 2 (WITH ORIGIN AND DESTINATION MARGINALS EQUAL
TO THE ORIGIN MARGINALS OF TABLE 2).

Category of father	Category of Respondent				
	1	2	3	4	5
1	.0871	.0283	.0491	.0076	.0063
2	.0267	.0347	.0652	.0135	.0079
3	.0509	.0603	.2158	.0562	.0486
4	.0082	.0138	.0570	.0328	.0192
5	.0055	.0110	.0448	.0208	.0286

tational techniques indentical to those used by Mosteller. The circulatory table for Table 1, presented as Table 6, necessarily shows as much total downward movement as total upward movement—that is, the upward or downward movements of average prestige, etc., for a society are eliminated. But there is remarkable similarity, as well, between corresponding frequencies of movement from class i to class j and from j to i. In fact, it is not possible to reject the hypothesis that the proportion moving from i to j is equal to the proportion moving from j to i, for any pair of i and j. We shall postpone further discussion of this concept for a later paper.

Kahl (1957) and Matras (1961) added information beyond that which has already been introduced to separate the effects of differential fertility and change in occupational distribution in the amount of mobility each effect "forces," subject to the important assumption that the labor force is replaced by generations rather than continuously. We feel this kind of analysis is most useful in consideration of a single pattern, although Matras has projected the effects over several generations. Three distributions—that of the labor force at a point in time t_0 (assumed to be the distribution of fathers), that of the labor force at time t_1, and the origin distribution of those persons who are in the labor force at t_1 are compared. The index of dissimilarity computed for the first and third distributions gives the proportional shift from fathers' distribution to the origin distribution of their sons, due entirely to differential fertility. The index computed for the first and second distributions gives the proportional shift from the distribution of the labor force at t_0 to that at t_1. The index computed for the second and third distributions (the destination and origin distributions of the usual mobility table) gives the net shift from origin to destination due to combined effects. Each of these indices gives the proportion of persons in each case who are "forced" to move. Matras found that for a gross three-way classification in Western countries and Japan, the residual amount of movement is remarkably constant (Matras, 1961). For United States data from Kahl (1957) giving class-specific net reproduction rates for eight occupational groups and $t_0 = 1920$, $t_1 = 1950$, it was found that 23% of the movement in this interval was "forced." In an extension of the analysis, the present author has found that 84% of the forced movement is traceable to change in the occupational distribution, and only 16% to differential fertility. Furthermore, 89% of the forced movement occurred in categories in which the two effects "reinforced" one another, i.e., in which both effects stimulated movement into the category or stimulated movements out of the category. For only 11% of the sons did the effects partially "compensate" one another. This is a manifestation of the well-known inverse relationship between relative growth of class and class-specific birth rates in the United States.

The analysis in the preceding paragraphs is seriously flawed by the concept of the "generation" and the fact that the origin distribution of an intergenerational table does not comprise a distribution of the labor force at any point in time. But we believe this analysis is a good starting point for work which is yet to be done and, taken qualitatively, most of its conclusions are valid.

McFarland (1969a) has applied the uncertainty function for a set of categories, $H = -\sum_i p_i \log p_i$, to mobility tables, using a bivariate form for the function. The base of the logarithms is arbitrary, and since tables for base 10 are more easily found than tables for base 2, which is used in many applications, we shall (with McFarland) use base 10. Uncertainty is a non-negative function which is a maximum ($\log K$, where K is the number of categories) when the probability is uniformly dispersed over all categories, and in this event one will gain the greatest amount of information when the actual outcome is learned. Thus H is also a measure of information. It makes no use of any ordinal property of the variable being considered. McFarland found that H can provide for categorical data an alternative to the product-moment correlation, which requires (as a minimum) continuity. In the context of occupational mobility, the level of uncertainty about destination, given origin, is an indicator of the "permeability" of the occupational structure as it affects the movement of persons in each origin.

We have recomputed the conditional uncertainty for each category in the five-category British table (see Column C of Table 5) to permit comparison with the quantities in Columns A and B of Table 5. Although inheritance-immobility and permeability may complement one another as theoretical concepts, the measures which have been associated with the concepts are far from complementary. In particular, H does not distinguish between changing category (disinheritance) or being immobile (inheritance); it can only measure departures from a uniform distribution over destinations (given origin). It is thus not inconsistent that an inverse relation between Column C and Columns A and B is lacking. But we do find it surprising that the uncertainty levels should be so nearly constant over origins (the maximum uncertainty over five destinations would be .70).

ORDINAL OR NOMINAL OCCUPATIONAL VARIABLE: SUCCESSIVE PATTERNS

It is quite possible that the superficially most sophisticated models in sociology are found in this area, due to the wholesale application of powerful techniques of mathematical statistics in an inappropriate way. The review of these models will therefore have a critical tone, and will emphasize the recent awareness of the difficulties.

Suppose that we had data concerning occupational group membership for a cohort of men at time t who were, say, age 20 to 24 at last birthday. Of this group, we shall say $n_i(t)$ were in category i at time t. If we followed the movement of those who survived five years, to time $t + 5$, we could readily compute transition rates $p_{ij}(t)$, the proportion of persons in category i at time t who are in category j at time $t + 5$; if $\mu_i(20)$ is the proportion of persons of age 20–24 in category i who will die in five years then $\sum_j p_{ij}(t) = 1 - \mu_i(20)$ for each origin i. And, by definition of these rates, $n_j(t + 5) = \sum_i n_i(t) p_{ij}(t)$ for each destination j. If we have K categories (including the employed and unemployed in each category) this activity can be represented by the matrix equation

$$(n_1(t+5), \ldots, n_k(t+5), d(t+5)) =$$

$$(n_1(t), \ldots, n_K(t), 0) \begin{bmatrix} p_{11}(t) & \cdots & p_{1K}(t) & \mu_1(20) \\ \vdots & & \vdots & \\ p_{K1}(t) & \cdots & p_{KK}(t) & \mu_K(20) \\ 0 & \cdots & 0 & 1 \end{bmatrix}$$

In abbreviated form, $\tilde{N}(t + 5) = \tilde{N}(t) \, \tilde{P}(t,20)$, where the $\tilde{N}$ (.) are row vectors. The far right entry in the row vector $\tilde{N}(t + 5)$ is the number of persons in the original population who have died by time $t + 5$. $\tilde{P}(t,20)$ is a $(K + 1) \times (K + 1)$ stochastic matrix (each entry is non-negative and the sum over each of its rows is unity).

The preceding is nothing more than a method for naming some data; it is not in any sense a model, for we have made no assumptions. If we followed the cohort for another five years, with complete data, we could write $\tilde{N}(t + 10) = \tilde{N}(t + 5) \, \tilde{P}(t + 5,25) = \tilde{N}(t) \, \tilde{P}(t,20) \, \tilde{P}(t + 5,25)$; we could, theoretically, describe the behavior of the cohort until it became extinct by the effect of a long sequence of transition matrices upon the original distribution vector. We would still not have a model.

We shall describe the assumptions concerning such a process that can be made to "permit" application of the theory of Markov processes. We characteristically have data on only two points in time, say t and $t + 5$, obtained from persons alive at time $t + 5$. If we (1) ignore mortality, in particular age- and origin-specific mortality, then we can incompletely describe the cohort's activities by the equation $\tilde{N}(t+5) = \tilde{N}(t)\ \tilde{P}(t)$. Here $\tilde{N}(t+5)$ and $\tilde{N}(t)$ are row vectors missing the last entry of $N(t+5)$ and $N(t)$, the decedents, and the matrix $\tilde{P}(t)$ is stochastic but is based just upon the surviving population at time $t + 5$. In order to project beyond time $t + 5$ we might assume that (2) all persons in the population are subject to the same set of transition rates during the interval. That is, they are *homogeneous* with respect to characteristics other than occupation (equivalently, occupational movement is determined solely by previous occupation). We might assume that (3) the incomplete matrices $\tilde{P}(t)$, $\tilde{P}(t+5)$, etc., are all equal: the transition matrices are *stationary*. Finally, we might assume that (4) only one's occupation 5 years previous is relevant to present occupation; there is no carry-over effect from earlier categories; this is the *Markovian* (first-order Markovian) property. Then the projection to time $t + 5s$ for integral positive s will be $\tilde{N}(t+5s) = \tilde{N}(t)\ \tilde{P}(t)^s$.

Perhaps the two greatest shortcomings of such an intragenerational projection are the concealment of the well-known reduction in mobility as a cohort ages and of the even better known extinction of the cohort for large s. When applied to *inter*generational movement, the model (5) ignores differential fertility and (6) assumes instantaneous replacement of one generation by another, rather than a fluid overlap of cohorts. More subtly, perhaps, stationarity ignores the impact of changes in the technology, etc., on the occupational distribution, and (1) and (5) ignore the effect (though slight, in the short run) of a changing age structure on occupational supply and demand. For further discussion, the reader is again referred to Duncan (1966).

Prais (1955) and Blumen, Kogan, and McCarthy (1955; partly reprinted in Lazarsfeld and Henry, 1966) were the first to apply the model of a first-order regular Markov process to mobility—the former to intergenerational movement, the latter to intragenerational movement. The motivation has largely been the convergence of the alleged process to a stable distribution which does not depend on the origin distribution (see Kemeny and Snell, 1960, chap. 4). As in stable population theory, this distribution should be viewed as a characterization or summary of the present rates rather than as a prediction; even so, the assumptions are of a much greater magnitude than in mathematical demography. Matras (1960) computed eventual distributions for several countries. Other authors, including Bartholomew (1967) have used the eventual occupational distribution to compute indices of mobility.

Attempts have been made to weaken the assumptions singly or in combinations. Since it has not thus far been possible to test each assumption separately, it may happen that some assumptions will prove justifiable in the absence of others, when more complete data are available. For instance,

Hodge (1966) has shown that the Markovian property (4) does not hold for certain inter- and intragenerational data. But McFarland (1970) has pointed out that if the data could be recognized to overcome a possible lumpability effect (Kemeny and Snell, 1960, chap. 6) the process might still come out Markovian. McFarland goes on, however, to argue that the above type of model must be rejected on other grounds.

Matras (1961) incorporated differential fertility in a paper discussed on page 270, and he has more recently (1966) proposed a way to overcome assumptions (1), (5), and (6) by using the growth matrix of the discreteage demographic model (see, for example, Keyfitz, 1969, chap. 2) to incorporate occupational category with age. Pullum (1968) has made the further bifurcation of the population into persons who have not yet assumed a first job and those who have (although the latter may at some time experience unemployment), which is essential to the evaluation of such a model, and building on Goodman (1968b) has given the form of the variance-covariance matrix of the age-occupational distribution, the eventual distribution, and the reproductive values of any category for any other category.

Another major improvement is a weakening of the homogeneity assumption, described in the "mover-stayer" model of Blumen, Kogan, and Mc-Carthy (1955). We can suppose that there are *two* kinds of persons for each origin: movers, who may change their category over time (but are not required to), and stayers, who are committed to that given category and will never move. If there are K categories, then the diagonal matrix S has, as diagonal entries, the proportion of stayers in each category; I-S will have as diagonal entries the proportion of movers in each category. If M is the stochastic matrix of transition probabilities for the movers, then the transition matrix P for the whole population will be given by $P = S + (I-S)M$. P will be known, but S and M will not be. However, reasonable estimates of these quantities can be obtained (Goodman, 1961). Projection over s intervals of time will then be estimated by the transition matrix $S + (I-S)M^s$. Blumen, Kogan, and McCarthy were able to improve their predictions remarkably through this change.

The mover-stayer model for one mobility pattern uses much different means of estimation of parameters, but is conceptually equivalent, with the difference that immobility for origin i does not require remaining in category i—it means staying within a region of i, as described earlier. The more restricted definition of immobility by Blumen, Kogan, and McCarthy does not require an ordering of categories. If the categories could be ordered, and if they could be constructed such that the boundaries were nearly equally permeable, then one could generalize to one kind of stayer and K-1 kinds of movers. The diagonal matrix S_0 would give the proportions of stayers in each category and the diagonal matrix S_i would give the proportions of persons in each category who *may* move, but by at most i categories; $\sum_i S_i = I$. If M_i were the transition matrix for i-movers then

$$P = S_0 + \sum_1^{K-1} S_i M_i.$$

Projection over s intervals of time would be estimated by the transition matrix

$$S_0 + \sum_1^{k-1} S_i M_i^s \ .$$

Estimation of parameters would not be easy but would, I believe, be possible. The matrix M_i would have zero entries in all cells more than i rows or columns off the main diagonal.

Blumen, Kogan, and McCarthy suggested a different kind of generalization, which is described more completely by Bartholomew (1968). For a given interval of time (say one year) the population may be heterogeneous according to the number of "decision points" at which the possibility of movement arises. Persons will be stayers except at these points, when they may or may not move. There are good reasons for supposing that the distribution of persons over numbers of decision points in a fixed time interval would be a Poisson distribution. Estimation methods and application of this generalization also have yet to be made.

It would also be possible to subdivide the act of changing category into stages, similar to stages in the adoption of an innovation, a change of attitude, etc. Only actual behavior would be recorded, of course, but the introduction of intermediate stages is attractive for sociological reasons and, mathematically, will yield better predictions (although more parameters are required, so improvement must be balanced against a loss in degrees of freedom). Mayer (1968), Conner (1969), and Goodman (1969b) have made some first steps in this direction.

Another distinct line of alteration of the basic model is elimination of the stationarity assumption. The most distinctive characteristic of a sequence of patterns for an age cohort is the decrease in movement with increased age. The most significant contribution to the incorporation into a model of this well-known trend is due to Mayer (1968). The modification is best made in conjunction with a continuous-time Markov chain (for mathematical background see, for example, Karlin, 1968, chaps. 7 and 8). The discrete-time chain imposes upon movement an artificially static implication; movement can of course occur at any time during an interval, and any time or (concomitant) aging effect is continuous (just as under a constant Malthusian rate populations will grow by a continuous exponential, rather than by a discrete geometric function). Let $P(t)$ be a stochastic transition matrix with continuous entries defined for positive t, which describes how the distribution at time t can be obtained from that at time 0. Associated with such a matrix is an instantaneous generating matrix $A(t)$ (whose rows sum to zero) which is related to $P(t)$ by

$$P(t) = \exp \int_0^t A(s)\,ds$$

$$\text{or} \qquad P(t) = I + \sum_{k=0}^{\infty} \left[\int_0^t A(s)\,ds \right]^k / k!.$$

Methods exist for using an observed $P(t_0)$ to obtain $A(s)$ and thereby obtaining $P(t)$ for t other than t_0. It is easily shown that for a stationary process $A(s)$ must be a constant matrix, independent of time. Mayer has considered the case of $A(t) = Ag(t)$, in which all entries of the generator are modified by the same scalar function of time. If $g(t)$ is, in particular, a negative exponential, then the model is markedly improved, even though Mayer was handicapped in having to use a synthetic cohort for data. Further work with generators which depend upon time, in more complex ways, should be most fruitful.

McGinnis (1968) has suggested use of an enlarged transition matrix which records the number of intervals in which a person has resided in a category. This "Cornell Mobility Model" or "retention model of social mobility" includes the hypothesis that tendency to move declines with increased tenure. Simulation and geographical migration investigations, reported by McGinnis, support this hypothesis. Levine (1969) has used the Blumen, Kogan, and McCarthy occupational mobility data to show that a measure of immobility between pairs of categories decays inversely according to a power of the elapsed time over a two-year period (for each of three five-year age groups). Morrison (1967), using data on residential movement, found evidence that tenure and age interact in predicting movement. Fairly neat analytical forms may be obtained by thus considering higher-order Markov chains for several age groups. Investigations of this sort clearly face severe challenges in terms of technique and availability of data.

Social reality should be further approached by a combination of the weakening of the stationarity and homogeneity assumptions. For example, the parameter of the Poisson distribution over decision frequencies, discussed above, could be made a decreasing function of time (the age of the cohort). It should be clear that any intragenerational model which does not stratify by age, at least, permits a great amount of confounding of the nonhomogeneity and nonstationarity implicit in actual mobility.

CONCLUSION

Although the models and methods described in this paper are fairly sophisticated, most readers will have observed that they are strictly demographic in nature. Without exception, they could have been rephrased for regional or residential mobility or for movement through any set of categories. In other words, there is no distinctive use of nonascriptive variables, such as educational aspiration, self-esteem, etc. The overriding view has been of occupational categories as entities which persist over time, the movement through and between them governed by each individual's history within the set of categories, and selected demographic characteristics. It is surprising that with such a skeletal view of social mobility we are able to detect patterns and regularities.

There are many questions about social mobility, however, to which this structural, demographic approach can never yield answers. Many answers probably lie in an extension of the Blau and Duncan (1967) use of a continuous prestige scale. In particular, we could take as the components of an analysis (a) a bivariate or trivariate status vector, in which the aspects of status are kept separate, to allow for the possibility of status inconsistency; (b) evaluation of this vector over a long period of time for each individual, tracing out his career, beginning with first job; (c) parallel to this time series, another vector function of time recording theoretically relevant variables which change over time; and (d) for each individual a vector of background characteristics, such as parental statuses and education, standing prior to the two time series. The choice of variables and postulated links could be evaluated with methods of econometrics, going beyond the linear model. It is not clear how most of the specific methods we have encountered in this paper, however, could be extended to incorporate continuous characteristics of individuals without becoming hopelessly complex.

But there is a desirable complementarity between use of the nominal-ordinal variable of occupational category and use of a continuous (perhaps multivariate) variable of prestige or status. The former is far better able to integrate movement with changes in demographic supply and in technological demand, by the use of persistent categories. On the other hand, the latter, by re-standardizing the individual's statuses at each time interval against the distribution of these statuses over the whole population, can describe how it may happen that a person who has held the same occupation through his whole career may actually have declined in prestige and been downwardly mobile, for example. There are other complementarities.

Finally, there is a great need in future work with models of the type discussed in this paper, as in all mathematical models in social science, for more careful interpretation of the substance of the findings. If, for instance, it is discovered that a cohort's instantaneous transition matrix is modified by a simple function of the cohort's age, then it remains to be found why all the opposing factors involved blend into this particular regularity, rather than another, and how the parameters of this pattern distinguish one cohort from another. It is only by this kind of careful conjunction of a mathematical framework with a social substance that useful future models can, in fact, be generated.

REFERENCES

Bartholomew, D. J.
1967 Stochastic Models for Social Processes. New York: Wiley.

Beshers, J. M. and E. O. Laumann
1967 "Social distance: a network approach." American Sociological Review 32: 225–236.

Blau, P. M. and O. D. Duncan
1967 The American Occupational Structure. New York: Wiley.

Blumen, I., M. Kogan, and P. J. McCarthy
1955 The Industrial Mobility of Labor as a Probability Process. Ithaca: Cornell Studies of Industrial and Labor Relations, Vol. 6.

Carlsson, G.
1958 Social Mobility and Class Structure. Lund, Sweden: W. K. Gleerup.

Conner, T. L.
1969 "A stochastic model for change of occupation." Unpublished manuscript, Michigan State University.

Duncan, O. D.
1966 "Methodological issues in the analysis of social mobility." In N. J. Smelser and S. M. Lipset (eds.), Social Structure and Mobility in Economic Development. Chicago: Aldine.

Glass, D. V. (ed.)
1954 Social Mobility in Britain. Glencoe, Ill.: The Free Press.

Goodman, L. A.
1961 "Statistical methods for the mover-stayer model." Journal of the American Statistical Association 56: 841–868.
1965 "On the statistical analysis of mobility tables." American Journal of Sociology 70:564–585.

Goodman, L. A.
1968a "The analysis of cross classified data: independence, quasi-independence, and interactions in contingency tables with or without missing entries." Journal of the American Statistical Association 63:1091–1131.
1968b "Stochastic models for the population growth of the sexes." Biometrika 55:469–487.
1969a "How to ransack social mobility tables and other kinds of cross-classification tables." American Journal of Sociology 75:1–40.
1969b "On the measurement of social mobility: an index of status persistence." American Sociological Review 34: 831–850.

Hodge, R. W.
1966 "Occupational mobility as a probability process." Demography 3:19–34.

Kahl, J. A.
1957   The American Class Structure. New York: Rinehart.

Karlin, S.
1968   A First Course in Stochastic Processes. New York: Academic Press.

Kemeny, J. G., and J. L. Snell
1960   Finite Markov Chains. Princeton: D. Van Nostrand.

Keyfitz, N.
1968   Introduction to the Mathematics of Population. Reading, Mass.: Addison-Wesley.

Lazarsfeld, P. F., and N. W. Henry
1966   Readings in Mathematical Social Science. Chicago: Science Research Associates.

Levine, J. H.
1967   "Measurement in the study of inter-generational status mobility." Ph.D. thesis, Department of Social Relations, Harvard University.
1969   "Decay analysis of a coefficient of labor immobility." Unpublished manuscript, University of Michigan.

McFarland, D. D.
1968   "An extension of conjoint measurement to test the theory of quasi-perfect mobility." Michigan Studies in Mathematical Sociology, Number Three, University of Michigan.
1969a "Measuring the permeability of occupational structures." American Journal of Sociology 75:41–61.
1969b "Social distance as a metric." Unpublished manuscript, University of Michigan.
1970   "Intra-generational social mobility as a Markov process: including a time-stationary Markovian model that explains observed declines in mobility rates over time." American Sociological Review 35 (June).

McGinnis, R.
1968   "A stochastic model of social mobility." American Sociological Review 33:712–722.

Matras, J.
1960   "Comparison of intergenerational occupational mobility patterns." Population Studies 14:163–169.
1961   "Differential fertility, intergenerational mobility, and change in the occupational structure." Population Studies 15:187–197.
1967   "Social mobility and social structure: some insights from the linear model." American Sociological Review 32:608–614.

Mayer, T. F.
1967   "Birth and death process models of social mobility." Michigan Studies in Mathematical Sociology, Number Two, University of Michigan.
1968   "Age and mobility: two approaches to the problem of non-stationarity." Michigan Studies in Mathematical Sociology, Number Six, University of Michigan.

Morrison, P. A.
1967   "Duration of residence and prospective migration: the evaluation of a stochastic model." Demography 4:559–560.

Mosteller, F.
1968   "Association and estimation in contingency tables." Journal of the American Statistical Association 63:1–28.

Prais, S. J.
1955   "The formal theory of social mobility." Population Studies 9:72–81.

Pullum, T. W.
1964   "The theoretical implications of quasi-perfect mobility." Unpublished manuscript, The University of Chicago.
1968   "Occupational mobility as a branching process." Unpublished manuscript, The University of Chicago.

Rogoff, N.
1953   Recent Trends in Occupational Mobility. Glencoe, Ill.: The Free Press.

Simon, H. A.
1957   Models of Man. New York: Wiley.

Svalastoga, K.
1959   Prestige, Class and Mobility. Copenhagen: Gyldendal.

White, H. C.
1963   "Cause and effect in social mobility tables." Behavioral Science 8:14–27.
1968   Opportunity Chains: Theory, Models and Data for Mobility. Unpublished manuscript, Harvard University.